DISCRD £6.50

127 270

D1461525

MACMILLAN STUDIES IN TWENTIETH-CENTURY LITERATURE

Anne Wright
LITERATURE OF CRISIS, 1910–22

Further titles in preparation

Series Standing Order

If you would like to receive future titles in this series as they are published, you can make use of our standing order facility. To place a standing order please contact your bookseller or, in case of difficulty, write to us at the address below with your name and address and the name of the series. Please state with which title you wish to begin your standing order. (If you live outside the UK we may not have the rights for your area, in which case we will forward your order to the publisher concerned.)

Standing Order Service, Macmillan Distribution Ltd, Houndmills, Basingstoke, Hampshire, RG21 2XS, England.

D. H. Lawrence
New Studies

Edited by

Christopher Heywood

**MACMILLAN
PRESS**

Editorial matter and Chapter 8 © Christopher Heywood 1987; Chapter 1 © Colin
Holmes 1987; Chapter 2 © R. P. Draper 1987; Chapter 3 © Neil Roberts 1987; Chapter 4
© Ian MacKillop 1987; Chapter 5 © Michael Bentley 1987; Chapter 6 © Andrew Peek
1987; Chapter 7 © Roger Ebbatson 1987; Chapter 9 © Henry Schvey 1987; Chapter 10 ©
Emile Delavenay 1987; Chapter 11 © Annemarie Heywood 1987

First edition 1987
Reprinted 1988

Published by
THE MACMILLAN PRESS LTD
Houndmills, Basingstoke, Hampshire RG21 2XS
and London
Companies and representatives
throughout the world

Typeset in Great Britain by
Vine & Gorfin Ltd,
Exmouth, Devon

Printed in Great Britain by
Antony Rowe Ltd
Chippenham

British Library Cataloguing in Publication Data
D. H. Lawrence: new studies. — (Macmillan
studies in 20th-century literature
1. Lawrence, D. H. — Criticism and
interpretation
I. Heywood, Christopher
823'.912   PR6023.A93Z/
ISBN 0-333-30922-7

Contents

vi   *Contents*

Preface and Acknowledgements

Most of these essays began as contributions to a lecture series commemorating the half-century of D. H. Lawrence's death. The series was arranged and delivered in Sheffield in the Division of Continuing Education of Sheffield University during 1979/80. Another commemoration, the centenary of his birth in 1885, has intervened, but still the need persists from the time of the lecture series to relate Lawrence's writings to some of the specific problems, events, lines of argument, and themes, of his age. His novels, poems, essays, letters and travels were an expression of a society as much as of an individual artist's impulses and impressions. Many details of the movements leading to the formation of his works have been lost, but many can still be retrieved by research and inquiry. The essays pursue their writers' discoveries, insights and preoccupations, without addressing themselves to any prescribed limit or plan.

The essays printed here make no attempt to cover all the works, and they do not present a coherent view. At times they present conflicting, or complementary, views of the same text or set of problems. No effort is made here to reconcile discordant views. They register, rather, the tensions inherent in the works themselves. The tendency of *The Rainbow* and *Women in Love* to dominate the discussion reflects the key position of the novels which began as 'The Sisters' in the unfolding of Lawrence's art and ideas. These essays trace some of the landmarks in the rise and fall of a great creative achievement.

Thanks are due to the contributors for their patience in awaiting the results of arrangement and editing, which took longer than had been expected. Occasional notes in the text point to the writers having altered or developed the views given in the original series. The Division of Continuing Education at Sheffield University and the Department of English Literature at Sheffield University are thanked for arrangements leading to the presentation and collecting of these essays. The essay by Professor Delavenay replaces the paper orginally given in the series. The essay by Henry Schvey was first given at the 1980 International Conference of the British Comparative Literature Association at the

University of Kent at Canterbury. The organisers are thanked for the arrangements leading to the presentation of this paper. A special note of thanks goes to Julia Steward and Valery Rose, for their long-suffering patience, good humour, and skilled assistance, during the editorial work.

All quotations from the various works by D. H. Lawrence are published by permission of Laurence Pollinger Ltd, on behalf of the Estate of the late Frieda Lawrence Ravagli, who are warmly thanked for advice, assistance and co-operation. The following collections are thanked for having consented to the publication of the works by Oskar Kokoschka appearing in the essay by Henry Schvey: Öffentliche Kunstsammlung, Kunstmuseum Basel (for *Die Windsbraut*, 1914); the Museum of Modern Art, New York (for *Hans Tietze and Erica Tietze-Conrat*, 1909). The following are thanked for permission to reproduce graphic material included in the essay by Annemarie Heywood: Frobenius-Institut, Frankfurt-am-Main (Figure 6, from Leo Frobenius, *Kulturgeschichte Afrikas*); Newnes Books and Photographie Giraudon, Paris (Figure 7, from Geoffrey Parrinder, *African Mythology*); Souvenir Press (Figures 5 and 8, from Joseph O. Campbell, *The Masks of God*, III; *Occidental Mythology*); Thames and Hudson (Figures 4, 9 and 10, from Stanislas Klossewski de Rola, *The Secret Art of Alchemy*). The editors of the following journals are thanked for permission to reprint essays first published by them: *Etudes Anglaises*, for the essay by Christopher Heywood; *Literature and History*, for the essay by Colin Holmes; *Notes and Queries*, and the D. H. Lawrence Society and the *D. H. Lawrence Journal*, for the essay by Andrew Peek.

Every effort has been made to trace all the copyright-holders, but if any have been inadvertently overlooked, the publishers will be pleased to make the necessary arrangements at the first opportunity.

List of Abbreviations

The following abbreviations are used throughout in references to commonly cited works by or about Lawrence, and identify the editions specified below. Wherever possible, references to these works are given in the text.

AR	*Aaron's Rod* (Harmondsworth: Penguin, 1950).
CL	*D. H. Lawrence: Collected Letters*, ed. Harry T. Moore, 2 vols (London: Heinemann, 1962).
CP	*The Complete Poems of D. H. Lawrence*, ed. V. de S. Pinto and W. Roberts (Harmondsworth: Penguin, 1977).
ET	Jessie Chambers, *D. H. Lawrence: A Personal Record by E.T.* (London: Frank Cass, 1965).
F	*Fantasia of the Unconscious/Psychoanalysis and the Unconscious* (Harmondsworth: Penguin, 1971).
Hardy	*Lawrence on Hardy and Painting*, ed. H. W. Davies (London: Heinemann, 1973).
K	*Kangaroo* (Harmondsworth: Penguin, 1950).
KL	*The Quest for Rananim: D. H. Lawrence's Letters to S. S. Koteliansky*, ed. George J. Zytaruk (Montreal and London: McGill-Queen's University Press, 1970).
LCL	*Lady Chatterley's Lover* (Harmondsworth: Penguin, 1960).
Letters I	*The Letters of D. H. Lawrence*, ed. James T. Boulton, vol. 1 (Cambridge: Cambridge University Press, 1979).
Letters II	*The Letters of D. H. Lawrence*, ed. George J. Zytaruk and James T. Boulton, vol. 2 (Cambridge: Cambridge University Press, 1981).
Nehls	*D. H. Lawrence: A Composite Biography*, ed. Edward Nehls, 3 vols (Madison, Wis.: University of Wisconsin Press, 1957–9).
Ph	*Phoenix* (London: Heinemann, 1936).
PhII	*Phoenix II*, ed. W. Roberts and Harry T. Moore (London: Heinemann, 1962).
PhS	*D. H. Lawrence: A Selection from 'Phoenix'*, ed. A. A. H. Inglis (Harmondsworth: Penguin, 1971).
R	*The Rainbow* (Harmondsworth: Penguin, 1966).

SL   *Sons and Lovers* (Harmondsworth: Penguin, 1952).
WL   *Women in Love* (Harmondsworth: Penguin, 1982).
WP   *The White Peacock* (Harmondsworth: Penguin, 1950).

In some essays references to certain other works appear in the text. The notes to the essays in question identify these works.

Notes on the Contributors

Michael Bentley is Senior Lecturer in History at the University of Sheffield. His publications include *The Liberal Mind 1914–29* and *High and Low Politics in Modern Britain*. He is currently writing a study of nineteenth-century political history.

Emile Delavenay is Honorary Professor at the University, Nice, where he held the Chair of English until his retirement in 1974. He has held numerous posts in England, France and elsewhere, including positions with the BBC and the United Nations. His publications include *D. H. Lawrence: The Man and his Work* and *D. H. Lawrence and Edward Carpenter*.

R. P. Draper is Professor of English at the University of Aberdeen. His numerous studies of Lawrence and other writers include *D. H. Lawrence* and *D. H. Lawrence: The Critical Heritage*.

Roger Ebbatson is Senior Lecturer in English, Worcester College of Higher Education, and was previously Senior Lecturer at the University of Sokoto, Nigeria. His publications include *Lawrence and the Nature Tradition* and *The Evolutionary Self*.

Annemarie Heywood is Senior Lecturer at the University of Namibia, and was previously Lecturer in English at the University of Ife, Nigeria. She has been a postgraduate student and teaching assistant at the University of Sheffield and has published several studies on African literature.

Christopher Heywood is Senior Lecturer in English Literature at the University of Sheffield and was Professor of English at the University of Ife, Nigeria, 1966–8. He has published *Perspectives on African Literature* and *Aspects of South African Literature*. He is currently working on a study of the Victorian novel.

Colin Holmes is Reader in Economic and Social History at the University of Sheffield. His publications include *Immigrants and Minorities in British Society*, *Anti-Semitism in British Society*, *John Bull's Island* and *Immigrants and Refugees in Britain 1871–1971*.

Ian MacKillop is Lecturer in English Literature at the University of Sheffield, where he specialises in eighteenth-century literature and in film. His publications include *The British Ethical Societies.*

Andrew Peek is Senior Lecturer in the School of General Studies at the Tasmanian State Institute of Technology, and has been a Lecturer in English at the University of Ife, Nigeria, and the Australian National University.

Neil Roberts is Senior Lecturer in English Literature at the University of Sheffield. He is the author of *George Eliot: Her Beliefs and Her Art* and *Ted Hughes: A Critical Study*, as well as various studies of modern literature.

Henry Schvey is Lecturer in English at Leiden University, and has been Visiting Professor at Webster University, St Louis, Missouri. His publications include *Oskar Kokoschka: The Painter as Playwright.*

1

Lawrence's Social Origins

COLIN HOLMES

What were the social origins of D. H. Lawrence? Was he from a
proletarian background? Or was this a myth which at times he found
convenient to cultivate? Have we believed too much of what he said
about these matters? And has the time come to demolish the views which
are held regarding his social background?[1]

My interest in this is not accidental. I know Lawrence country. For
me, as for him, it constitutes 'the country of my heart'[2] and, like
Lawrence, I went to university in Nottingham, 'that dismal town'[3] – not
to the 'ugly neo-Gothic building' in Shakespeare Street[4] which opened
its doors in 1881, but to that lighter University on the hill, 'Nottingham's
New University' built 'grand and cakeily'[5] above its lake and near to
Jesse Boot's Beeston. In my years there the memory of Lawrence was
undergoing a revival and his stature as a writer was in the process of
being reassessed. The scandal of the elopement with Frieda Weekley had
faded with the passing years and, in the University, Vivian de Sola Pinto
was trying to re-establish Lawrence's literary importance free from such
personal considerations. It was in fact a time of considerable activity in
Lawrence studies. In 1960 the University held its Lawrence Exhibition[6]
and in the same year Professor Pinto gave evidence in the court case over
Lady Chatterley's Lover. Along with other critics, he testified to
Lawrence's literary genius and played a part in releasing the author's
work from the problems of censorship which had bedevilled it since the
Rainbow case in 1915.[7] Throughout the late 1950s and early 1960s, in line
with this growing interest, there seemed to be a procession of research
students making a pilgrimage to the English Department at Nottingham,
anxious to discuss central, interstitial and vestigial aspects of
Lawrence's life and thought. To us, the undergraduates, it seemed that
an enthusiastic industry was at work.

Most thinking students were aware of all this, but in the Sub-
Department of Economic and Social History there was a link of a
different kind with this activity. The head of the Sub-Department –
Departmental status came in 1962 – was J. D. Chambers.[8] At this time

1

Chambers was in charge of a small, energetic school which was rapidly
establishing its name in the growing discipline of economic and social
history. But there was more to Chambers than the academic historian.
He was the brother of Jessie Chambers, the Miriam of *Sons and Lovers*.
The small, round-faced, booted child on the family photographs, the
Hubert of *Sons and Lovers*, was now lecturing to us on the Industrial
Revolution. And in the course of his lectures he suggested that it would
be rewarding for an economic and social historian to analyse
Lawrence's work, to test it with the rigour which might be applied to any
other historical source.[9] Lawrence had a great deal to say about the
processes of industrialisation and the social consequences which grew
out of the transformation of England from an agrarian to a 'mechanical
disintegrated, amorphous'[10] industrial society. Growing up in
Eastwood he saw every day a blend of the old and the new. The
blackened pit tips where the earth's core accumulated on the surface and
the iron headstocks below which men were taken into an underground
world rose stark and sudden among such stretching woodlands and country
fields. Through the clash of such visual symbols Lawrence could hardly
fail to be aware of the impact of industrialisation. On a more animate
level, the sight of colliers in their pit dust spilling into Eastwood when
their shift was over was another permanent feature of the industrial
landscape.[11] But familiarity does not necessarily lead to accuracy, and in
1960 Chambers made it clear in his seminars on the Industrial
Revolution – a course for third-year undergraduates – that he was
deeply dissatisfied with the analysis presented by Raymond Williams in
Culture and Society, in which Lawrence was described as a perceptive
critic of industrialisation.[12]

Any attempt at a full discussion of Lawrence's critique of
industrialisation would be a formidable undertaking and is best left for
another occasion. Instead I want to restrict myself here to a study of
Lawrence's social origins; in particular, I intend to discuss George
Watson's recent opinions on this, in the course of which he draws upon
Chambers's knowledge and recollections of Lawrence's early life.[13]
Watson's work has shown a clear tendency to cross traditional academic
boundaries in pursuit of the past, and his peppery, iconoclastic raids
have been concerned to overturn current orthodoxies, particularly those
derived from the writings of the political Left.[14] As a historian I want to
question his argument on Lawrence's origins and, at the same time,
indicate some of the dangers which can arise when academic boundaries
are crossed.

The usual view of Lawrence's background derives from Lawrence himself, who wrote, 'I was born among the working classes and brought up among them'; he went on to comment that he was in fact 'a man from the working class'.[15] This view has become widely accepted. While Marxist critics of the inter-war years, such as Christopher Caudwell, could refer to Lawrence as a bourgeois artist, this constituted an attack upon his ideas rather than a reference to his social origins.[16] Indeed, the belief that Lawrence had a working-class background became part of the accepted version of his life. E. M. Forster could refer to him as of the working class in an obituary notice in 1930,[17] and a similar belief was apparent at a later date in F. R. Leavis's discussion of Keynes and Lawrence in Cambridge.[18] Indeed, 'By the 1950s', Watson has written, 'the myth had taken up its lodging in academe.'[19] Richard Hoggart in *The Uses of Literacy*[20] and Raymond Williams in *Culture and Society*[21] both viewed Lawrence's origins in this light and, still more recently, Terry Eagleton in *Criticism and Ideology* has referred to Lawrence as 'of proletarian origin'.[22] It is this strand of opinion which Watson attempts to overturn.

Watson's argument can be summarised as follows. Lawrence was 'the son of a contractor in a Nottinghamshire coal mine and of a former schoolmistress of some cultivation and social standing'. Consequently, it is argued, 'The common assertion that his father was a miner, though not false, is misleading in context; he was not by the period of Lawrence's upbringing dependent upon wages, being in charge of a group of miners, and his income was good.'[23] Furthermore, it is claimed, 'If his manners were rough and at times even wild, this needs to be measured against the superior existence his wife created in Eastwood for the sons who, as she successfully resolved, would never work in a mine.' This is the first salvo of the counter-attack.

The next barrage comes via J. D. Chambers, described as 'the brother of Jessie Chambers and himself a social historian' who knew Lawrence 'intimately in his youth'.[24] According to Chambers – and Watson uses this in his evidence – it was simply untrue to say that the Lawrence family had lived in poverty. Lawrence's father was 'a highly skilled man, bringing home good money, occupying a house with a big window and separate "entry" of which the Lawrences were immensely proud, and handing over to his wife enough money to give three of their five children a good education'.[25]

In view of this the working-class origins of Lawrence are regarded by Watson as without foundation and he is particularly keen to emphasise that after the age of six Lawrence left 'the mean terraced house marked as his birthplace' and 'lived in a superior residence on the hill until he

was eighteen'.[26] And going to Nottingham High School for the best type
of local education, and thence to the University in Nottingham and a
schoolmaster's post in Croydon, and marrying the daughter of a
German aristocrat were, in a sense, part of a progression away from the
wage-earners, whose lives, it is argued, Lawrence had observed rather
than experienced.

According to Watson, therefore, Lawrence was never outside the
middle class, although at no point is any clear indication given of what
Watson regards as the determinants of class position. And, in order to
explain why the myth of Lawrence's social origins should have arisen,
Watson refers to the possibility that in his later years 'the humbler status
of his father came to look disputatiously convenient' to Lawrence.
Indeed, 'men sometimes discover in their middle years that an origin
they once found disadvantageous can be turned to an unlooked-for
account'.[27]

In considering this counter-interpretation it has to be admitted
straightaway that when his son David Herbert was born in 1885 Arthur
Lawrence was not just a day-wage collier, and any account which
assumes that he was is undoubtedly mistaken. In that sense alone we
need to take Watson's argument seriously. But Watson's own position is
unsatisfactory both with regard to his discussion of the nature of Arthur
Lawrence's work and his suggested wage-earning capacity.

Lawrence's father, we are told by Watson, was a contractor, in charge
of men and not dependent upon wages.[28] In more conventional terms, he
was a 'butty'. Butty work, which is still in need of close academic study,
was subject to great regional variations and different practices prevailed
among and within pits in the same area. But oral historians, using
collective memories of miners, are in the process of reconstructing the
historical patterns of the butty system and the essential features it
contained. From this work it becomes clear that there were broadly two
kinds of butty. There was the sub-contractor or 'big butty', who
contracted with the owners to extract a certain amount of coal in return
for an agreed payment and who then proceeded to recruit workers and
provide the working capital to achieve this. In this case we are referring
to a self-employed man who also employed wage labour. But in the
course of the nineteenth century this type of man became less significant
as mining life became increasingly regulated and responsibility for
working conditions became more centralised and organised. In such
circumstances the contractor or the 'little butty' remained important,
but his role was significantly different from that of the sub-contractor.
The 'little butty' was a superior workman who oversaw the working of a

stall, a place of work at the coalface, and was responsible for getting out the coal. For this he collected the wages for the coal extracted by the stall and proceeded to distribute part of the payment to the men who worked under him, who were, like himself, employees of the coal owners. In this work situation he was closely supervised. Whichever system operated it allowed for corruption. Details of the financial arrangements which butties, big and little, had with the owners were often secret and a source of tension and suspicion. 'Good' – in other words, docile – butties would be favoured with stalls which guaranteed high productivity, while recalcitrant men such as Arthur Lawrence could be given difficult parts of the pit to work. Furthermore, an inevitable consequence of so splitting the workforce – with men working under butties, while the butties also encountered managerial discrimination – was that the butty system operated generally as an agency of management control.[29]

So much for the general picture. But what of Brinsley? As yet we have no detailed study of this particular pit. Nevertheless, from evidence that does exist, it can now be reported with confidence that Lawrence's father was a 'little butty' at Brinsley. He worked his stall in conjunction with another butty and two or three day-wage workers, and was himself entirely dependent upon wages. This is quite different from the image of the self-employed Lawrence that Watson is keen to stress.[30] Moreover, being an independent-spirited man, Arthur Lawrence was seldom guaranteed a good stall. Evidence suggests that he gave not an inch to the owners; he showed no signs of bowing before authority, even if docility held out the prospect of material benefits. He did not share a consciousness with the pit owners, nor did he find it with his family. His sense of belonging came when he was with his fellow colliers. In view of all this, how much remains of the new image of Arthur Lawrence in which we are asked to believe?[31]

In trying to establish a new image of Lawrence's background, Watson also contends that Arthur Lawrence earned 'good money'. Ada Lawrence gives a quite different picture, one more in line with the traditional view of the Lawrence household:

We were always conscious of poverty and the endless struggle for bread. Perhaps many other children of mining folk knew frequently enough that they had not enough to eat. We were conscious of more. The anxieties of our mother were shared by us. She never concealed the fact that she had not enough money to clothe and feed us as adequately as she wished. The sight of father coming up the field at midday took all the pleasure from our games. It meant that on Friday night he would be short on half a day's pay. I don't remember him giving mother more than thirty-five shillings a week. So much was rare. The usual amount was twenty-five. The rent was five shillings and the rates were extra. She baked the bread, made what clothes she could for us and schemed day and night so that we should have enough to eat. It was the terrible indignity of such poverty that embittered my brother so much.[32]

But we do not know if Arthur Lawrence handed over all his wages, and, since his earnings would have been cyclical, we should be cautious about accepting Ada's statement too readily. However, we are equally unable to accept uncritically Watson's claim that Lawrence's father earned good money. This suggestion is derived from Chambers and for a historian it is surprisingly vague. We simply do not know whether it is the relative or absolute level of earnings to which reference is being made. In fact, we cannot make any direct, positive statement about the earnings of Lawrence's father, since the wage sheets at Brinsley have disappeared. But, if we scrutinise what is known of earnings in the Nottinghamshire coalfield, it can be claimed on good authority that, although he would have been among the more highly paid manual workers, in no circumstances would he have drawn 'what might be described as a middle class income'.[33]

Nevertheless, it might be argued that the Lawrences could hardly have moved to better housing if Arthur Lawrence had not been earning a good wage. And Watson does in fact make this point. In reply it should be said that, if anyone wishes to develop this kind of argument, the first requirement is to provide accurate information on the moves undertaken by the Lawrences – and this Watson fails to do. The moves during Mrs Lawrence's life were from Victoria Street down to the Breach, up to Walker Street and then, after the death of Ernest Lawrence, in 1904–5, to Lynn Croft. Watson's account, which implies that movement was from the Breach – where he seems to believe that Lawrence was born – up the hill towards better property, is a simplification of events.[34] While it is true that in the course of time the Lawrences did move into a better type of property, it is not possible to draw firm conclusions from this about Arthur Lawrence's earning-power. For instance, there is evidence, of a personal kind, that the migration up the hill was achieved at the cost of a good deal of sacrifice. Mabel Collishaw, one of Lawrence's contemporaries in Eastwood, unsuspectingly provided evidence on this when she wrote,

Mr Lawrence was a very boastful man and a very careless one when working in the mine. As a direct consequence, he had many accidents. My father was the sick visitor for the Foresters lodge, and it was a part of his duty to pay benefits and take care that the miner's wife and children had food if the husband was seriously injured. On one occasion, Mr Lawrence broke his leg and had to be taken to the hospital in Nottingham. As they were carrying him out of the house he said to his wife:-

'Don't let the children starve. Cut that large ham behind the pantry door.'

Father opened the door to see if they had meat but the only food was bread.[35]

This was designed to give an insight into the psychology of Lawrence's father. But it revealed more than that. It also suggested that the Lawrences could have their 'superior residences' (anyone who has *seen* them will recognise that there are overtones in this which should be resisted) at a cost of doing without certain other things. In this instance it seems that food was skimped for the sake of a house. It is also worth bearing in mind the following recollection, again from Collishaw:

When his parents moved from the Breach to Walker Street, it was a great lift for the family, for we who lived on Lynn Croft never, as a rule, mixed with the children of the Breach. The first thing Mrs Lawrence did was to buy new lace curtains for the bay windowed 'parlour' . . . . My sister and I were passing as she was hanging up the curtains threaded on a tape and Bertie stood proudly beside her. When he saw me coming, he held the curtain for the side window high up. His looks said, 'You boast about your curtains on a bamboo pole. Now we have some too!' He nearly cried when he came out to play and said, 'I don't care! We will have a proper pole some day!'[36]

Collishaw's recollection is concerned with the social distinctions which existed in Eastwood, and these clearly stayed with her. It was also intended to throw light on Lawrence's character. But once again it was revealing in a different sense. One could move to Walker Street and have the house but, at the same time, it was necessary to economise on the bamboo pole.

Apart from the move into better types of property, the drive towards respectability was also evident within the Lawrence's household. This is presumably part of the 'superior existence' to which Watson refers,

attributing an influence here to Lydia Lawrence. Although it is not
clearly spelt out, the assumption behind such a statement is that Mrs
Lawrence was the wife of a high earning miner and had the resources
with which to satisfy the refined tastes she had formed before her
marriage. But we need to be careful about jumping to such conclusions
and should bear in mind the well-known Northern saying about 'lace
curtains and nothing for breakfast'. In other words, it was not unusual
for a home to be built up through saving and sacrifice rather than a high
level of earnings, and there is evidence that such forces were present in
the Lawrence family. In describing the home Ada Lawrence recalled,

> We were proud of our front room or parlour with its well-made
> mahogany and horse-hair suite of furniture – the little mahogany
> chiffonier and the oval Spanish mahogany table which my mother
> insisted on covering with a fawn and green tapestry tablecloth to
> match the Brussels carpet. Here again were oleographs heavily
> framed in gilt, and the family portrait in the place of honour over the
> mantelpiece.
>
> Although so unpretentious there was something about our house
> which made it different from those of our neighbours. Perhaps this
> was because mother would have nothing cheap or tawdry, preferring
> bareness.[37]

Further confirmation that the 'superior existence' of the Lawrences came
through self-help and sacrifice rather than earning-power is provided by
the careers of the Lawrence children. The drive towards respectability
maintained by Mrs Lawrence was reflected in her ambitions for them,
which resulted in their all being placed in clerical or teaching careers.
There is firm evidence that the economic foundations for this came
through sacrifice rather than the 'good money' earned by Lawrence's
father.[38]

So where does this leave us? 'There is no real evidence', Watson tells
us, 'that Lawrence was never outside the middle class, as that phrase is
most commonly understood, at any time in his life.'[39] In this view
Lawrence's father was a self-employed contractor; he earned good
money; on the basis of this the Lawrences could enjoy a 'superior
existence' in Eastwood. In reply to this it has been argued here that
Watson has misunderstood the kind of work in which Arthur Lawrence
was engaged. Lawrence's father was an employee of the Barber, Walker
Company and it is Watson's ignorance of the butty system which has
resulted in his major misjudgment. Furthermore, Watson has produced

no evidence, other than Chambers's comment, made without access to any wage sheets, to substantiate his claim that Lawrence's father earned 'good money'. He has also failed to recognise that the moves of the Lawrence family to better properties within Eastwood – a place with which Watson is clearly unfamiliar – and other aspects of their 'superior existence' can be accounted for by quite different influences from those which he has suggested. Thus, each point of Watson's argument can be refuted or contested.

But it would be unwise, having countered Watson's argument, to insist that Lawrence's social background was typically working-class. Lawrence's father, even though he enjoyed some status in the mining community as a result of his role as a little butty, was working-class. His market situation was that he was a miner in receipt of wages – on which the family was solely dependent – and that he was reliant upon the pit-owners for employment. He could read only with difficulty and could only just sign his name. His culture was of a non-literate kind. In terms of such economic and cultural indices he could hardly be described as other than working-class. It would strain the bounds of social analysis to argue otherwise. But the Lawrence family was made up of more than Arthur Lawrence. It is also necessary to take account of the strong mother figure, Lydia Lawrence, who played a critical role in the family and on the development of the Lawrence children. We have already noticed her commitment to respectability, her striving to 'get on' and her consequent worship of the lean goddess, abstinence. In this she was displaying her attachment to the virtues worshipped in Samuel Smiles's catechism, and such qualities helped to secure her children against a working-class future. But these were not the only values she brought to the household. She also injected into it other cultural influences. She read a good deal, wrote poetry, insisted on standard English and refused to make any concession to the local dialect. The result was that the home contained the culture of Lawrence's father, which Lawrence came to regard as 'the old instinctive, sensuous life of pre-industrial England', and that of a woman who was keen on self-improvement and who had been a pupil teacher and possibly a governess in the South before straitened family circumstances brought her to Nottingham as a lace-drawer.[40]

In other words, colliding planes of consciousness were present and Lawrence was tossed between opposing sets of influences. And, as Lydia Lawrence took a grip on the family, as the children were turned against their father, Arthur Lawrence expressed himself increasingly in the company of his fellow miners in the local public houses. Consequently, the gap in the family widened. This was the crucible in which D. H. Lawrence was born, through which he lived and which he remembered in his poem 'Red Herring', which appeared in 1929 in *Pansies*. Watson's interpretation of this poem is that it provides further evidence for his case that Lawrence was 'outside the working class'. But it is a mistaken insistence upon this view, based mainly upon his distorted conception of the work of Lawrence's father, which prevents Watson from making the poem a central feature in his analysis of Lawrence's social origins. 'Red Herring' is in fact a hymn to social and psychological marginality, to the in-between. What is being suggested here – and Lawrence's poem underlines the claim – is that Lawrence was born into a working-class home, in terms of his father's occupation, but it was one full of aspirations derived from Lydia Lawrence. In other words, it was a household in which the children were oriented towards a future life outside the working class. It was because of this that the Lawrence children experienced problems of ultimate social identification. 'Red Herring' remains as the clearest testimony of this, and consequently it is worth extracting from it its salient message:

> My father was a working man
> and a collier was he . . .
> My mother was a superior soul
> a superior soul was she,
> cut out to play a superior role
> in the god-damn bourgeoisie.
>
> We children were the in-betweens
> little non-descripts were we,
> indoors we called each other *you*
> outside, it was *tha* and *thee*.
>
> But time has fled, our parents are dead
> we've risen in the world all three;
> but still we are in-betweens, we tread
> between the devil and the deep sad sea.[41]

(*CP*, pp. 490–1)

   This consideration of Lawrence's social origins has turned principally upon a discussion of Watson's *Encounter* article, and in conclusion I want to set his work in a wider context. Watson's writing is patently ideological in character. His pen has been used to label Marx and Engels as 'racialists', and in various writings he has displayed a clear relish for taking an intellectual swipe at anything socialist.[42] It is no surprise that he finds *Encounter* a congenial home for his material, and, in pursuit of Lawrence's origins, his reliance upon the testimony of J. D. Chambers has brought about an interesting fusion of academic forces. Chambers himself was a leading representative of the optimistic school of economic and social history which exercised a powerful influence upon the academic history world of the 1950s and 1960s. As a young man he had been a near-convert to Marxism under the influence of Maurice Dobb's *Capitalist Enterprise and Socialist Progress* (1925) – he once described its author as probably the cleverest man of his generation – and he devoted the rest of his life, after the trauma of near-conversion, to an attack upon the Marxist historical position while simultaneously having the highest regard for individual Marxists.[43] In general terms the consequence of this was an emphasis upon certain positive favourable trends within the process of industrialisation and a minimising of the conflict inherent in such a traumatic change.[44] What we have, then, in the *Encounter* article is the merging of two strands of thought drawn from literature and history which are hostile to socialist opinion, in an attempt to construct a different picture of Lawrence's origins from that which has been widely accepted – particularly on the Left.[45] But, it has been argued here, it is a picture which is ultimately unconvincing.

A failure along these lines is not a cause for rejoicing. In spite of all the attention which has been lavished upon Lawrence, much yet remains to be done. If we restrict ourselves to the kind of work which would benefit from an intercommunion of the disciplines of history and literature, the opportunity still exists for a full-scale examination of his writing in the light of what we know about the economic and social history of the period through which Lawrence lived and the area where he was born. Furthermore, there is still historical evidence as yet unused – and, indeed, unseen – on Lawrence's problems with the censor.[46] There is also, I suspect, a need for a re-evaluation of Lawrence's socio-political philosophy, free from the distortions to which it has been subjected by the categorisation of his thought outside its appropriate context.[47] In all these instances, a cross-fertilisation of history and literature is capable of yielding fresh insights into Lawrence's life and work. But the rigours and pitfalls of interdisciplinary work need to be constantly kept in mind, and in this respect the *Encounter* analysis of Lawrence's origins is a reminder not only of the potential harvest, but also of the actual dangers, when academic boundaries are crossed in the reconstruction of the past. However, a failure should not deter us; we should press ahead, confident that the fruits of such an enterprise can be considerable.[48]

12   *D. H. Lawrence: New Studies*

NOTES

Professor J. T. Boulton, Dr J. A. Morris and Dr D. E. Martin have read this paper. I am grateful to them, but the final responsibility for the arguments presented here remains mine.

1.   As suggested by George Watson in 'D. H. Lawrence's Own Myth', *Encounter*, Dec 1976, pp. 29–34, repr. in Watson, *Politics and Literature in Modern Britain* (London: Macmillan, 1977) pp. 110–19. The reviewer of Watson's book in *The Times Literary Supplement*, 21 July 1978, p. 826, found the chapter on Lawrence unconvincing but was unable to bring evidence to bear in order to substantiate his disquiet.
2.   Letter to Rolf Gardiner, 3 Dec 1926, *CL*, pp. 950–3.
3.   See 'Nottingham's New University', *CP*, pp. 488–9.
4.   V. de S. Pinto, *Reginald Mainwaring Hewitt (1887–1948): A Selection from his Literary Remains* (Oxford: Blackwell, 1955) p. 18.
5.   See 'Nottingham's New University', *CP*, pp. 488–9.
6.   V. de S. Pinto, *D. H. Lawrence after Thirty Years* (Nottingham: University of Nottingham, 1960). For an earlier appreciation by Pinto of Lawrence see V. de Sola Pinto, *Prophet of the Midlands* (Nottingham: University of Nottingham, 1951).
7.   C. H. Rolph, *The Trial of Lady Chatterley* (Harmondsworth: Penguin, 1961) pp. 73–83.
8.   On Chambers see the obituary in *The Times*, 15 Apr 1970. He provides some background on his family in Nehls, III, 531–629.
9.   A theme he developed in his seminars on the Industrial Revolution with third-year undergraduates in 1960.
10. Raymond Williams, *Culture and Society* (Harmondsworth: Penguin, 1961) p. 201.
11. Such scenes are captured in the works set in the area, in particular *The White Peacock* (1911), *Sons and Lovers* (1913) and *Lady Chatterley's Lover* (1928). See also his essay 'Nottingham and the Mining Countryside', *New Adelphi*, June–Aug 1930, pp. 255–63. For later academic comment, see A. R. and C. P. Griffin, 'A Social and Economic History of Eastwood and the Nottinghamshire Mining Country', in *A D. H. Lawrence Handbook*, ed. Keith Sagar (Manchester: Manchester University Press, 1982) pp. 127–63. See also G. Holderness, *D. H. Lawrence: History, Ideology and Fiction* (Dublin: Gill and Macmillan, 1982) ch. 2, pp. 48–94.
12. Although the standard-of-living debate generated considerable interest in the late 1950s, there was very little discussion of literary evidence. For some later critical comment on literary sources as aids in understanding the industrialisation process in Britain, see J. M. Jefferson, 'Industrialisation and Poverty in Fact and Fiction', in *The Long Debate on Poverty* (London: Institute of Economic Affairs, 1972) pp. 189–238.
13. See the Introduction by J. D. Chambers to *ET*, 2nd edn (London: Cass, 1965); and J. D. Chambers, 'Memories of D. H. Lawrence', *Renaissance and Modern Studies*, XVI (1972) 5–17.

14. A selection of his work is collected in Watson, *Politics and Literature in Modern Britain*. For his early attempt to blend history and literature, see George Watson, *The English Ideology* (London: Allen Lane, 1973).

15. This remark appeared in Lawrence's autobiographical sketch and can be found in *D. H. Lawrence: Selected Literary Criticism*, ed. A. Beal (London: Heinemann, 1963).

16. C. Caudwell, 'D. H. Lawrence: A Study of the Bourgeois Artist', repr. in S. E. Hyman, *The Critical Performance* (New York: Random House, 1956) pp. 153–73.

17. *D. H. Lawrence: The Critical Heritage*, ed. R. Draper (London: Routledge and Kegan Paul, 1970) pp. 332ff.

18. F. R. Leavis, 'Keynes, Lawrence and Cambridge', *Scrutiny*, XVI (1949) 242–6; repr. in Leavis, *The Common Pursuit* (London: Chatto and Windus, 1952) pp. 254–60 (p. 258).

19. Watson, *Politics and Literature in Modern Britain*, p. 32.

20. Richard Hoggart, *The Uses of Literacy* (Harmondsworth: Penguin, 1959) p. 33.

21. Williams, *Culture and Society*, p. 205.

22. Terry Eagleton, *Criticism and Ideology* (London: New Left Books, 1976) p. 157.

23. Watson, *Politics and Literature in Modern Britain*, p. 30.

24. Ibid.

25. See J. D. Chambers, Introduction to *ET*, p. xv. In *Renaissance and Modern Studies*, XVI, 7, Chambers placed greater emphasis on the variable levels of butty pay, depending on whether the butty obtained a good stall (section of the coalface) on which to work. Watson does not stress this qualification and his work does not recognise this change of emphasis.

26. Watson, *Politics and Literature in Modern Britain*, p. 30.

27. Ibid., p. 33.

28. Ibid.

29. R. Goffee, 'The Butty System in the Kent Coalfield', *Bulletin of the Society for the Study of Labour History*, no. 34 (Spring 1977) p. 42, notes the need for further research into the butty system. Jessie Chambers (*ET*, p. 16) mentions that a contribution to the Congregational chapel in Eastwood could secure a better type of stall. Hence the chapel's nickname, the 'Butty's Lump'. For a discussion of the butty system at Brinsley, see C. P. Griffin, 'The Social Origins of D. H. Lawrence: Some Further Evidence', *Literature and History*, VII (1981) 223–7.

30. See Griffin, 'The Social Origins of D. H. Lawrence'.

31. Nehls, I, 21 (evidence of Hopkin) and 10 (evidence of Ada Lawrence) provides evidence on Arthur Lawrence which supports my argument. For an affirmation of Lawrence's working-class origins, see *Letters*, I, p. 6.

32. Nehls, I, 16–17. For one particularly poor week, see G. Neville, *A Memoir of D. H. Lawrence*, ed. C. Baron (Cambridge: Cambridge University Press, 1981) p. 49.

33. See Griffin, 'The Social Origins of D. H. Lawrence'. For a recent loose acceptance of the Lawrences' evidence see Philip Callow, *Son and Lover* (London: Bodley Head, 1975) pp. 26–7.

14   *D. H. Lawrence: New Studies*

34. Watson, *Politics and Literature in Modern Britain*, p. 30.
35. Nehls, III, 31.
36. Ibid., p. 30.
37. Ibid., p. 9. See G. D. H. Cole, *A Short History of the British Working-Class Movement, 1789–1937* (London: Allen and Unwin, 1960) pp. 152ff. for the ambience of self-improvement after the mid nineteenth century.
38. Harry Moore, *The Intelligent Heart* (Harmondsworth: Penguin, 1960) pp. 43 and 46; and Nehls, III, 605. See *ET*, p. 75, for evidence of Lawrence saving up to pay for himself at University College, Nottingham. Ada Lawrence (*ET*, pp. 16–17), comments upon her mother's careful management.
39. Watson, *Politics and Literature in Modern Britain*, p. 32.
40. Pinto, *Prophet*, pp. 7–8 refers to cultural differences. For a recent discussion, see R. Spencer, *Lawrence Country* (London: Cecil Woolf, 1979) pp. 56–83.
41. On marginality see, *inter alia*, H. F. Dickie Clark, *The Marginal Situation* (London: Routledge and Kegan Paul, 1966). Although Mrs Lawrence had well-authenticated interests in literature, this does not mean that she would have approved of the precarious financial literary life which D. H. Lawrence pursued. Her concern was for her children to acquire professional respectability and security. In fact, Lawrence defied the career expectations of both his parents. See Graham Holderness, 'Lawrence, Leavis and Culture', *Working Papers in Cultural Studies* University of Birmingham, no. 5 (Spring 1974) pp. 94–6. Lawrence's marginality is hinted at but not directly mentioned in Graham Hough, *The Dark Sun* (London: Duckworth, 1956) p. 90. Most of the themes referred to in this categorisation of Lawrence are touched upon in Brian Jackson, *Working-Class Community* (London: Routledge and Kegan Paul, 1968) pp. 15–17. For Watson's passing reference to 'Red Herring', see *Encounter*, Dec 1976, pp. 32–3. Moore, *The Intelligent Heart*, p. 27, argues that Lawrence exaggerates the class differences within his family, noting that Arthur Lawrence had 'no genuine seasoned proletarian heritage'. But this underplays the fact that for D. H. Lawrence the crucial issue was the immediate one, that his father and mother represented opposing cultures derived from their different occupational backgrounds.
42. See Watson's article 'Race and the Socialists', *Encounter*, Nov 1976, pp. 15–23.
43. Referred to in 1960 in Chambers's third-year seminars on general economic history. The major fruit of this research was his paper 'Enclosure and Labour Supply in the Industrial Revolution', *Economic History Review*, V (1952–3) 319–43. On Dobb, see the obituary in *The Times*, 19 Aug 1976.
44. A point emphasised by a former Nottingham student, G. E. Mingay, in 'The Contribution of a Regional Historian: J. D. Chambers 1898–1970', *Studies in Burke and his Time*, XIII (1971) 2007. The same point is made but from a differing ideological viewpoint by F. K. Donnelly in 'Ideology and Early English Working-Class History: Edward Thompson and his Critics', *Social History*, no. 2 (May 1976) pp. 219–38.
45. In the words of Watson, *Politics and Literature in Modern Britain*, p. 32,

the belief that Lawrence had working-class origins amounted to 'a standard intellectual socialist myth by the 1950s'.

46. Nehls, III, xxi, refers to the withholding of Metropolitan Police material on the exhibition of Lawrence's paintings which was raided in London in 1929.
47. J. R. Harrison, *The Reactionaries* (London: Gollancz, 1966), needs careful watching in this connection. See the wise and cautionary general remarks in Hough, *The Dark Sun*, p. 239.
48. For an affirmative general comment on the intercommunion of the disciplines and the need to perceive society as an interconnecting totality, see R. H. Tawney, 'Social History and Literature', in Tawney, *The Radical Tradition*, ed. Rita Hinden (London: Allen and Unwin, 1964) pp. 183–4. Watson, in *Politics and Literature in Modern Britain*, p. 9, acknowledges the risks of any enterprise which defies conventional boundaries.

2

The Poetry of
D. H. Lawrence

R. P. DRAPER

As Richard Hoggart pointed out some time ago (in a review of *The Complete Poems* published in the *Listener*, 29 October 1964), there is a wide variety of tone in Lawrence's poetry, but in the main it falls into two kinds: the vatic or rapturous (which Hoggart calls the 'prophetic or mystical voice') and the more down-to-earth, colloquially familiar voice of his working-class background. Some readers might wish to identify the dialect poems as belonging to a third kind; and yet a fourth group – nostalgic in tone and *fin de sièce* in style – might be found in the early poems written on the theme of the mother and about Lawrence's relationships with the soulful women he knew before he met Frieda. But the dialect poems and the poems of the colloquially familiar voice, especially as this is expressed in *Pansies* and *Nettles*, are similar in attitude and manner (it is in *Pansies* that the actual use of dialect reappears after a period of several years' absence), and many of the early poems, though the variation of theme and mood is such as to make generalisation more hazardous, share the rapt, incantatory rhetoric of 'Almond Blossom' and 'Bavarian Gentians'. Throughout his poetic career both the vatic and the colloquial are present in varying degrees; and this would seem to be so because they represent the two poles of a basic Lawrencean duality which gives rise to action and reaction – a poetry of alternating moods – but also to a poetry in which Lawrence seeks to establish a connection between the two.

In certain poems the struggle to effect such a connection betrays itself in a faltering eagerness which inevitably topples over into failure, yet gives the verse a touching liveliness half redeeming the lack of success. An example is 'Virgin Youth', a poem of adolescent sexuality in which the first embarrassed stirring of the phallus provokes contradictory and unreconciled attitudes, with corresponding shifts and slides of tone. It begins with a comment on those revelatory moments (they are new, and therefore revelatory, to the adolescent) when normal consciousness,

16

symbolised by daylight vision and speech, is superseded by the instinctual movement of desire:

> Now and again
> The life that looks through my eyes
> And quivers in words through my mouth,
> And behaves like the rest of men,
> Slips away, so I gasp in surprise.
>
> (*CP*, p. 38)

This initiates a stirring of the unconscious rhythms – what Lawrence elsewhere calls the 'dark gods' – before which the 'I' of the poem stands trembling with a quasi-religious awe. A sense of divinity is aroused, and this, it seems, needs to be expressed either in terms of the negative attributes of mysticism ('without sound, / Without eyes, without hands'), or the positive symbolism of the Old Testament:

> Yet, flame of the living ground
> He stands, the column of fire by night.
>
> (*CP*, p. 39)

The biblical 'column of fire' is also, however, the absurdly erect penis, which, like the John Thomas of Lady Chatterley's gamekeeper, is a perky, independent creature. The very force which is felt as the overwhelming power of the unconscious is also regarded as the agent of a comic and slightly embarrassing physical reaction with a will of its own like an impudent collier who will not show respect to his 'betters':

> Then willy nilly
> A lower me gets up and greets me;
> Homunculus stirs from his roots, and strives until,
> Risen up, he beats me.
>
> (*CP*. p. 39)

Later the futility of the risen penis that cannot 'ply' its 'twofold dance' in 'the womanly valley' (another metaphor awkwardly compounded of both symbolism and euphemism) becomes an expression of the pain of frustration; and finally the 'I' asks pardon for his failure to have the courage of his desire, while at the same time offering the excuse that it is society ('the hosts of men') which denies him the chance.

The confusions and stylistic inconsistencies of this poem, like its rather inept use of rhyme, can be attributed quite simply to the immaturity of a poet who is the victim of an unresolved ambiguity in his responses to his own sexuality; but the way of making it a better poem would not have been for the poet to focus his attention on a single, isolated response. There is, as it happens, a short earlier version of 'Virgin Youth' (printed by Pinto and Roberts in Appendix III of *The Complete Poems*) which concentrates more exclusively on the rhapsodic passion of the desire-flooded body, and as a result is a more single-minded and unified poem. In this version there is less apparent uncertainty of tone – no disconcerting 'willy nilly', no 'homunculus', and no comic self-questioning. The inclusion of such elements in the revised version adds a complication which undermines the unity of the poem, but at the same time increases its psychological interest. They suggest a greater determination to be frank and honest and a more critical attitude, taking into account the simultaneous presence of wonder and mocking doubt in the poet's response to his experience. The transitions made necessary by the introduction of this more complex material are awkwardly managed, and the new inconsistencies fail to achieve an aesthetically satisfying resolution; but the revised version none the less constitutes a more attractive and memorable poem than the simpler, more coherent original.

The popular notion that Lawrence has a narrow sex-obsessed range is not true of his novels, stories or plays, and, if anything, is even less true of his poetry. The early work is often tinged with an Edwardian preciousness, but even the casual reader cannot miss the variety of subjects and stances which the poet is exploring. He calls on the full range of his experience, including not only the love affairs with Jessie, Louie, Helen and others, but also the relationship with his mother, and his college and teaching experiences. Poems such as 'The Wild Common', 'Love on the Farm' and 'Snap-Dragon' are in one sense concerned with nascent sexuality, but their contact with the world of external nature is detailed and immediate; and the self-discovery which is their theme extends to a realization of hidden instinctual forces of which sex is only one manifestation. The dialect poems (notably 'The Collier's Wife') are astonishingly impersonal dramatisations of communal material in which Lawrence becomes the spokesman for a particular kind of working-class experience; and, different again, a whole group of underrated poems record his reactions to London and its suburbs – an urban environment alien to the industrial–pastoral world of Eastwood, but revealing to the young provincial a range of cosmopolitan possibilities which tantalise his imagination.

In some of these poems Lawrence can be seen in the act of wondering at the disparate nature of his experience, and seeking for a form capable of linking his scattered impressions together with the haphazard, yet organic, connectedness which they have in actual life. Here he is as 'modern' in his disconcerting juxtapositions as T. S. Eliot or Virginia Woolf. Unlike them, however, he emphasises continuity rather than discontinuity – not the fragmentariness of a disintegrated conscious-ness, but the flexibility of a stretched awareness and its plastic adaptability to what may seem logically and rationally discrete areas of experience.

'Embankment at Night, Before the War: Outcasts' is just such a flawed, but interestingly experimental, poem. The very naïveté of its language and structure helps one to see its constituent elements more clearly. To begin with, there is the word-painting of a verbal Whistler who finds a new kind of beauty in the rapprochement between art and nature divined in a city nightscape. The brilliantly illuminated trams passing over the Thames bridge create an artificial, yet curiously natural-seeming, glamour, as emphasised by the slightly strained 'bridge–midge' rhyme and, in the last line of the following passage, by the conjunction of the river's dark tidal movement with the man-made light glancing on its surface:

> Under the bridge
> Great electric cars
> Sing through, and each with a floor-light racing
>   along at its side.
> Far off, oh, midge after midge
> Drifts over the gulf that bars
> The night with silence, crossing the lamp-touched tide.
>
> (*CP*, p. 144)

This imagist painting is followed by a change of focus to the outcasts sleeping beneath the bridge, 'Packed in a line with their heads against the wall'. The intention is perhaps to stir the reader's conscience and make him sympathetically aware of the 'wastrels' who are ignored by the electrically lit city and its theatre-goers passing by under their umbrellas. Very little is done, however, to emphasise the sense of social injustice – though it is implicit in the emotional colouring of such phrases as 'huddled rags' and 'low black heap', and more explicit in the line, 'The white bare bone of our shams'. What is more prominent is the imaginative curiosity playing over the beauty-in-ugliness of the sleepers:

> Eloquent limbs
> In disarray,
> Sleep-suave limbs of a youth with long, smooth thighs
> Hutched up for warmth; the muddy rims
> Of trousers fray
> On the thin bare shins of a man who uneasily lies.
>
> > (*CP*, p. 145)

Compassion dissolves into the aesthetic pleasure derived from a carefully composed picture somewhat too self-consciously 'eloquent'; but the search for a new kind of picturesque has its compensations. The eye is stimulated, and relations are perceived which hold out the possibility of an original conception of the elements composing the picture.

  Gradually it becomes apparent that the realism is not enlisted primarily for social criticism, but is part of an effort to penetrate the psychological aspects of the experience more deeply. The bridge itself becomes a funereal 'pall' covering 'this human blight', and the indifferent theatre-goers defend themselves from the Circean spell of recognition by

> Holding aloft their umbrellas that flash and are bright
> Like flowers of infernal moly.
>
> > (*CP*, p. 146)

The mythological dimension thus introduced is a shade pretentious. It does not yet seem to be an organic part of a total vision; but the direction in which Lawrence is trying to move the poem is apparent. Out of an aesthetic reshaping of the experience he is trying to conjure a deeper awareness of it, and relate it to a wider, more evocative context. Most ambitiously of all, the final lines seek to combine the pictorial and the psychological in a comment on the relationship between light and dark:

> The factories on the Surrey side
> Are beautifully laid in black on a gold-grey sky.
> The river's invisible tide
> Threads and thrills like ore that is wealth to the eye.
>
> And great gold midges
> Cross the chasm
> At the bridges
> Above intertwined plasm.
>
> > (*CP*, p. 146)

This does not come off, but the attempt is interesting. The pictorial contrasts arrest our attention, and the juxtaposition of the midge-like trams with the hidden tidal movement of the river achieves an authentically Lawrencean effect.

There is a similarity here between the poetry and those passages in the novels where Lawrence tries to combine symbolism and realism in a new and revealing relationship. It is perhaps only a hint, or at best an unrealised potentiality, in 'Embankment at Night', but in such a poem as 'The North Country', which reads as almost a variant of certain pages in *Women in Love*, the similarity becomes virtual identity. Its vision of 'the man-life north imprisoned' in a purple landscape is at one with the blackened, corrupt Derbyshire countryside and the machine-enchanted people which both attract and repel Gudrun (in the chapter of *Women in Love* titled 'Coal-Dust'). Likewise, the hypnotic rhetoric – which some readers find so irritating in the novels, and which becomes a marked feature of much of the later poetry – is already present in the incantatory repetitions of 'The North Country':

> The air is *dark* with north and with sulphur,
>   the grass is a *darker* green,
> And people *darkly* invested with purple move palpable
>   through the scene.
>   (*CP*, p. 148; emphasis added)

The stress on 'dark' in these two lines passes over into 'gloom' in the next stanza, and the words 'north' and 'purple' become the key to more iterative rhetoric as the poem progresses. A booming resonance and somnambulistic motion in the second and third stanzas, created by further hypnotic repetitions, produce drugged cadences which aptly express the 'moaning of sleep-bound beings in travail that toil and are will-less there / In the spellbound north'; and, though the poem ends with the apocalyptic suggestion of a pent-up force that will burst out at last, the dominant impression remains that of a land and its people in a machine-induced trance.

Such poetry represents a significant advance in Lawrence's ability to fit language to his vision, and the fact that it runs parallel with great mythopoeic passages in the novels (and in the short stories, too) is indicative of a unified development of his sensibility and creative powers. But it also brings with it a danger which is greater for the poetry than it is for the prose. In Lawrence's prose the seductive spell of the rhetoric is counteracted by the wider context of human activity and the links with traditional realism which, notwithstanding the intensity of his vision and the technical originality which accompanies it, he still maintains in his novels and stories. The poetry, however, with its greater lyrical independence, is more able to withdraw into itself. On occasion it moves so deep into its vision world that, like the poetry of Baudelaire, to which the rhetoric of 'The North Country' is heavily indebted, it becomes absorbed in its own sonorous music. It then runs the risk of losing that balance between the ordinary and the exotic which is of peculiar importance to Lawrence.

As a critic, Lawrence recognised this danger, and his recognition led him to value the achievement of poetry below that of the novel. In his essay 'Why the Novel Matters' he claims that the novel covers a more variable and flexible range than any other form of expression, including poetry. It is the supreme medium for 'man alive'. This is why he himself is a novelist; and 'being a novelist', he says, 'I consider myself superior to the saint, the scientist, the philosopher, and the poet, who are all great masters of different bits of man alive, but never get the whole hog.' (*Ph*, p. 535). This essay must be regarded as to some extent polemical. The poet is obviously not as limited as Lawrence here represents him. That he sets the poet in such a light is almost certainly part of his reaction against a particular kind of poetry, and a kind which he himself often wrote, especially in his earlier volumes. But that is not his own best poetry. Lawrence is most successful, and most his individually distinctive self, in the poetry where he tries to 'get the whole hog'. This involves connecting the disturbing beauty of the visionary poetry with more familiar experience – and, often enough, with more sceptical attitudes to which the symbolic world is profoundly hostile. The result is a poetry which evokes something of a contradictory critical response. On the one hand, it has a particular kind of energy and imaginative appeal, deriving from the advances which are made into the symbolic territory towards which 'The North Country' points, expressed in its own incantatory rhetoric and highly characteristic verbal music. In this respect it is a poetry which denounces our familiar world and seeks to draw us with hypnotic power towards a superior, more life-enhancing alternative, demanding not only an attitude of sympathetic responsiveness, but a positive commitment to the revolutionary values which the poetry embodies. Frequently, however, a dramatic strategy is adopted which involves a voice resisting this appeal; and, though the 'meaning' of the poem may imply the subjugation of the resistant voice, and the recognition that it is damaging to the humanity for which the poem is arguing, the very presence of that voice is an extremely important addition to the tonal range of the whole poem. This is not merely a question of aesthetic satisfaction (though aesthetic satisfaction is certainly enhanced by the incorporation of a variety of sounds and rhythms which provide symphonic contrast to the resonant visionary music). The extension of the tonal range is an extension of the poem's meaning. It keeps different areas of experience alive and in touch with each other, thus implying a greater flexibility of attitude than either the visionary rhetoric or the sceptical opposition could achieve by itself. The poem's whole is thus greater than its parts, even though its purpose seems to include the triumph of one part over another.

The most obvious example of this process at work is 'Snake'. The 'I' of that poem is the nexus of two voices, one persuading him that the snake is 'a king in exile, uncrowned in the underworld, / Now due to be crowned again', the other rejecting in the name of 'human education' the seductive blandishments of the pro-snake voice. As far as its argument is concerned, the poem is certainly on the side of the snake. The language is loaded in its favour. Not only is the snake 'like a god', 'like a king', but the sympathetic feelings which it arouses ('I felt so honoured', for example) are given approval, while the revulsion which it excites is condemned as an inferior, even unnatural response induced by conscious training:

I thought how paltry, how vulgar, what a mean act!
I despised myself and the voices of my accursed human education.

(CP, p. 351)

Viewed in the context provided by the rest of Lawrence's writings, the snake is readily identified as a representative of those unconscious forces which he persistently commends as life-affirming, and the persona's rejection of the snake is part of that hyperconsciousness which Lawrence deplores, the root evil of modern Western civilisation. In its total effect, however, the poem, *qua* poem, transcends its 'message', indispensable though the message is to the poem's vigour and capacity for arresting our attention. The experience of reading the poem is an experience of fluctuation between the two opposite poles, and its language is a corresponding alternation – or even, at times, interpenetration – of two different styles. The 'snake' style is a powerfully evocative, repetitive, incantatory rhetoric. The following passage, for example, makes full use of all the traditional resources of alliteration, assonance, repetition (or near-repetition) of words, and repetition of parallel (or near-parallel) syntactical structures, with particular emphasis on continuous forms in

'-ing', which add to the overall hypnotic effect a sense of continuity that seems timeless, or at least immune from the time-ridden preoccupations and anxieties of human life:

> He lifted his head from his drinking, as cattle do,
> And looked at me vaguely, as drinking cattle do,
> And flickered his two-forked tongue from his lips,
>   and mused a moment,
> And stooped and drank a little more,
> Being earth-brown, earth-golden from the burning
>   bowels of the earth
> On the day of Sicilian July, with Etna smoking.
>
> (*CP*, p. 349)

In sharp contrast are the interjections of the 'voice of my education', quite bare of the colour and seductive rhythms associated with the snake, and the abrupt, staccato style used to express the action of throwing the log:

> I looked round, I put down my pitcher,
> I picked up a clumsy log
> And threw it at the water-trough with a clatter.
>
> (*CP*, p. 351)

These represent a stylistic antithesis to the repetitive rhetoric of the poem, its incompatible polar opposite. And yet, despite their seeming incompatibility, there is a link between the two styles. A carefully premeditated complex syntax is alien to both; each is based on a loose, co-ordinate, polysyndetic sentence structure, casual in manner and informal in movement. Moreover, occasional phrases infiltrate the pro-snake rhetoric which might seem discordant with it and risk toppling it over into absurdity, but which in some curious way are none the less perfectly acceptable. This is the case, for example, with the phrase 'Seeming to lick his lips' in the following passage:

> He drank enough
> And lifted his head, dreamily, as one who has drunken,
> And flickered his tongue like a forked night on the air, so black;
> Seeming to lick his lips,
> And looked around like a god, unseeing, into the air,
> And slowly turned his head.
>
> (*CP*, p. 350)

The commonplace 'lick his lips' is an incongruous, slightly ridiculous touch in this otherwise richly evocative passage. Yet it comes off – partly because of the continuity provided by kindred sounds in the rhetorical sequence, 'lifted his . . .flickered his . . . lick his lips . . . looked . . . like . . . his head'; and partly because of the suggestion which it carries that the snake, in spite of his opposition to 'accursed human education', has something in common with general humanity. (This suggestion is also kept alive elsewhere in the poem by such linguistic details as the regular use of 'he' rather than 'it' for the snake, the comparison of the snake to 'a god' and 'a king', and the reference to the snake's hole as 'the dark *door* of the secret earth'.)

'Snake' thus offers the reader a paradox: it is a dialectical poem working through contrasting styles which voice antithetical attitudes to life, and yet there is also important common ground between the two styles. It is not, however, a poem of paradox in the seventeenth-century 'Metaphysical' manner. When the poem is considered as a whole it is the common ground rather than the clashing opposites which seems most significant. Although the title points to the snake, and within the poem the snake is presented sympathetically while the observer, the authorial 'I', is criticised for his 'pettiness', the 'I' is as much a part of the whole poem as the snake – and arguably more. The snake is summoned not to displace the 'I', but to be recognised as an essential, if neglected, element in the potentially fuller life of that 'I'. And what the fuller life is we must judge, not by what we are told the snake represents, but by the sense of balance which emerges from the commerce between the opposed styles of the poem. The snake embodies something within the 'I', a suppressed part of the persona's own humanity without which he must fail to realise himself, and the poem stirs awareness of the need for reintegration of the snake-element into a larger humanity; but the real achievement of the poem is the relationship which it establishes between its opposites and the example it thereby offers of a whole rather than divided being.

Certain poems, not necessarily the best, make this flexible relationship their own theme. It is adumbrated in 'Bei Hennef', spelt out in 'The Evangelistic Beasts', and used as a constant springboard for satire in *Pansies*, *Nettles* and 'More Pansies'. Of 'The Evangelistic Beasts' 'St Matthew' is the most explicit. Matthew is a man; he will be lifted up by the Saviour, but he will be set down again on 'The crumbling, damp, fresh land, life horizontal and ceaseless'. He does not belong permanently to a state of spiritual exaltation, nor, by implication, permanently to 'the avenues where the bat hangs sleeping, upside-down':

> But I, Matthew, being a man
> Am a traveller back and forth.
>
> (*CP*, p. 323)

As in 'Snake', there is a reaction against the spiritualised pole to which, in Lawrence's view, man is excessively drawn, and this gives the poem its necessary point of attack. But the more important purpose of the poem is to keep man free in a basic detachment, to let him continue his travelling back and forth rather than to urge him finally towards some alternative goal. And, if we turn to those poems in which Lawrence does show himself at his best, those in which he realises his own special poetic self, it will be found that, notwithstanding a surface energy of involvement and commitment, the clue to their success lies in an underlying detachment.

Lawrence's greatest poems are generally about non-human life, but, as with 'Snake', despite their titles, humanity often proves to be their real subject. Again as with 'Snake', humanity emerges via the style, i.e. through that concert of voices which creates the distinctively Lawrencean tone. 'Fish', for example, is a poem which takes as its subject the elusive otherness of fish life; but the rhetorical negatives which purport to separate the fish from the sentimental intimacies of human living and loving give, by so doing, satirical emphasis to those very qualities:

> But oh, fish, that rock in water,
> You lie only with the waters;
> One touch.
> No fingers, no hands and feet, no lips;
> No tender muzzles,
> No wistful bellies,
> No loins of desire,
> None.
>
> (*CP*, p. 335)

It is a cool, ironic poem (except towards the end, when it becomes both more didactic and less alert and alive), concerned with the satisfying imagination of a sexuality freed from the clichés and overworked emotions associated with the intercourse not only of men and women, but also of beasts and even snakes ('Even snakes lie together'). The independence of the fish gives a sense of delighted release from the overheated involvements of human love; but the poem's underlying preoccupation is human inflexibility and the need for greater freedom.

Similarly, the Tortoise sequence of poems is concerned with an animal sexuality which seems absurdly remote from the human variety, but actually derives both its comedy and tragedy from continual analogy with human mating. These poems express what Lawrence seems to want to express in certain parts of *Lady Chatterley's Lover*, but fails to bring off there – the insistent, virtually tyrannical force of the sexual drive which can make the human beings under its influence seem both beautiful and ridiculous. In *Lady Chatterley* he can at best only alternate a mood of disenchanted ridicule (haunches prancing in the act of love) with one of healing and purifying passion, while the novel's basically romantic didacticism ensures that it is the latter which triumphs. In the Tortoise poems, however, the contradictory moods exist simultaneously: sex is at once a crucifixion, a Dionysiac rapture, and an absurd, ignominious compulsion (though still recognised as something touchingly intimate). The language in which it is expressed is an appropriately tender-ridiculous series of paradoxes, summed up representatively in 'Tortoise Gallantry' by the characterisation of the tortoise lover as

> Stiff, gallant, irascible, crook-legged reptile,
> Little gentleman,
> Sorry plight,
> We ought to look the other way.
>
> (*CP*, p. 363)

A tortoise is the subject, but his predicament becomes a very human comment on a very human dilemma.

With poems such as 'Peach' and 'Bat' the Lawrencean manner is so elusive as to run the risk of being mistaken for slightness and triviality. Both are poems, however, in which the medium is the message. 'Bat' is an imagistic poem, it images the effect of an evocative newness of vision expressed in disconcertingly familiar terms:

> Swallows with spools of dark thread sewing the shadows together.
> . . .
> A twitch, a twitter, an elastic shudder in flight
> And serrated wings against the sky,
> Like a glove, a black glove thrown up at the light,
> And falling back.
> . . .
> Wings like bits of umbrella.
> . . .

Hanging upside down like rows of disgusting old rags
And grinning in their sleep.

(*CP*, pp. 340–2)

From all this the bat emerges as a creature that is weird, yet memorable; obnoxious, yet understandable; and, if not lovable, at least in some curious way acceptable. It becomes, as the snake does, an extension of human experience, but without the same visionary dimension. The value of the experience consists in the articulation of it: the stretching of the imagination to create those bizarre images, and the plasticity of rhythm and syntax which allows them to emerge in such a convincingly dramatic way.

'Peach', too, is imagistic and dramatic, but with more emphasis on its implicit debate. An unspecified interlocutor – the 'you' of the first line, and the person to whom the peach stone is handed in the last – is present throughout as target for the poem's seeming whimsicality. The typically contrasted voices are unusually marked here. The middle section, on the sensuous qualities of the peach, is a highly elaborate piece of rhetorical parallelism:

Why so velvety, why so voluptuous heavy?
Why hanging with such inordinate weight?
Why so indented?

Why the groove?
Why the lovely, bivalve roundnesses?
Why the ripple down the sphere?
Why the suggestion of incision?

while other lines drop to a deliberately off-hand, prosaic flatness: 'I am thinking, of course, of the peach before I ate it' and 'And because I say so, you would like to throw something at me' (*CP*, p. 279).

If there is a message it is that the natural is unpredictably organic, not 'round and finished' like the man-made billiard ball. But the human and the natural are not fundamentally at variance. The contrast is rather between the vitally human and the deadening influence of the self-consciously human, the poem itself, with its elusive, flickering rhythms and changeable style, being an expression and examplification of what it is to be vitally human. On the surface whimsical and inconsistent, its unity consists in its faithfulness to the shifting tones and accents of 'the whole man'.

The nearest Lawrence comes to a formal, critical manifesto for this kind of poetry is in the Introduction to the American edition of *New Poems* (1920). There he rejects what he calls the 'exquisite finality, perfection' of poetry which belongs either to the future or the past, and makes a claim instead for a poetry of process, of 'the immediate present':

> But there is another kind of poetry: the poetry of that which is at hand: the immediate present. In the immediate present there is no perfection, no consummation, nothing finished. The strands are all flying, quivering, intermingling into the web, the waters are shaking the moon. There is no round, consummate moon on the face of running water, nor on the face of the unfinished tide. . . . There is no plasmic finality, nothing crystal, permanent. . . . If you tell me about the lotus, tell me of nothing changeless or eternal. Tell me of the mystery of the inexhaustible, forever-unfolding creative spark. Tell me of the incarnate disclosure of the flux, mutation in blossom, laughter and decay perfectly open in their transit, nude in their movement before us. (*CP*, p. 182).

His own best poetry in the years immediately following this manifesto is a remarkable realisation of what is there announced. It is a poetry which captures the very quick of changeableness; its 'strands are all flying'; it not merely tells, but re-creates, 'the incarnate disclosure of the flux'. It is perhaps the very highest achievement in the whole body of Lawrence's poetry. There is, however, some shift of emphasis in the poems he wrote during the last years of the 1920s – the poems edited and posthumously published by Aldington and Orioli under the title 'Last Poems'.[1] Many of these form a series of meditations and variations on the theme of death. Lawrence himself was a recurrently sick man at this period with very clear intimations of his own approaching end, and the impetus which this gives to his treatment of the theme is self-evident. It is not, however, a new theme for him. It is one which had occurred frequently in his earlier work and which is particularly noticeable in the letters he wrote during the 1914–18 war. His letter, for example, of 9 November 1915, written to Lady Cynthia Asquith from Garsington Manor, Oxfordshire, strikingly anticipates the seasonal imagery and even some of the phrasing of 'The Ship of Death':

> When I drive across this country, with autumn falling and rustling to pieces, I am so sad, for my country, for this great wave of civilisation, 2000 years, which is now collapsing, that it is hard to live . . . the past, the great past, crumbling down, breaking down, not under the force

of the coming buds, but under the weight of many exhausted lovely yellow leaves, that drift over the lawn, and over the pond, like the soldiers, passing away, into winter and the darkness of winter – no, I can't bear it. For the winter stretches ahead, where all vision is lost and all memory dies out.   (*Letters*, II, pp. 431–2)

What lies behind this letter is the thought not of personal death, but of the death of European civilisation, with its – from Lawrence's point of view – excessive emphasis on mental consciousness. The war seemed to Lawrence a part of this death movement, involving destruction and annihilation which has an awful air of finality about it, but as the autumnal imagery implies, is not ultimately final. New life lay hidden in the wintry bleakness, and – since winter must precede spring, is, indeed, a condition of renewal – the destructive movement was therefore to be welcomed. This apocalyptic, destructive–creative view of contemporary civilisation did, however, pose a problem for Lawrence which was never clearly resolved in his work. It is formulated in the poem 'To Let Go or to Hold On – ?' (published July 1929), where alternative responses to the death movement are contemplated. One possibility is to swim with the ebbing tide:

> Shall we let go,
> and allow the soul to find its level
> downwards, ebbing downwards, ebbing downwards to the flood?
>
> (*CP*, p. 428)

The other possibility is to resist, and call for one last effort to bring about a change:

> Or else, or else
> shall a man brace himself up
> and lift his face and set his breast
> and go forth to change the world?
>
> (*CP*, p. 428)

Choice between these alternatives is never actually made. Throughout the poem variations on the possibilities continue to be entertained, always in the interrogative form, and the climax is a recapitulation of the choice:

> Must we hold on?
> Or can we now let go?
>
> (*CP*, p. 429)

The conclusion of the poem, however, is yet to come; and it takes the form of one further, tantalising question: 'Or is it even possible we must do both?' (*CP*, p. 429).

To do both is not a possibility but an impossibility – a seemingly illogical ducking of the issue. But it is a vital illogicality, in line with the illogicality which informs the best of Lawrence's poetry. It expresses the contradictoriness which most readers can recognise as part of their own experience when they are faced, for example, with the impossibility of believing that mankind will act sanely enough to prevent his annihilation by his own weapons of mass destruction, and yet feel compelled to live and act from day to day in the hope that sanity will prevail. Such a reaction is of a piece with the contradictory voices incorporated in such a poem as 'Peach'. The poem 'To Let Go or to Hold On – ?', however, lacks the stylistic balance of 'Peach'. It is far more convincing, i.e. more poetically persuasive, when contemplating the possibility of collapse rather than the possibility of holding on. Then it acquires the incantatory seductive power of the Lawrencean rhetorical voice:

> Tell me first, O tell me,
> will the dark flood of our day's annihilation
> swim deeper, deeper, till it leaves no peak emerging?
> Shall we be lost, all of us
> and gone like weed, like weed, like eggs of fishes,
> like sperm of whales, like germs of the great dead past
> into which the creative future shall blow strange,
>   unknown forms?

(CP, p. 428)

The resemblances to the 'Last Poems' also become more marked. For this, both with its strengths and limitations, is the dominant voice of Lawrence's final poems on death.

The two most celebrated – and deservedly so – are 'Bavarian Gentians' and 'The Ship of Death'. In these poems repetition is almost exclusively incantatory. The reiterated, slightly modified phrases lead the reader towards a trance-like condition of acquiescence in the universal death process. On the positive side, the rhetoric is creative in that it induces a relaxation of the will without which, for Lawrence, the detachment from the old, exhausted civilisation necessary for the renewal hinted at the end of 'The Ship of Death' would be incomplete and therefore ineffective. By comparison with *Birds, Beasts and Flowers*, however, these poems are less complex and their rhythms narcotic. They are spells to induce the reader, and the poet himself, to accept the inevitable. In the finest possible sense of the phrase they are death-bed poems.

Of course, such a generalised impression does not do justice to the more detailed texture of his poetry. Tensions exist within the language and imagery of 'The Ship of Death', as they do in the earlier poems of process. These are, however, on a smaller scale, and they constitute only a minor, muted part of the total effect. Thus the furnishing of the little ship, 'with its store of food and little cooking pans / and change of clothes' (*CP*, p. 719), is a reminder of the commonplace world of eating and dressing in contrast with the surrounding imagery of autumnal decay and annihilating floodwaters. Such hints of warmth and intimacy certainly provide a welcome relief from the tense, hieratic mood pervading most of 'The Ship of Death'; but, even so, they lack the conversational familiarity of 'Bat' and 'Peach'. In 'The Ship of Death' language is raised to a more sombre plane. Speech is addressed to the reader, and the poet communes with himself, but invariably with a sense of gravity – even, in a way that is unusual for Lawrence, with a touch of literary self-consciousness. (Hence, for example, the Shakespearean allusiveness of 'And can a man his own quietus make / with a bare bodkin?')

The opening of 'Bavarian Gentians', with its easy, relaxed 'Not every man has gentians in his house' is again an echo of the earlier Lawrence; but this poem, too, quickly turns from the recognisable world and speech of everyday to enraptured concentration on the subtly changing 'blaze of darkness' into which the flower is transformed. By a remarkable originality in the varying of his verbal material, coupled with an equally original adaptation of the Pluto-Persephone myth, Lawrence draws the reader down a spiral of descent into his own mysterious underworld where the laws of daylight reality no longer apply, where darkness itself is a kind of illumination, and death a creative marriage feast. The last line ('among the splendour of torches of darkness, shedding darkness on the lost bride and her groom') is magnificent, but as remote as it could be from the first – and from the Lawrence of earlier days.

Exception must also be made for particular poems such as 'Red Geranium and Godly Mignonette' with its delightfully down-to-earth conception of divinity; and for 'The Greeks are Coming' and 'Middle of the World', which evoke a pre-Christian world with the same unpretentious ease that Lawrence believed that world itself possessed. But these poems *are* exceptions; the norm of 'Last Poems' is the tone and mood of 'Bavarian Gentians' and 'The Ship of Death'. Beautiful as these poems are, they represent what must be recognised as a departure and decline from that flexible commerce between vatic and colloquial which gives the *Birds, Beasts and Flowers* volume its special status. It is in this poetry that Lawrence realizes his wish to communicate 'the Whole Man', and in so doing successfully transcends his own limitations. It is a poetry less obviously experimental than that of many more determinedly 'modernist' poets, but more genuinely fresh and new; and so much a purely personal achievement that it is perhaps impossible for others to imitate. That Lawrence himself seemed to lose touch with it in his very latest work is perhaps an indication of how much it depended on the sensitive awareness of a vitally alert imagination plying confidently on the complete range of experience. Once some of that vitality was gone, though the imagination remained potent, the essential flexibility was lost, and without it Lawrence's poetry could not continue to perform its unique balancing-act.[2]

NOTES

1. The volume was called *Last Poems* (1932), but divided into two sections under the headings 'Last Poems' and 'More Pansies'. The distinction is broadly valid, but some of the 'More Pansies' poems clearly overlap with those in the 'Last Poems' section, just as some of the poems included in the *Pansies* volume of 1929 do.

2. For my modified view of *Last Poems* and 'The Ship of Death', see my book *Lyric Tragedy* (Macmillan, 1985) ch. 7, 'D. H. Lawrence: Tragedy as Creative Crisis'.

3

Lawrence's Tragic Lovers: The Story and the Tale in *Women in Love*

NEIL ROBERTS

A part of our received wisdom about *Women in Love* is that the novel enacts a tragedy, at the centre of which is the character of Gerald Crich. As Pritchard explicitly puts it, 'Gerald is the tragic hero of *Women in Love*'.[1] The imaginative breadth and power of the final episodes in the Alps, the complex and convincing sense of Gerald's representativeness, above all the fact that unlike most Lawrencean antagonists he has a large measure of certain indispensable human qualities, undoubtedly make the word 'tragedy' seem appropriate – perhaps uniquely so in Lawrence's *oeuvre*. And yet one finds in many commentaries a surprisingly bland acknowledgement that Gerald is *manipulated* by his author in a way that discredits him. The following passage, for example, occurs in Pritchard's study one page before the statement that Gerald is a tragic hero:

> Lawrence makes Gerald less complex and initiate in corruption than he was before, and clumsy and insensitive, in order to emphasise Loerke's nature; Gerald becomes for Gudrun the epitome of the brute and mechanical, while he becomes obsessed with desire for sexual self-obliteration in her. She turns to Loerke . . . .[2]

Much the same point is made by Colin Clarke when he remarks that earlier in the novel Birkin is the more innocent, whereas later 'it is Birkin who has to explain Loerke's significance to Gerald, whose earlier capacity for subtle knowledge in corruption seems to some extent to have deserted him'. Clarke sees the Gerald of the final episodes as 'just a little of a *Dummkopf*' and explains that 'the reason for this toning down is clear enough: a distinction needs to be drawn between Gerald's limited perversity and Loerke's far subtler capacities'.[3]

On such a reading it appears that Lawrence may interfere as he pleases with the imagined reality of his characters, for the sake of the thematic development, and still have the credit of a tragic artist. This seems to me unlikely. But before looking further into the particular case we need to be clearer about what, when discussing Lawrence, we might mean by 'tragedy'.

The most immediate stimulus to the rethinking of *Women in Love* behind my essay was Michael Black's humane and intelligent book *The Literature of Fidelity*, a study of love in several great European writers, in which Lawrence is a key figure. One of Black's chapters is entitled 'Lawrence and "that which is perfectly ourselves" '. The phrase comes from the 'Mino' chapter of the novel, in which Birkin, rejecting Ursula's demand for love, says, 'there needs the pledge between us, that we will both cast off everything, cast off ourselves even, and cease to be, so that that which is perfectly ourselves can take place in us'. It is needless to discuss the obvious objection to this passage, that you might conceive of the self as an onion, in which layer after layer can be cast off until there is nothing left. Such metaphysical speculations would be unprofitable. Lawrence is obviously making metaphysical assumptions, but I think it is reasonable to take him pragmatically on his own terms, and that the reality of the kind of radical personal reassessment Birkin is talking about is borne out by experience. But if we do take Lawrence on his own terms we still have to ask some important questions. It is easy to read the novel in a way which assumes that those who succeed in throwing off their ordinary selves are those who are creatively fulfilled, and those who don't succeed are the ones who meet some kind of personal disaster. On the one hand, Birkin and Ursula; on the other, Gerald, Gudrun and Hermione. Such a reading takes for granted – and Birkin in putting his case seems to take for granted – that 'that which is perfectly ourselves' is good.

But suppose it isn't? Suppose that what our ordinary selves hold down is something monstrous and destructive? Another of Michael Black's key works is *Phèdre*, and he argues that Racine would have responded to Birkin's words in just this way: that in the play the self that the heroine releases is effectively symbolised by the monster that destroys Hippolytus.[4]

There is another remark by Lawrence that has a close bearing on Birkin's statement. It comes at the end of the Preface to his play *Touch and Go* – in which, incidentally, the main characters of *Women in Love* reappear: 'The essence of tragedy, which is creative crisis, is that a man should go through with his fate, and not dodge it and go bumping into an accident. And the whole business of life, at the great critical periods of mankind, is that men should accept and be at one with their tragedy' (*PhII*, p. 293). This, I admit, is an obscure corner of Lawrence, but it provides a conveniently concise crystallisation of the more extended discussion of tragedy – the 'war with God' in Sophocles and Shakespeare as opposed to the lesser, socially determined tragedy of Hardy and Tolstoy – in the *Study of Thomas Hardy* (*Ph*, pp. 419–20). I don't think it is cheating to see a parallel between 'going through with your fate' and 'letting that which is perfectly ourselves take place in us'. Fate is, after all, largely an internal matter. Now, the word 'tragedy' would have no meaning if our fate, or our perfect self, were something reliably good, and if going through with our fate were sure to result in creative fulfilment.

I now want to turn to Gudrun, and to quote a passage from the novel in which a character is, I think, allowing that which is perfectly herself to take place in her. It is from the 'Water-Party' chapter, and Gudrun has just chased away Gerald's herd of cattle:

> 'You think I'm afraid of you and your cattle, don't you?' she asked.
>
> His eyes narrowed dangerously. There was a faint domineering smile on his face.
>
> 'Why should I think that?' he said.
>
> She was watching him all the time with her dark, dilated, inchoate eyes. She leaned forward and swung round her arm, catching him a blow on the face with the back of her hand.
>
> 'That's why,' she said.
>
> And she felt in her soul an unconquerable lust for deep brutality against him. She shut off the fear and dismay that filled her conscious mind. She wanted to do as she did, she was not going to be afraid. . . .
>
> 'You have struck the first blow,' he said at last, forcing the words from his lungs, in a voice so soft and low, it sounded like a dream within her, not spoken in the outer air.
>
> 'And I shall strike the last,' she retorted involuntarily, with confident assurance. He was silent, he did not contradict her.
>
> She stood negligently, staring away from him, into the distance. On the edge of her consciousness the question was asking itself, automatically:
>
> 'Why *are* you behaving in this *impossible* and ridiculous fashion?'
>
> But she was sullen, she half shoved the question out of herself. She could not get it clean away, so she felt self-conscious.
>
> (*WL*, pp. 236–7)

Gudrun's words and actions here are coming from her unconscious, unrecognised self. Her conscious self can only look on in amazement and embarrassment. And what these words and actions signify is that Gudrun is fated to see other people as a threat to herself, and intimate relationships as a battle. This is suggested in the opening chapter, when the two sisters walk through the mining town, and Gudrun cannot bear the proximity of the common people. It is still more strikingly indicated in the extraordinary scene in the hotel in the Alps, when Gudrun, seated at a mirror, sees Gerald standing behind her and cannot bring herself to turn round and face him.

Gudrun leaves Gerald for Loerke, the 'negation gnawing at the roots of life' as Birkin calls him, because Loerke unlike Gerald understands this fact about her innermost self and will enter into a relationship based on recognition of it.

How should Gerald hope to satisfy a woman of Gudrun's calibre? Did he think that pride or masterful will or physical strength would help him? Loerke knew a secret beyond these things. The greatest power is the one that is subtle and adjusts itself, not one which blindly attacks. And he had understanding where Gerald was a calf. He, Loerke, could penetrate into depths far out of Gerald's knowledge. Gerald was left behind like a postulant in the ante-room of this temple of mysteries, this woman. But he, Loerke, could he not penetrate into the inner darkness, find the spirit of the woman in its inner recess, and wrestle with it there, the central serpent that is coiled at the core of life.

What was it, after all, that a woman wanted? Was it mere social effect, fulfilment of ambition in the social world, in the community of mankind? Was it even a union in love and goodness? Did she want 'goodness'? Who but a fool would accept this of Gudrun? This was but the street view of her wants. Cross the threshold, and you found her completely, completely cynical about the social world and its advantages. Once inside the house of her soul, and there was a pungent atmosphere of corrosion, an inflamed darkness of sensation, and a vivid, subtle, critical consciousness, that saw the world distorted, horrific.

What then, what next? Was it sheer blind force of passion that would satisfy her now? Not this, but the subtle thrills of extreme sensation in reduction. It was an unbroken will reacting against her unbroken will in a myriad subtle thrills of reduction, the last subtleties of analysis and breaking down, carried out in the darkness of her, whilst the outside form, the individual, was utterly unchanged. even sentimental in its poses. (*WL*, p. 549).

In *River of Dissolution* Colin Clarke quotes Lawrence's essay 'The Reality of Peace': 'There is a natural marsh in my belly, and there the snake is naturally at home . . .' and summarises the burden of the essay: 'if the snake is not acknowledged he will declare himself with a peculiar, foul virulence. So it is with Egbert [in "England My England"], who begins now to be identified with the principle he has denied.'[5] The serpent declares himself with a most foul virulence in Gudrun, but not because she fails to acknowledge him. True, Lawrence writes, shortly after the passage quoted, 'All this Gudrun knew in her subconsciousness, not in her mind', but he nowhere suggests that the 'obscene religious mystery of ultimate reduction' between her and Loerke would be less obscene if she were conscious. And Loerke himself, the 'gnawing little negation', is perfectly conscious of the serpent.

The simple repression theory of the essay is not borne out by the novel. Indeed the second part of that essay from which Clarke's quotation comes, is (unlike the marvellous first part) not Lawrence at his most cogent. He instructs the serpent to 'keep to your own ways and your own being. Come in just proportion, there in the grass beneath the bushes where the birds are' (*Ph*, p. 679). This is a feat more easily accomplished in the rhapsodic mode of the essay than in life or an imaginative creation such as Gudrun.

Throughout the novel Lawrence communicates a respect for Gudrun that he does not seem to have for Gerald. The phrase 'a woman of Gudrun's calibre' comes from Loerke, implicitly endorsed by the author; earlier Birkin has said to Gerald, 'Do you think you can hire a woman like Gudrun Brangwen with money? She is your equal like anything – probably your superior' (*WL*, ch.16). (Gerald's implausible demur on this point, coming after the statement in chapter 8 that 'He wanted to come up to her standards, fulfil her expectations', is an example of the manipulation of his character.) A part of this respect for Gudrun is shown in the way that she, with Ursula and Birkin, shares a part of the novel's vision. There are places, notably the beginning of the 'Water-Party' chapter, in which we see events through Gudrun's eyes, not just in order that we learn something about her, but because she has perceptions that the novelist shares.

> People were standing about in groups, some women were sitting in the shade of the walnut tree, with cups of tea in their hands, a waiter in evening dress was hurrying round, some girls were simpering with parasols, some young men, who had just come in from rowing, were sitting cross-legged on the grass, coatless, their shirt-sleeves rolled up

in manly fashion, their hands resting on their white flannel trousers, their gaudy ties floating about, as they laughed and tried to be witty with the young damsels.

'Why,' thought Gudrun churlishly, 'don't they have the manners to put their coats on, and not to assume such intimacy in their appearance.'

She abhorred the ordinary young man, with his hair plastered back and his easy-going chumminess.

Hermione Roddice came up, in a handsome gown of white lace, trailing an enormous silk shawl blotched with great embroidered flowers, and balancing an enormous plain hat on her head. She looked striking, astonishing, almost macabre, so tall, with the fringe of her great cream-coloured vividly-blotched shawl trailing on the ground after her, her thick hair coming low over her eyes, her face strange and long and pale, and the blotches of brilliant colour drawn round her.

'Doesn't she look *weird*!' Gudrun heard some girls titter behind her. And she could have killed them.

'How do you do!' sang Hermione, coming up very kindly, and glancing slowly over Gudrun's father and mother. It was a trying moment, exasperating for Gudrun. Hermione was really so strongly entrenched in her class superiority, she could come up and know people out of simple curiosity, as if they were creatures on exhibition. Gudrun would do the same herself. But she resented being in the position when somebody might do it to her. (*WL*, pp. 223–4)

The sharp, disgusted recoil of Gudrun's response is more intense than we might expect if Lawrence were to describe these things directly, but there can be no doubt that he participates in her reaction.

If Gudrun is a tragic figure, the crisis of her tragedy lies beyond the novel's scope: I am not proposing her as a companion for Phèdre and Lady Macbeth. But her inner development does correspond, more closely perhaps than any other of his characters, to Lawrence's account of the tragic process. She does 'go through with her fate'. If her self-consciousness, hypercritical mentality and inability to love are especially characteristic of the phase of civilisation Lawrence lived through, I can find no suggestion that her 'self' is socially conditioned in any escapable sense. There is no potential being that she fails to grow into, nothing more perfectly herself than the 'central serpent'. And if her story is not a tragedy she at least provides a test for the integrity of the character whose tragedy does reach its crisis – Gerald.

Another enormously influential part of our received wisdom is that *Women in Love* is essentially a diagnostic novel: that it is an investigation of industrial civilisation, and a study of some human aberrations as responses to social ideals which Lawrence felt to be antipathetic to life. The structure of contrasted sexual relationships, the personal contrasts of Ursula and Gudrun, the hortatory nature of Birkin's relationship to Gerald, all support this view. The qualified success of Ursula and Birkin's love and the disaster of Gudrun and Gerald's invite the reader to make judgements on their respective ways of living, and inspire comments such as this by F. R. Leavis: 'I will consider the treatment of Gerald Crich's case. There we have peculiarly well exemplified the way in which, in Lawrence's art, the diagnosis of the malady of the individual psyche can become that of the malady of a civilisation.'[6] Taking issue with this view is a delicate matter, since much of our debt to Lawrence concerns his critique of civilisation and this critique enters into a great deal of what is vividly imagined in Gerald – such as his treatment of the horse in the 'Coal-Dust' chapter. However, in so far as the medical language used by Leavis is appropriate, it clearly implies a causal understanding of Gerald's condition and the possibility of a 'cure', there being, in contrast to Gudrun, a potential self that he fails to grow into for reasons clearly articulated in the novel.

Gerald is the one character in the book for whom we are given a set of conditioning circumstances, and there is no doubt that his family is such as to engender a 'malady' in its children. But his awesome, demonic quality, what makes him the compelling figure he is, fit to be thought of in tragic terms, is hardly the necessary product of any set of circumstances:

> But about him also was the strange, guarded look, the unconscious glisten, as if he did not belong to the same creation as the people about him. Gudrun lighted on him at once. There was something northern about him that magnetized her. In his clear northern flesh and his fair hair was a glisten like cold sunshine refracted through crystals of ice. And he looked so new, unbroached, pure as an arctic thing. Perhaps he was thirty years old, perhaps more. His gleaming beauty, maleness, like a young good-humoured, smiling wolf, did not blind her to the significant, sinister stillness in his bearing, the lurking danger of his unsubdued temper. (*WL*, p.61)

The association of Gerald with ice and the magnetic pole does not merely subject him to a symbolic–diagnostic pattern. It alerts us, from

the very beginning, to something dangerously elemental in him –
something not to be explained by reference to his family or to industrial
civilisation, nor to be cured.

In the first version of his essay on Poe, Lawrence distinguishes
between the *tale*, such as Poe's, and the *story*. 'A tale is a concatenation
of scientific cause and effect. But in a story the movement depends on
the sudden appearance of spontaneous emotion or gesture, causeless,
arising out of the living self.' All that is best and most distinctive in
Lawrence corresponds to what he calls the 'story': such stories as 'You
Touched Me' and 'The Horse Dealer's Daughter', in which the strangest
events carry conviction despite the reader's being unable to give an
explanation for them. In *Women in Love* this is true of Birkin's stoning of
the moon (of which critics share essentially the same admiration, despite
giving opposed interpretations), the 'Rabbit' episode, the quarrel in
'Excurse' and everything concerning the child Winifred, as well the
episodes that I have already discussed, in which Gudrun figures.

I think there is a relationship between this and the experience of
tragedy, as well as Lawrence's own account of tragedy in the *Touch and
Go* Preface. The great tragic heroes have this element of unknowable-
ness, which makes their tragedies a repeatedly new experience. This is
one reason why one feels that a play such as *Coriolanus* is not in the
same class as the great tragedies: the hero, though a perfectly convincing
character – in some ways perhaps more 'convincing' than Hamlet – is
too clearly defined and limited, and therefore knowable.

Gerald's death in the Alps is the tragic consummation of the
elemental inhuman 'something' that is embodied in his very flesh –
tragic because he has not the inhuman self-sufficiency to belong entirely
outside 'the same creation as the people about him'. This, however, is
not what Birkin thinks when he sees Gerald metamorphosed into a
block of ice:

> With head oddly lifted, like a man who draws his head back from an
> insult, halt haughtily, he watched the cold, mute, material face. It had a
> bluish cast. It sent a shaft like ice through the heart of the living room.
> Cold, mute, material! Birkin remembered how once Gerald had
> clutched his hand with a warm, momentaneous grip of final love. For
> one second – then let go for ever. If he had kept true to that clasp,
> death would not have mattered. Those who die, and dying still can
> love, still believe, do not die. They live still in the beloved. Gerald
> might still have been living in the spirit with Birkin, even after death.
> He might have lived with his friend, a further life.

(*WL*, pp. 581–2)

The end of *Women in Love* is so moving that critical objections can seem impertinent. It is entirely appropriate that Birkin should feel this about the death of his friend, but is it so appropriate, that this feeling should also have the force of authorial judgement? One could not, I think, sustain a claim that Birkin's feelings are entirely dramatised here, and that Lawrence is dissociated from them. The judgement that the hero had failed to be true to himself – to the implicitly more authentic self expressed in 'that clasp' – would sound obtrusive at the end of most tragedies, and is obviously opposed to Lawrence's own understanding of tragedy. There is a powerful impulse in the novel (expressing itself most damagingly in the manipulation noticed but apparently condoned by Pritchard and Clarke) to deny that Gerald has gone through with his authentic fate, to see his calamity as the result of a curable 'malady' that he perversely chose to foster.

I believe that Birkin is wrong in judging that love for himself would have cured Gerald. The main text for this judgement is the offer and refusal of '*Blutbrüderschaft*'[8] in chapter 16 (immediately before the conversation in which Gerald so inconsistently questions Gudrun's superiority). Gerald unsettles Birkin by telling him, 'I'm never sure of you. You can go away and change as easily as if you had no soul.' What prompts this comment is, in fact, the characteristic that Birkin is most concerned to cultivate himself, the independence and integrity of spirit that he insists on in his arguments with Ursula:

> He knew Birkin could do without him – could forget, and not suffer. This was always present in Gerald's consciousness, filling him with bitter unbelief: this consciousness of the young, animal-like spontaneity of detachment. It seemed almost like hypocrisy and lying, sometimes, oh, often, on Birkin's part, to talk so deeply and importantly. (*WL*, p. 277)

After a pause in the conversation, during which 'each man was gone in his own thoughts', Birkin, 'with quite a new happy activity in his eyes', makes the '*Blutbrüderschaft*' proposal: 'We ought to swear to love each other, you and I, implicitly, and perfectly, finally, without any possibility of going back on it.' Gerald, though pleased and aroused by the proposal, refuses to commit himself:

> 'We'll leave it till I understand it better,' he said, in a voice of excuse.
> Birkin watched him. A little sharp disappointment, perhaps a touch of contempt, came into his heart.

'Yes,' he said. 'You must tell me what you think, later. You know what I mean? Not sloppy emotionalism. An impersonal union that leaves one free.'

They lapsed both into silence. Birkin was looking at Gerald all the time. He seemed now to see, not the physical, animal man, which he usually saw in Gerald, and which usually he liked so much, but the man himself, complete, and as if fated, doomed, limited. This strange sense of fatality in Gerald, as if he were limited to one form of existence, one knowledge, one activity, a sort of fatal halfness, which to himself seemed wholeness, always overcame Birkin after their moments of passionate approach, and filled him with a sort of contempt, or boredom. It was the insistence on the limitation which so bored Birkin in Gerald. Gerald could never fly away from himself, in real indifferent gaiety. He had a clog, a sort of monomania.

(*WL*, pp. 278–9)

Before commenting on this episode I want to mention the relevant observations of two other critics. Pritchard argues,

Forgotten is the thought that love – for women – is horrible. He even suggests *Blutbrüderschaft*, the mingling of blood – an equivalent of sexual union. Gerald, apprehensive of how significant it might be for him, fatally declines the relationship, which is presented in terms of 'an impersonal union', with the overtly homosexual feeling played down.[9]

Pritchard's implication seems to be that Birkin or Lawrence is dishonest about the relationship proposed to Gerald, and that it is a holiday from the difficulties of Birkin's relations with women. If so, it is hard to see why Gerald's refusal is 'fatal'. The idea that the '*Blutbrüderschaft*' is an escape from the difficulties of sexual love is corroborated by Daleski:

Though Birkin strenuously opposes (albeit not always successfully) Ursula's efforts to make him declare his love for her, since the word is tainted in his mind with connotations of 'mingling and merging', he proposes a swearing of love as the oath of brotherhood. In other words, the typically 'male' desire for a 'melting into pure communion', for a 'fusing together into oneness', is allowed only in relation to a man; for in such a relation, it seems, there is no defensive compulsion, as there is in regard to a woman, to realise the 'otherness' of the partner.[10]

I do not think that there is any disguised homosexuality in Birkin's offer. The language of the wrestling-match is sensuous but not erotic; there is no 'sexual' excitement in its rhythms. It is unlike the bathing scene in part *II*, chapter 8, of *The White Peacock* – perhaps because the Lawrence who had written the Prologue to *Women in Love* was sufficiently aware of his own homosexuality to be able to control its expression. But I do agree with Pritchard and Daleski that the simple offer of 'love' to Gerald is inconsistent wth Birkin's expressed beliefs about love, and I think Gerald is right to be suspicious. Gerald only sees the obvious inconsistency of the man with 'animal-like spontaneity of detachment' suggestion that they 'swear love to each other . . . without any possibility of going back on it'. He does not see the deeper, really dangerous inconsistency. Simple, committed love is possible between heterosexual men, but not between an emotionally dependent 'wanting' man such as Gerald and a man who almost obsessively hates and fears dependence. 'A clog, a sort of monomania' might be an unsympathetic description of Birkin's resistance to Ursula's 'love': we might expect him to respect Gerald's wariness. That Lawrence shares his contempt is undeniable, and symptomises an arid, blinkered impatience with Gerald's tragic fate.

The young Lawrence could not forgive Conrad 'for being so sad and for giving in' (*CL*, p. 152). Gerald has long reminded me more of Conrad's distorted idealists than of any other character in Lawrence. One could make quite separate links with Kurtz, Charles Gould and perhaps Jim. Lawrence was wrong to call Conrad's pessimism 'giving in', and in the *Study of Thomas Hardy* there is, as Raymond Williams has said,[11] an ambiguity in his attempt to combine a Nietzschean (and Conradian?) tragic–affirmative pessimism with a belief in 'the *morality* of nature or of life itself' (*Ph*, p. 419; emphasis added). The ambiguity is contained in one sentence when he says of Oedipus, Hamlet and Macbeth, 'But being, as they are, men to the fullest capacity, when they find themselves, daggers drawn, with the very forces of life itself, they can only fight till they themselves are killed, since the morality of life, the greater morality, is eternally unalterable and invincible' (*Ph*, p. 419). In the work of the great tragic dramatists, whose authority he cannot deny, he celebrates tragic rebellion. But, if we reflect that the passage quoted here is a fair account of Gerald Crich, we have to notice that the weight falls heavily on the second half of the sentence, and remember the 'fatal halfness' to which Birkin attributes Gerald's refusal of '*Blutbrüder-schaft*'. 'The morality of life' can too easily become a stick with which to beat the tragic potential out of a character. Lawrence does that, as a critic, notoriously with *Anna Karenina*, and as a novelist he tries his best to do it to Gerald.

NOTES

1. R. E. Pritchard, *D. H. Lawrence: Body of Darkness* (London: Hutchinson, 1971) p. 105.
2. Ibid., p. 104.
3. Colin Clarke, *River of Dissolution: D. H. Lawrence and English Romanticism* (London: Routledge and Kegan Paul, 1969) p. 83.
4. Michael Black, *The Literature of Fidelity* (London: Chatto and Windus, 1975) p. 62.
5. Clarke, *River of Dissolution*, p. 117
6. F. R. Leavis, *D. H. Lawrence, Novelist* (Harmondsworth: Penguin, 1964) p. 158.
7. D. H. Lawrence, *The Symbolic Meaning*, ed. Armin Arnold (Arundel: Fontwell, 1962) p. 118.
8. Lawrence's version of *Blutsbrüderschaft* is cited here.
9. Pritchard, *Lawrence: Body of Darkness*, p. 97.
10. H. M. Daleski, *The Forked Flame* (London: Faber, 1965) p. 184.
11. Raymond Williams, *Modern Tragedy* (London: Chatto and Windus, 1966) p. 124.

4

Women in Love, Class War and School Inspectors

IAN MACKILLOP

While Ursula Brangwen struggled through her last months as a pupil teacher of Standard Five at St Philip's School her family went up in the world. Her father gave up his job as a lace-designer to become a peripatetic handiwork instructor, a new post created by Nottingham Education Committee. He was to spend two days a week at the forward-looking Grammar School at Willey Green. The family moved to the suburbs of the nearby colliery town, Beldover, where, said a friend, they would be among the élite. 'They would represent culture. And as there was no one of higher social importance than the doctors, the colliery managers, and the chemists, they would shine, with their Della Robbia beautiful Madonna, their lovely reliefs from Donatello, their reproductions from Botticelli' (*R*, p. 427). There may have been no one of higher social importance in Beldover, but beyond the grimy small town there was, of course, county society. It was some years before the Brangwens made an awkward début there. Ursula had taken her BA at the University College in Nottingham, where Gudrun went to art school; she had returned to Willey Green Grammar School as a class-teacher and Gudrun had gone to London. It was during one of Gudrun's visits home that the other élite favoured the family with an invitation: the local industrial magnate opened his summer lakeside party to the rising professional class of Beldover, inviting for the first time the staff of the Grammar School and his senior managers. So Will Brangwen, hot, exasperated and feeling not at all like a gentleman, stepped out to the great house, with his wife (who took it all in her stride) and two teasing daughters. Ursula and Gudrun had already scaled higher social pinnacles. In an earlier chapter of *Women in Love* we see them as house guests at Breadalby, the home of Hermione Roddice and her brother Philip, a Liberal MP. This was their second visit, and their presence slightly puzzled the son of the industrial magnate, who is also a guest:

'Who are those two Brangwens?' Gerald asked.
'They live in Beldover.'
'In Beldover! Who are they then?'
'Teachers in the Grammar School.'
There was a pause. . . .
'And what's the father?'
'Handicraft instructor in the schools.'
'Really!'
'Class-barriers are breaking down!'
Gerald was always uneasy under the slightly jeering tone of the other.
'That their father is handicraft instructor in a school! What does that matter to me?'   (WL, p. 150)

It does not need to be argued that a major subject of Lawrence's Brangwen novels, from which these cameos are taken, is the meaning of class friction; it is a necessary part of his study of a dying culture. He began Women in Love in 1913 and it was altogether rewritten and finished in Cornwall in 1917: during the months of composition 'I read Thucydides . . . when I have the courage to face these wars of a collapsing era, of a dying idea.' Gudrun Brangwen was nauseated by the denizens of the dying culture: 'There was Shortlands with its meaningless distinction, the meaninglessness of the Criches. There was London, the House of Commons, the extant social world. My God!' Lawrence took pains over this social world: 'It was only through such people could one discover whither the general run of mankind . . . was tending.' We find in Women in Love all kinds of class friction between 'such people' and their inferiors.[1]

In this essay I hope to throw light on one aspect of class war in Women in Love, a particular skirmish in the world of teachers. The contestants are the Brangwen sisters and Hermione Roddice, representing the new class of professional teachers and a segment of the Liberal intelligentsia; alongside them is Birkin, 'one of the school-inspectors of the county'. I shall spend less time on war within the novel than outside it. What interests me is the way in which the knot of conflict among these characters illustrates a conflict in the real world of England before the First World War: I shall lift a corner of the fiction and show the history beneath it. I should say immediately that it is the history and not Marx from which 'class war' (in my title) is taken. This word was used in a parliamentary episode in 1911, when a scandal broke concerning the role and opinions of school-inspectors. C. P. (later Sir Charles)

Trevelyan, a Liberal MP and Parliamentary Secretary to the Board of Education, had to defend his department against the charge of 'stirring up a state of class war'. The scandal led to the removal to other offices of both the Permanent Secretary and the President of the Board of Education (Sir Robert Morant and Walter Runciman). When this happened Lawrence himself was teaching at Davidson Road Boys' School in Croydon (he was there from 12 October 1908 to 8 November 1911). If I were concerned with point-by-point historical accuracy in *Women in Love* I should be tempted to relate the Inspectorate scandal to the arrival of Philip Roddice in chapter 8, bringing news from the House of Commons that 'there had been a split in the Cabinet; the Minister for Education had resigned owing to adverse criticism'. But I am less interested in what Lawrence 'must have known' in detail than in his general alertness to the kind of problems that were abundantly illustrated by the Inspectorate scandal – or, to give it its recognised title, the Case of the Holmes Circular.[2]

The Case of the Holmes Circular was all about an issue which at first glance appears unexciting, the respective merits of government inspectors (HM inspectors) and those appointed by local education authorities. But it 'humbled the government' (said the *Saturday Review*), moved Morant and Runciman from the Board, generated at least one book, and filled the Albert Hall with protesting teachers. It also has some features of a detective story, because the Circular disappeared and eluded historians until 1978. The document is called after its author, Edmond Gore Alexander Holmes, Chief Inspector for Elementary Schools. It was dated 6 January 1910, entitled, drily enough, 'Memorandum by Mr. E. G. A. Holmes on the Status, Duties &c., of Inspectors employed by Local Education Authorities'. It was headed 'strictly confidential' and only after Holmes's retirement in November 1910 was it 'leaked' by a Conservative MP, who embarrassed the Liberals by quoting it in the House of Commons on 21 March 1911. A furore ensued, after which it was ordered that the Circular be 'withdrawn', which it was so successfully that later researchers (myself included) were baffled in their attempts to find it in the Public Record Office and in the library of the Department of Education and Science until a historian of education (with me on his heels) unearthed it among the Runciman papers in the University library of Newcastle-upon-Tyne. Actually the document once discovered proved disappointing (a cry of sour grapes?), containing little more than the abbreviated versions which had been quoted in Parliament and in 1912 by F. H. Hayward in his *Educational Administration and Criticism: A Sequel to the 'Holmes Circular'*.[3]

We can understand the significance of the Circular if we pay some attention to the career of its author, E. G. A. Holmes. Holmes was an unusual man who arrived at some insights into the British educational system not dissimilar to those expressed by Lawrence in *The Rainbow*. So he bears witness to some of Lawrence's discoveries; but equally he is symptomatic of some phenomena of which Lawrence is deeply critical in *Women in Love* and in his essay 'Education of the People', written in 1918 for (but not published in) *The Times Educational Supplement*.

Edmond Holmes was an Irishman, Oxford-educated, taking a double First in Greats. He was appointed HM Inspector of Schools soon after coming down in 1874. In his autobiography, *In Quest of an Ideal* (1921), he remarks bitterly that 'I was really nothing more than an examiner of young children (who ought never to have been examined by an outsider) and an assessor of Government grants (which ought to have been paid on an entirely different principle).' This 'principle' had operated for less than ten years, since Robert Lowe's Revised Code of Grants of 1862 had established the method of 'payment-by-results', enabling schools to draw a capitation grant calculated against the performance of pupils as tested by such inspectors as Holmes. This code was made to work harder and faster by the provisions of the Education Act of 1870, which stimulated the addition of nearly 5000 more schools to the English system. More inspectors were required (thus Holmes's appointment) and they had to do a new kind of work. Instead of acting in an advisory capacity, the Inspectorate had to carry out what Matthew Arnold called 'a vast system of minute local examinations' and, in another place, 'a game of mechanical contrivance in which the teachers will and must more and more learn how to beat us'. In the year of the class-war accusations Holmes published a book of educational theory called *What Is and What Might Be: A Study of Education in General and Elementary Education in Particular* (1911), in which he describes the payment-by-results era and the confusion that was caused by the eventual abolition of the Revised Code:

> For a third of a century (1862–1895) the 'Education Department' did everything (or nearly everything) for the teacher; then, after having for thirty-three years deprived the teachers of almost every vestige of freedom, the Department suddenly reversed its policy and gave them in generous measure the boon which it had so long withheld. . . . A man who had grown accustomed to semi-darkness would be dazzled to the verge of blindness if he were suddenly taken out into broad daylight.

This is what was done in 1895 to the teachers of England, and it is not to be wondered at that many of them have been purblind ever since. For thirty-three years they had been treated as machines, and they were suddenly asked to act as intelligent beings.

Without the Revised Code teachers were at a loss, inheritors of an authoritarian system but without the awesome annual inspection acting as a goad. The children became slack and the teachers (I continue to paraphrase Holmes) stayed in their ruts. Things were made worse by the inspecting officers appointed by the school boards, many of whom had been successful headmasters under the old régime, whose disciplined pupils had earned good grants for their school in the annual inspections.

The Education Department scourged the teachers and the children with whips. The local inspectors scourged them with scorpions. The paralysing effect of such a régime on all who came under it can be better imagined than described. And the worst of the paralytics was the inspector himself. He lived in his own past, and he required all the teachers in his district to live there with him.[4]

These local 'paralytics' came to obsess Holmes. He was promoted to Divisional Inspector in 1903, based in Newcastle-upon-Tyne, and became Chief Inspector for Elementary Schools in 1905 soon after which he asked his divisional team to report on the 'paralytics': in November 1906 he circularised his colleagues on the matter. In 1908 he sought information through a questionnaire: it was the result of this that he wrote up in the notorious Circular of January 1910. Its tone is that of a man having his last stab before retirement at a subject which had long exasperated him.[5]

At its simplest the message of the Circular is that elementary schools were plagued by the attentions of inspectors who were stupid and common. It states that nearly all the 123 local inspectors in Great Britain were former elementary-school teachers. Only two or three of these had the correct 'antecedents', 'i.e. have been educated first at a Public School and then at Oxford or Cambridge', thus capable of 'freshness and originality', 'a broad view of things'. (If we accept the Prologue to *Women in Love* Birkin was one of these: 'He was a fellow of Magdalen College, and had been, at twenty-one, one of the young lights of the place ... his essays on education were brilliant, and he became an inspector of schools.') The remaining inspectors stereotyped routine, and perpetuated cast-iron methods. They and the system they ran were 'vicious' (the word is used three times in a document of about 1000 words): they tried, hopelessly, to survey a wide field of action from a well-worn groove. One of the specific conclusions of the Circular was that 'The £500 which is being spent on one Oxford man in East Sussex, is being laid out to infinitely better advantage than the £900 a year which is being spent on three ex-elementary teacher inspectors in Durham County.' It is hardly surprising that Durham County considered legal action against the Board of Education when the Circular was made public.[6]

Made public it was in the House of Commons on 14 and 21 March 1911. Samuel Hoare, Conservative MP for Chelsea, quoted liberally from the Circular and proceeded to make hay of a Liberal administration that was proposing reform of the House of Lords. C.P. Trevelyan, Parliamentary Secretary at the Board of Education, had described the Liberals' plans for the Lords in these terms: 'What was happening was not mere indignation, not a mere party cry; it meant a revolt of the common man against the privileged man. The real inner meaning of what the Liberal party were doing was to provide new machinery of government by common men who feel the pinch of life.' The 'common men' could take little comfort from the Holmes Circular, said Hoare: how could the Liberals have one policy for the country and another for its administration? Runciman, President of the Board, was baited mercilessly. Steam built up outside Parliament. On 17–20 April 1911 the National Union of Teachers (NUT) held its annual conference; it deplored the Circular's attitude to local inspectors and, on another tack, which we shall soon see to be significant, moved that HM Inspectorate should be open to all irrespective of their 'antecedents'. The NUT published a series of protest leaflets (including *A Plot against Elementary School Children*) and announced a demonstration at the Albert Hall on 13 May whose theme was to be the exclusion of the common man, without 'antecedents', from the higher posts in public service. By 8 May nearly all seats were sold, and in the end 10,000 tickets in excess of the Hall's capacity were ordered. The affair rumbled on at Westminster. In the debate on the education estimates on 13 July, Runciman took pains to show that his Inspectorate appointments had regard to experience and not 'antecedents'. He was attacked by several distinguished former pupil teachers. Trevelyan concluded the debate apologetically and announced that the Circular had been withdrawn; he probably cursed Holmes his pension. Runciman was soon to resign, followed in November by the more important figure, Permanent Secretary Sir Robert Morant. As autumn drew on, Morant's attention was more than once claimed by a framed print of Kipling's 'If' on the wall of his office. In the long run the teaching-profession scored a victory. Its efforts over the Circular bore fruit after strong submissions to the Royal Commission on the Civil Service of 1912–14, after which the Board's Inspectorate was reorganised to allow appointment of former elementary-school teachers and stricter requirements of teaching-experience were made of inspectors.[7]

It would be foolish to dismiss Holmes as a simple snob. His work as a social critic in *What Is and What Might Be* has been praised, rightly, by no less a historian than E. P. Thompson, who relates it to Lawrence: it is 'a quite devastating attack upon the entire educational process . . . a criticism which takes us directly to that other devastating treatment of Board School education, the chapter entitled "The Man's World" in *The Rainbow*'. There were teachers like Mr Harby and doubtless some 'vicious' local inspectors. Thus far Holmes endorses Lawrence. But if we look a little closer at Lawrence's pictures of school life we shall find in him appreciation of elements in the predicament of teachers of which Holmes was unconscious. In 'Education of the People', written in 1918, he describes the 'vile and false position' of the elementary-school teacher. He is

insulted from above and from below. Comes along an inspector of schools, a university man himself, with no respect for the sordid promiscuity of the elementary school. For elementary schools know no remoteness and dignity of the rostrum. The teacher is on a level with the scholars, or inferior to them. And an elementary school knows no code of honour, no *esprit de corps*. There is the profound cynicism of the laundry and the bottle-factory at the bottom of everything. How should a refined soul down from Oxford fail to find it a little sordid and common?

The elementary school-teacher is in a vile and false position. Set up as representative of an ideal which is all toffee, invested in an authority which has absolutely no base except in the teacher's own isolate will, he is sneered at by the idealists above and jeered at by the materialists below, and ends by being a mongrel who is neither a wage-earner nor a professional, neither a head worker nor a hand worker, neither living by his brain nor by his physical toil, but a bit of both, and despised for both. He is caught between the upper and nether millstones of idealism and materialism, and every shred of natural pride is ground out of him, so that he has to die or to cultivate some unpleasant *suffisance* which makes him objectionable for ever.

Holmes bridled at the 'unpleasant *suffisance*'. He appears not to have grasped that it derived from a real problem of professional status. The teachers' predicament can be expressed in a practical question: why should he or she be held fixed in a sphere, 'between the upper and nether millstones', with no chance of becoming a member of HM Inspectorate? By the time of the Circular teachers had been systematically deprived of such prospects for decades: indeed, the chances of transfer from the elementary school of the local inspectorate to HM Inspectorate had *declined* since the Education Act of 1902. What we have already seen of the effect of successive Education Acts on school life has made Holmes's attitude comprehensible; but we need to go further to see long-term causes of resentment that sanctioned talk of class-war in the immediately pre-War years.[8]

The Act of 1870 confirmed a two-tier system of inspection, by HM Inspectorate and school board. Long before it, and before the Revised Code, teachers who were certificated by the state had only the most remote hopes for promotion into HM Inspectorate. One historian quotes a statement of 1853 that boys in an attorney's office could aspire to the Woolsack, but no teacher could expect to become an HM inspector. The Newcastle Commission of 1858 was firm about such pretensions: inspectors should be fitted by training and *social position* to be able to communicate with school-managers and the clergy. Former teachers made slight inroads into the Inspectorate after the Revised Code when, in 1863, HM inspectors were allowed to engage local assistants (called always 'Mr', never 'Esq.'). But they could not be appointed to the full inspectorate, and all other appointments had to be made below the age of thirty (thirty-five in 1886), so excluding experienced teachers. The establishment of a lower grade of inspector in 1882 made little difference. It was not until the Cross Commission of 1888 thoroughly investigated the workings of the Education Acts that the recommendation emerged that HM Inspectorate should be open to former elementary teachers; between 1894 and 1902 six such men were appointed. But in 1902 the situation worsened.

The Education Act of 1902 marked the ascendancy of Robert Morant at the Board of Education. He was widely experienced in educational administration; he had set up a schooling-system in Siam and worked on the presentation to Parliament of the recommendations of the Bryce Commission on secondary education. By private secretaryships he had risen to Acting Secretary at the Board of Education towards the end of 1902, just before the passing of the Act to which he had contributed much; for it was Morant who had discovered that the school boards were breaking the law by providing secondary education, which discovery proved to be the lever by which the proposals of the new Act (transferring authority from school boards to county councils) came into being. This Act unified English education by bringing under a single authority the schools run by the boards and the ones run by religious denominations. Once it was passed Morant set about a process of educating the new local authorities, issuing codes and suggestions.[9]

The traditional role of the Board of Education had been to find the means by which government could get good educational value for money. After 1902 the task of the Inspectorate was 'to watch, encourage, warn, co-ordinate' (to quote the Board of Education report of 1905). Morant inherited a second-rate Inspectorate, so he appointed intelligent Oxbridge men with little or no teaching experience. No further steps were taken to provide an upward route to the Inspectorate from the classroom. Indeed, the Inspectorate became so securely 'establishment' that even the public schools allowed themselves to be inspected. The general view of teachers caught between the 'upper and nether millstones' was well put in 1914 by the President of the NUT: 'I still resent the insistence of the Board of Education which forced me into its mould, and then declared that mould to be a poor thing by shutting the door against me and my colleagues.'[10]

So far we have seen that Holmes and Lawrence made similar discoveries about school life under (well under) the Board of Education; but that Holmes was indifferent to a real social predicament experienced by teachers. *Women in Love* has disappeared from view in a welter of facts about Acts, codes and commissions. I suggest that these facts show that those young teachers who stepped out with slightly affected assurance into county society near Beldover were at a key point of friction in the pre-war class structure. I shall now turn to Holmes's positive opinions about education, because I believe they illustrate another kind of conflict: this is to be found in some of the arguments about education in *Women in Love*.

Teachers, said Lawrence in 'Education of the People', were caught between the upper and nether millstones of *idealism* and *materialism*: they were trapped ideologically as well as professionally. Now, Holmes was very much the 'Whitehall idealist' – witness his autobiography, *In Search of an Ideal*. What Holmes sought and spoke out for was 'self-expression'. Lawrence himself appears to have been highly proficient at stimulating the imagination of his pupils, so his rather dry comments on 'self-expression' have some authority. 'Here was a pretty task for a teacher: he was to make his pupil *express himself*. Which *self* was left vague ... the responsibility for all this foolery was heaped on the shoulders of that public clown, the elementary school-teacher.'

Holmes discovered 'self-expression' at the foot of the South Downs shortly before his retirement. At this Sussex Damascus he experienced a two-fold conversion: he realised that children could be taught without imposition by encouraging their growth and he found what he called a new sense of 'kinship with my kind'. In his years at the Board Holmes had evolved a form of humanism, described in two books which attempted to reconcile the religious traditions of East and West called *The Creed of Christ* (1905) and *The Creed of Buddha* (1908). He argued that both figures were agnostic, naturalist, humanist, spiritualist and idealist; the Buddha was here wedded to an Arnoldian Christ: he called both 'agnostic' in the sense that they either kept silent about the ultimate mysteries of existence or spoke of them in the medium of poetry, 'the only medium in which the letter counts for nothing and the spirit has free play'. The 'kinship' he discovered in Sussex, at the little school run by a headmistress he calls 'Egeria', was democratic, undermining 'my belief in the congenital inferiority of the lower to the upper classes'. He describes the conversion in *In Quest of an Ideal*:

I believed that the life of the spirit, the inner life, the life of devotion to the Whole, was the real life. And I believed that this inner life was an adventure into the infinite, an eternal movement towards an unrealisable ideal – an ideal which owed to its infinitude its authority and its magnetic force. But what were all these beliefs worth if I did not hold them on behalf of my fellow men as well as of myself?

It was with this faith – and this unfaith – in my heart that I entered Egeria's school. Then and there my eyes were opened. What had hitherto prevented me from realising my kinship with my kind was my belief in the congenital inferiority of the lower to the upper classes. In the presence of Egeria's pupils this belief proved to be a mere superstition; and the resultant barrier between my soul and the soul of Humanity melted away. The activity, the versatility, the all-round capacity of the children could not fail to impress me. But the school had other distinctive features which impressed me even more. Allowed to energise freely, the children were radiantly happy in their school life.

Egeria's teaching methods are described, with rather more eloquence than information, in *What Is and What Might Be*. And here, it seems to

me, there is a remarkable resemblance between Holmes's educational
idealism and that of Hermione Roddice in *Women in Love* as expressed
in her rows with school-inspector Birkin in the Willey Green classroom
and at Breadalby. Both Holmes and Hermione believe in 'growth' and
distrust instruction. Both are rhapsodically non-utilitarian. 'There *can*
be no reason,' says Hermione, 'no *excuse* for education, except the joy
and beauty of knowledge in itself. . . . Vocational education *isn't*
education, it is the close of education' (*WL*, pp. 140–1). For both,
knowledge must be 'real'. At Willey Green Grammar School Hermione
asks Birkin whether children should really be roused to consciousness:

> 'They are not roused to consciousness,' he said, 'consciousness comes
> to them, willy-nilly.'
> 'But do you think they are better for having it quickened,
> stimulated? Isn't it better that they should remain unconscious of the
> hazel, isn't it better that they should see as a whole, without all this
> pulling to pieces, all this knowledge?'
> 'Would you rather, for yourself, know or not know, that the little
> red flowers are there, putting out for the pollen?' he asked
> harshly. (*WL*, p. 89)

Holmes is as fastidious as Hermione about 'knowledge':

> There are, of course, many cases in which the conscious acquisition of
> information is a necessary stage in the acquisition of knowledge. But
> in all such cases, if the information acquired is to have any educative
> value, it must be allowed to sink down into the subconscious strata,
> whence, after having been absorbed and assimilated and so converted
> into knowledge, it will perhaps reascend towards the surface of the
> mind, just as the leaves which fall in autumn are dragged down into
> the soil below, converted into fertile mould, and then gradually lifted
> towards the surface; or as the fresh water that the rivers pour into the
> sea has to be slowly absorbed into the whole mass of salt water before
> it (or its equivalent) can return to the land as rain.

Holmes is here elaborating the Arnoldian concept of *inwardness*, but
with a glutinousness of expression that gives it, to my mind, a self-
regarding quality very much in tune with Hermione's over-bearing
spirituality. Holmes has, of course, none of Birkin's 'harshness' – or
practical sense: he scarcely ever considers the relation of Egeria's scheme
to adult life or to the social organism as a whole. At one point he

remarks that the good things of life may not be available to all, but is dubious about their redistribution, an idea which he ascribes to persons 'known as *Socialists*', whom he reproves for the mistake of trying to effect collectivism before the standard of reality has been changed. There are limits to kinship with his kind.[11]

Politically progressive and educationally progressive ideas may only appear to belong in the same mental package: it is only superficially tempting to equate ideas of creativity and imaginative liberation with ideas of social democracy. We find in Holmes a facile allegiance to Froebelianism (the 'growth' idea) combined with insuperable class prejudice: on his own confession he spent a career convinced that the lower classes are congenitally inferior to the upper, and one in which he was persistently agitated by hostility to the lower-middle-class professional man, or intellectual. We have seen that this hostility was institutionally enforced. Lawrence has a reputation for anti-democratic thinking. We better appreciate its complexity if we understand the forms and the context in which some democratic ideas were available to him. To this end my essay has been directed – with a specific hope that future editions of *Women in Love* may advert us to the significance of the roles of teacher and inspector in the novel, and perhaps to the historical analogues to Hermione's thinking. Again I insist that I have been concerned with milieu in general and not with Lawrence's actual relations with members of the educational profession: of that more could be said. We should include a reference to an encounter which amusingly did *not* take place. When HM inspector visited Davidson Road Boys' School he declined an invitation to enter Lawrence's classroom: 'I have no intention of being pilloried in some book', he said.[12]

NOTES

1.   Some of the material in this essay has appeared in another form under the hand of the present author in *Moirae: Journal of the School of Politics, Philosophy and History, Ulster College, the Northern Ireland Polytechnic*, 3 (1978). For 'class barriers' and 'the extant social world', *see WL*, chs 8 and 29. For the 'dying idea', see letter to Barbara Low, May 1916, *CL*, p. 454. For the period of composition of the novel and the reference to 'such people' (quoted in Carswell's *Savage Pilgrimage*) I am indebted to Charles L. Ross, 'From "The Sisters" to *The Rainbow* and *Women in Love*: A Textual and Critical History, 1913–1917' (unpublished DPhil thesis, Oxford 1973).

2. On the period at Davidson Road Boys' School, see Harry T. Moore, *The Priest of Love: A Life of D. H. Lawrence*, rev. edn (London: Heinemann, 1974) pp. 88, 132. On Trevelyan and class war see *Hansard*, 5th ser., XXVIII, col 615.

3. The Holmes Circular was published in full with commentary by Peter Gordon in the *Journal of Educational Administration and History* (University of Leeds), X, no. 1 (1978) 36–40.

4. For the history of education I lean heavily on the following (of which the first three are informative about Holmes): John Leese, *Personalities and Power in English Education* (Leeds: E. J. Arnold, 1950); Asher Tropp, *The School Teachers: The Growth of the Teaching Profession in England and Wales from 1800 to the Present Day* (London: Heinemann, 1957); Bernard M. Allen, *Sir Robert Morant: A Great Public Servant* (London: Macmillan, 1934); W. H. G. Armytage, *Four Hundred Years of English Education* (Cambridge: Cambridge University Press, 1964; 2nd edn 1970); E. L. Edmonds, *The School Inspector* (London: Routledge and Kegan Paul, 1962). The quotations from Holmes are taken from Edmond Holmes, *What Is and What Might Be* (London: Constable, 1911) pp. 7, 111; and Edmond Holmes, *In Quest of an Ideal* (London: R. Cobden-Sanderson, 1920) pp. 62, 119–20. Arnold is quoted in Leese, *Personalities and Power*, p. 93; and Armytage, *Four Hundred Years*, p. 125.

5. On Holmes's investigation, see Allen, *Sir Robert Morant*, p. 254.

6. For the Circular, see n. 3; for the Prologue to *Women in Love*, see *PhII* p. 94. The response of Durham County is shown in its Education Committee Minutes of 4 Oct and 29 Nov 1911.

7. For the parliamentary debates, see *Hansard*, 5th ser., XXIII, cols 277–8 (Hoare quotes the Circular, and Trevelyan on reform); XXVIII, cols 495–577 (Runciman in estimates debate); XXVIII, cols 614–16 (Trevelyan's apology). The NUT response is quoted from various pamphlets and press releases in its library: curiously and characteristically, its publication called *The 'Holmes–Morant' Circular* cannot be found either in this or in the British Library. For the sequel to the rumpus and Morant's last days at the Board, see Tropp, *The School Teachers*, p. 202; Allen, *Sir Robert Morant*, pp. 262–3; and Edmonds, *The School Inspector*, p. 146.

8. For Thompson on Holmes, see E. P. Thompson, *Education and Experience*, Fifth Mansbridge Memorial Lecture, Leeds (1968) pp. 15–16. Lawrence on the teacher quoted from *Ph*, pp. 589–90.

9. See Tropp, *The School Teachers*, pp. 40–1, 58, 72, 119. The rise of Morant after 1902 is traced by Allen.

10. On the new role of the Board and restriction of teachers, see Leese, *Personalities and Power*, p. 231; and Tropp, *The School Teachers*, p. 195.

11. The teachers' 'pretty task': *Ph* pp. 594–5. Quotations from Holmes from *In Quest of an Ideal*, pp. 123, 125, and *What Is and What Might Be*, pp. 55, 287–8; from *Women in Love*, chs 8, 3.

12. See Moore, *The Priest of Love*, p. 93.

5

Lawrence's Political Thought: Some English Contexts, 1906–19

MICHAEL BENTLEY

From the point of view of the historian of British political thought, Lawrence's writing asks three questions. It seems important to be clear, in the first place, whether the material contains anything so cerebral or systematic as to constitute evidence of coherent thinking, as opposed to shafts of intuitive insight unconnected one with another and irreducible to a speculative pattern. In so far as thought of this kind is detectable, the question arises, second, of the nature and extent of its political ingredient and especially of the latter's hortative aspect. And if both questions yield intelligible answers a third problem will present itself in the requirement to assess the degree to which Lawrence's political thought can be said to display an English conditioning in the pre-Lorenzo years. It has to be said that even these crass approaches place some strains on the techniques of mere historians: it soon becomes plain that only an application of literary, anthropological and psychological analyses are likely to make possible a rounded response. No such comprehension will be feasible, personal inadequacies apart, within the confines of a short essay. It may be thought helpful if one attempts nevertheless to offer a few reflections from a perspective which is not common in studies of Lawrence. Doubtless conclusions will remain elusive – the climate of Lawrence criticism suggests that they can hardly turn out otherwise – but some of the significant questions may be sufficiently refined for those with greater literary expertise to further the inquiry through their own mode.

Surrender in the face of Lawrence's continuing refusal to coagulate is a tempting option at the outset. Before the fiction begins even to focus, hesitations creep over one about what the noise 'Lawrence' ought to be taken to denote.[1] His life was so patently a succession of crossed thresholds that one wonders whether to speak of a single Lawrence between the dates covered by this essay is not to miss a number of covert identities. 'Lawrence was Lawrence before 1912'; perhaps this offers some reassurance.[2] Yet the senses in which such certainties are valid may be as unimportant as they are undeniable. The arrival of Frieda and the explosion of Lawrence's erotic genius mark, after all, a real-enough divide. So does, a little earlier, the death of his mother in pulling apart the fabric of the consciousness that had lain behind *The White Peacock* and producing the 'tear in the veil' (*SL*, p. 495) through which Lawrence felt his life would thenceforth drift. The war brought in 1914, of course, a further separation from all that had gone before and one that Lawrence himself conceived to be fundamental. All his writings concur in stressing that 1916–17 were in particular years resembling a watershed, throwing everything into strange channels, 'as if the Current of life was dividing now and carrying some definitely one way, others definitely in a quite different direction' (*KL*, p. 116).[3] Nor was Lawrence merely diverging from previously parallel courses; he was also becoming painfully aware of the irrelevance, perhaps the unreality, of his past. Witness the miserable Christmas he spent with his 'people' in 1915 and his hatred for their 'pure' pastness, 'without mitigation' (*KL*, p. 61).[4] The grey coffin that slipped into the sea in 1919 was, that is to say, one of many jettisoned by Lawrence after his departure from Eastwood.

How damaging this fragmentation may be to an evaluation of the stability of Lawrence's political thought is not easy to assess. There are certainly grounds for believing that its effects can be exaggerated. Beside the commonplace that all critical thinkers shed their skins occasionally may be placed the thought that Lawrence's understanding of what thought entailed was one which disdained geometry and integration. Antinomies often struck Lawrence as evidence of resource rather than grounds for criticism. This is not to espouse the romanticism of inter-war critics who liked to see in Lawrence a preference for Life over tedious logic;[5] it is simply to recall that the universe which Lawrence built around himself was emphatically post-Bergsonian and carried implications about the limits of ratiocination as a tool of ontological inquiry.[6] Knowledge of the world reached Lawrence through nerve and sensation as much as through syllogism, and within this understanding Berkeley came off as badly as Russell. What might be transmitted through these unfamiliar channels included 'an ancient sort of root-knowledge' (*K*, p. 145), 'mindless, progressive knowledge through the senses, knowledge arrested and ending in the senses' (*WL*, p. 330).[7] To this extent Eliot's notorious complaint that Lawrence did not know how much he did not know loses its punch. The point is that Lawrence did not care to know what Eliot required him to know. 'I am so sure of what I know', he wrote to Lady Ottoline Morrell in 1915, '. . . that I am sure I am stronger in the truth, in the knowledge I have, than all the world outside that knowledge' (*CL*, p. 351). And here at least he had been consistent since his early days. At Nottingham he had spurned the prescribed course reading – 'systematic reading be damned!' – and despised what he took to be second-hand knowledge lifted from other writers.[8] It followed that Lawrence's thought was never going to be based on a collection of admired texts or on a series of deductive procedures applied to stated premises.

So far as the political dimension of his thought is concerned, however, the immediate impression is one of patent paucity. Take away *Kangaroo* and some pieces from the *Phoenix* collection and surprisingly little direct comment on politics is evident. Indeed, there are obvious senses in which Lawrence is not a political novelist at all. He defends no single social class, supports no single political cause. He does not speak a language of international hope; but neither does he imply a national or sectional purpose. Any political theories he may hold are contaminated by a concept of art which can, for example, elevate a writer such as Eric Gill to a status greater than that of Marx or Whitehead,[9] and which can convince contemporaries that Lawrence's politics are turgid or half-baked. 'As an artist', Jessie Chambers wrote after Lawrence's death, '. . . he is superb, but when he assays to be a thinker I find him superficial and unconvincing and quite soon boring . . . his long arguments about aristocrats and democrats and the rest are only the dusty miles he covered in his pilgrimage.'[10] Miriam pokes through her original at such points, but the view is certainly understandable. When Lawrence himself relegated so much of his political observation to half lines of contextual *rapportage* or the vatic spiritualities of *Kangaroo*, it is hard to see the seriousness of any claim that he assumed a singular and interesting political position.

Quotidian politics do sometimes intrude. One recalls Leslie, the Conservative county councillor of *The White Peacock*, standing at a general election after the Liberal landslide win of 1906 and (quite plausibly) winning the seat back for the Conservatives (*WP*, pp. 330, 339, 346), or perhaps Gudrun's conviction that the Crich of *Women in Love* will one day follow a similar path (*WL*, p. 511).[11] *Aaron's Rod* has its whispers of the Sankey Commission beneath the discussion of mines nationalisation among the opera-goers (*AR*, p. 76).[12] *Kangaroo* contains allusions to the Irish Civil War, to President Wilson, and to Lloyd George and his symbolic ousting of Asquith, which sends Somers stalking the moors in despair: 'It is the end of England. It is the end of the old England. It is finished. England will never be England any more' (*K*, pp. 71, 250–1). Then there is the thematic concern with miners and their lives, 'the faces of the old men and the privations of the women', the 'cold, disheartening atmosphere of sorrow' – sentiments which lie behind the contempt which Lawrence heaps on paternalists such as the Duke of Portland with his comical 'model villages' (*WP*, p. 149).[13] Were there no strong counter-evidence, it would be possible to construct along these lines an account of Lawrence's political awareness which would go a considerable distance towards establishing his credentials as a reflector of contemporary political concerns if not as a consistent political theorist.

But for every snippet which implies such an awareness there are countless others which lead one in an opposite direction. If Lawrence occasionally reflected some newspaper-reading he also made no secret during the anguished years after 1915 of his unwillingness over long periods to face the newsprint which made him ill.[14] If Lloyd George was a devil and his deposition of Asquith a crime etched in Lawrence's consciousness, it was not so deeply etched that he could remember when it happened.[15] If there is a considerable documentation of strikes, it tends to be pluperfect registration that the event had been and gone. Working-class hardship is a matter for report – 'the day was just twelve hours long' (*SL*, p. 136)[16] – rather than a platform on which to build a case. Only in the instance of the elder Crich's lock-out at the pit is any searching examination made, and even then it is a depiction of personal tragedy rather than a social criticism (*WL*, pp. 297–9). The impassioned theorising of *Kangaroo* is not proof from confessions of political indifference from Somers (*K*, pp. 71–2). The fictionalised Frieda alleges that Somers has never cared for politics (*K*, p. 111). Politics in the eyes of the latter is a form of national book-keeping, a theme which Lawrence developed in an essay, 'Democracy', written at about the same time:

> You, you Cabinet Minister – what are you? You are the arch-grocer, the super-hotel-manager, the foreman over the ships and railways. What else are you? You are the super-tradesman, same paunch, same ingratiating manner, same everything. Governments, what are they? Just board-meetings of big businessmen. . . . But Ideal! An Ideal Government? What nonsense. . . .
>   Politics – what are they? Just another extra-large commercial wrangle over buying and selling – nothing else. Very good to have the wrangle. Let us have the buying and selling well done. But ideal!

Politics *ideal! Political Idealists!* What rank gewgaw and nonsense.
(*Ph*, pp. 701–3)

One is left with Green's conclusion that, at least so far as the immediate
political environment was concerned, Lawrence's mind developed a
series of resistances which made it impossible for him to acquire the
information necessary for precise commentary.[17]

It follows that to seek an English context for Lawrence's political
thought within the ephemeral happenings of contemporary politics is to
enter a *cul de sac*, certainly for the period before 1914. A more promising
avenue is opened if one seeks reflections on the English social structure
and the quality of Englishness. Everyone knows the Lawrence of
England, My England, and that knowledge is in itself sufficient to combat
the notion that Lawrence's social thought derives from traditionally
'English' attitudes. Whatever warmth he had generated for the idea of
aristocracy, Lawrence plainly felt no admiration for an elite composed
of Egberts with 'that fatal three pounds a week'.[18] Nor were his loathings
for the trappings of reaction a product only of the censorship and
humiliation that he experienced during the war. It is true that the
vocabulary of a nation 'finished', of dead dogs, of a people who have
'slopped and wobbled' is most frequent after 1915; but in sources as
early as *The White Peacock* one can find the 'crackling fires' of the
bourgeoisie 'sodded down with the sods of British respectability'.[19] So
that by the time of the Weekly imbroglio in 1912 any patience with the
English he had ever felt was gone:

> Curse the blasted, jelly-boned swines, the shiny, the belly-wriggling
> invertebrates, the miserable sodding rotters, the flaming sods, the
> snivelling, dribbling, dithering palsied pulse-less lot that make up
> England today. They've got white of egg in their veins, and their
> spunk is that watery it's a marvel they can breed. They *can* nothing but
> frog-spawn – the gibberers. God how I hate them! God curse them,
> funkers. God blast them, wish-wash. Exterminate them, slime.
> (*CL*, p. 134)[20]

The way was already clear for Lawrence's wartime responses and for his
determination to leave 'so meagre and paltry, . . . so unspiritual a
country' (*R*, p. 461).

Alienation itself supplies a context important to the understanding,
however, and the deduction ought not to be made that Englishmen and
English society did not find their way into Lawrence's thinking, despite

his tantrums. It was often noticed by others that Lawrence cherished a certain *calme anglais*, especially when he was presented with the alternative ambiences of Australia or Mexico. Indeed, Somers is himself described in *Kangaroo* as 'one of the most intensely English men England ever produced' (*K*, p. 247). As late as 1923, at a time when Lawrence could with difficulty forgive Europe but not England, Wytter Brynner found him 'stubbornly English' none the less with a continuing inability to 'shake off his island's hereditary sense of abiding social levels'.[21] Whether or not Lawrence was in the grip of such assumptions, it is clear that his social analyses are frequently set in an English context and often in a half-rural, half-urban one. It is clear also that his adumbration of the communities he knew was authentic and occasionally, as in the depiction of the Bestwood class system (*SL*, p. 69), masterly. The presupposition of the inquiry undertaken here is simply that insights of this kind had origins and consequences and that a fuller understanding of Lawrence's political thought requires their presence. Since narrative seems too blunt an implement for present purposes, it will be abandoned in favour of a concentration on three aspects of Lawrence's development: the contexts of his nascent socialism; the wartime period of reorientation and the contact, in particular, with Russell's reconstructionism; and the later development, finally, of a more emphatic and bizarre individualism.

Eastwood and Nottingham provided the milieux in which Lawrence came closest to developing a socialist position. Personal relationships were clearly important in bringing this about. His mother may, for example, have given Lawrence some mild political orientation: the mothers of *The White Peacock* and *Sons and Lovers* are progressives, readers of Morley's *Life of Gladstone*, givers of papers at the Women's Guild (*WP*, pp. 94, 150; *SL*, p. 68). On the other hand, the grievance which Paul Morel hurls at his mother during their most bitter quarrel is precisely that '*You* don't care about Herbert Spencer' (*SL*, pp. 260–1). It may be that from his family background with its imperatives and decencies Lawrence nevertheless took away at least that apologetic regard for English Liberalism – 'a slobbery affair, all sad sympathy with everybody' – which led him to believe that it remained 'true to its great creed' under Asquith's direction until the end of 1916 (*K*, p. 251). Outside the family circle were Willie Hopkin and Alice Dax, who opened up shelves of political literature and introduced him to some leading personalities of the Left who visited the study circle organised by the two Eastwood socialists. Ramsay MacDonald, Philip Snowden, Charlotte Despard, Annie Kenney, Margaret Bondfield and the Webbs are reliably reported to have visited the group. Another important name associated with the Eastwood group is Edward Carpenter.

Carpenter's relationship with Lawrence has assumed special interest since Professor Delavenay drew attention to it in 1971.[22] Whilst no great imagination is required to see obvious parallels between the two men (they were both libertarians, were both preoccupied by sexual mores and both rejected religion), Delavenay has gone much further in identifying Carpenter as a crucial context for an understanding of Lawrence. Indeed, it is part of Delavenay's contention that Lawrence almost certainly met Carpenter through the Hopkin–Dax network and that he had unquestionably read Carpenter's books; that Carpenter is the unacknowledged mediator of some of Lawrence's intellectual dispositions; and that between the end of 1912 and the end of 1916 Carpenter's influence reached a 'high-water mark'.[23] These contentions are patently of relevance to the concerns of this essay and the evidence on which they are based presumably merits critical consideration.

Criticism stumbles at once, however, over serious epistemological obstacles. In the first place it is apparent that Delavenay has employed an ethereal conception of what relevant evidence might be said to be. He disavows any straightforward 'factual approach' and prefers one that is supplemented by 'some sort of intuitive and interpretative reasoning',[24] though it is not consistently clear at which points this has been applied. To this extent the list of hard historical evidence which follows is susceptible to a significant margin of error. It seems none the less to contain the points on which Delavenay's position is made to rest:

(1) Millthorpe is thirty miles from Eastwood.
(2) Enid Hopkin Hilton said that Carpenter visited Eastwood.
(3) Willie Hopkin's name is in Carpenter's address book.
(4) Jessie Chambers said in 1935 that (i) Alice Dax owned most of Carpenter's books and that (ii) Lawrence read all Alice Dax's books.
(5) During the war Lawrence asked Hopkin to solicit support for the *Signature* from 'a few people in Sheffield'.

There are other points, doubtless intuitive and interpretative, such as the observation that the personality of Alice Dax and Blanche Jennings 'fits perfectly into the picture of Lawrence's interests,'[25] but these are left aside since it is not apparent which, if any, historical proposition they are intended to confirm.

Now it may be that literary evidence can sufficiently augment these points to make possible the construction of a case; but it seems plain that on historical grounds they are too fragile to support any weight. That Lawrence lived a comparatively short distance from Carpenter by itself says nothing. If Enid Hopkin says that Carpenter met Lawrence, Jessie Chambers, whose evidence Delavenay is happy to present, felt sure that he did not. Willie Hopkin's entry in Carpenter's address book confirms what no one wants to deny, that Carpenter knew of (and perhaps visited) the Eastwood circle. Jessie Chambers's assertion that Carpenter was read by Lawrence seems firm if circumstantial; but then Lawrence read many other socialists and may well – an intuitive or interpretative point – have concentrated on writers less outmoded. (Carpenter's political writing and best social criticism date from the early part of his career, except for a burst of enthusiasm for the politics of land in 1907–8; after 1890 his themes are mostly the sexual ones to which Lawrence was antipathetic.[26]) As for Lawrence's attempt to drum up support for his short-lived *Signature*, his mention of Sheffield is unstressed in the original and has to be placed in the context of his remark that he wants 'a few people anywhere'.[27] Moreover, the tone of Carpenter's letter to Hopkin when he returned a copy of the suppressed *Rainbow* gives no hint whatever that Carpenter was speaking of a man he knew.[28] Too much can easily be read into the capacity of the Dax–Hopkin circle to create contacts and acquaintances. It is noticeable, for example, that when in a letter of 1918 to Kotelianski Lawrence reflected on which socialists he would most like to know, his list contained two individuals – Snowden and Margaret Bondfield – who are supposed to have been introduced into the Eastwood underworld before the war (*KL*, p. 150). But, of course, most damaging of all to Delavenay's thesis is the stark fact that Lawrence nowhere, publicly or privately, refers to Carpenter; and the proffered explanation – that Carpenter was not prestigious enough to mention and/or that he was a defender of homosexuality[29] – seems weak in the presence of so complete a silence.

It should be stressed that this is not to question that Lawrence had come into contact with socialists at a formative moment in his life or that he had read many of their theorists – including, no doubt, Edward Carpenter. The outlook of the early years is certainly characterised by the 'passionate feeling for "the workers"' which Catherine Carswell erroneously took to be an enduring facet of Lawrence's *Weltan-schauung*.[30] Much of the reading on which this sentiment was based was done in Nottingham and Croydon rather than at Eastwood. It seems that during the second year of his college course Lawrence read widely in the philosophical literature of the nineteenth century (Carlyle, Mill,

Spencer, Huxley, William James). Among continental thinkers he read Schopenhauer, whom he liked, and Renan, whom he did not.[31] These writers find their way into the early novels, where Lawrence was not always innocent of a certain degree of *arriviste* name-dropping. The case of Spencer has been mentioned; Schopenhauer and James come into *The White Peacock* (*WP*, p. 75). Renan enters *Sons and Lovers* via Paul and Miriam, who are said to be at 'the Renan "Vie de Jésus" stage' (*SL*, p. 279); and Spencer reappears in *The Rainbow* (*R*, p. 90). It is likely that the political literature strewn about the first of Lawrence's novels also came to his attention during the Nottingham period and after. If one amalgamates the reading attributed to George Saxton and Lettie Beardsell, for example, the list comprises Blatchford, Masterman, Chiozza Money, Wells, Shaw, Neil Lyons and Querido. Of these Wells and Shaw fit the Nottingham–Croydon context.[32] Blatchford and Lyons, cleverly split between the two fictional characters, are probably one source, Lyons's life of Blatchford, which appeared in 1910, though Blatchford also wrote for the *New Age*, to which Lawrence subscribed for a time.[33] Which of Masterman's books Lawrence had in mind is unclear: an obvious candidate is *The Condition of England* (1909), or perhaps the earlier collection of essays *The Heart of the Empire* (1901), which Masterman edited. Granted Lawrence's interests and the aesthetic emphases of *The White Peacock*, however, it may be that Masterman's Introduction to the 1907 Cassell edition of Ruskin's *The Political Economy of Art* is more relevant. Chiozza Money poses fewer problems: his chapters on rural estates, his section on land rent and a chapter on depopulation make *Riches and Poverty* suitable background.[34] Equally, the Querido would have to be *Toil of Men*: all the other writings of this period were untranslated.[35] Similarly, the studiously throwaway reference to 'some work about Woman and Labour' in *The Rainbow* must refer to Olive Schreiner's book of that title, which Lawrence may have borrowed from Helen Corke.[36]

Reading apart, the move to Nottingham brought personal contacts which ought not to be forgotten. It is well known that Lawrence was profoundly unhappy in the Nottingham environment and put little faith in his teachers:

College gave me nothing, even nothing to do – I had a damnable time there, bitter so deep with disappointment that I have lost forever my sincere boyish reverence for men in position. Professors and the rest of great men I found were quite small men . . . all wind and quibbles, flinging out their chaffy grain to us with far less interest than a farmwife feels as she scatters corn to her fowls. . . . there are only four or five respectworthy people in the place, and only one or two whom I knew and felt superior to myself – I am speaking of professors.[37]

It appears, however, that Professor the Reverend John Elliotson Symes was among the chosen few.[38] Symes was Principal of Nottingham University College between 1890 and 1911 and was in a position significantly to influence the young Lawrence. None of the difficulties which dog the attempt to relate Lawrence to Carpenter, moreover, attends this connection: it is a matter of simple record that Lawrence knew Symes and was taught by him. And there are some grounds for believing that the early novels – and *The White Peacock* in particular – registered an awareness of themes which could not have been avoided at the hands of Symes.

Only the skeleton of Symes's biography is at present known; there has been no full-length study of him and it seems that no collection of unpublished material is extant.[39] After leaving Cambridge he spent some years as an extension lecturer, a period as a curate in Stepney and a year or so as a schoolmaster in Newcastle. In 1881 Symes was appointed to one of the four chairs established in the new University College of Nottingham. Although his designated field was English language and literature, Symes turned out to be a polymath who could teach all the arts subjects and political economy in addition. It was, indeed, in the latter field that Symes first made his mark nationally; in 1884 the pundit Goddard Orpen referred to him as 'a Political Economist of repute', and when his textbook on the subject appeared four years later that reputation was consolidated.[40] Already, however, Symes's tendencies towards the socialist position were creating friction within his own university. A pervasive anxiety concerned Symes's putative espousal of the ideas of Henry George, whom Symes had met during Henry George's lecture tour of Britain.[41] The lectures which Symes gave on the political economy of land and its taxation helped to stimulate resentments against him, so that, when he was dismissed in 1911 on the grounds of 'administrative incompetence', cynics could have been forgiven for believing the real reason to lie elsewhere.

Can any of this teaching, the question arises, be seen beneath the surface of Lawrence's early writing? It is at once evident that both *The White Peacock* and *Sons and Lovers* voice an interest in and knowledge of some notions central to contemporary political economy. There is an announcement of what was to be a lifelong contempt for *laisser-faire* complacency which could mean 'pulling the nipple out of your lips' and leaving you, the individual, the victim of an uncontrolled predator: 'they're free to charge and you're forced to pay' (*WP*, p. 78; *K*, pp. 15, 241). He sets his characters within a rural argument about rent and land nationalisation. In *The White Peacock*, George – is the name a coincidence? – has a father who reads books on the land question, engages in disputes with his squire over his rent and himself speculates in land during the years of his drunken decline (*WP*, pp. 74, 215, 338).[42] On the Leivers' farm, similarly, Paul observes, in the interstices of avoiding Miriam, that 'all the men, Mr Leivers as well, had bitter debates on the nationalization of land and similar problems' (*SL*, p. 195). Plainly such problems were part of a common currency, especially when Lawrence was writing *Sons and Lovers*, in the context of Lloyd George's land tax in the 1909 budget and the opening moves of the land campaign which he was soon to begin.[43] Yet it seems reasonable to suggest that Symes's message formed an important part of Lawrence's context at Nottingham which should not be ignored. If it is true that Lawrence never came into contact with any great thinkers, as Green suggests,[44] then the case is only strengthened for encompassing the smaller ones.

There were other socialist contexts, Shavian Fabianism, for example, and some representatives of the London Progressive Movement during the Croydon period. But their hold was tenuous. Perhaps Lawrence rejected Fabianism from the start, as Tiverton believes;[45] certainly he had moved out of its orbit by 1910. When his mother's last illness made it impossible for him to keep an engagement with Willie Hopkin in August of that year, Lawrence confided to him, 'I seem to have lost touch altogether with the old "progressive" clique: in Croydon the Socialists are so stupid and the Fabians so flat' (*CL*, p. 63).[46] This disenchantment was to grow stronger after 1912 despite the contact with socialists such as Jaffe which involvement with Frieda entailed. The political accents of *The White Peacock* and *Sons and Lovers* are mostly missing in *The Rainbow* and *Women in Love*, despite the agricultural context of the former and the opportunities for reflections on industrial civilisation offered by the latter. By the time of *Aaron's Rod*, socialist notions have been given a vibrant, post-revolutionary colouring and are advertised by unsympathetic characters; it tends to be a John Bricknell who is left 'talking rather vaguely about Labour and Robert Smillie and Bolshevism' (*AR*, p. 72). All that was left of the pre-war working-class language was a life-force vocabulary of eloquent eyes and tanned biceps. There was no longer any urge politically to ally with proletarian movements. From Sicily, Lawrence wrote to Kotelianski in 1920 telling

him how much he did not want to come home 'to be associated with
[Henry] Mond and Gilbert [Cannan] on a paper. What remaining belief
I had in Socialism dies out of me more & more as the time goes by.'
There was no attraction in communicating with the post-war masses.
'One ha[d] to be a Murry or a Squire or a Sassoon' (*KL*, p. 206).[47] The
spell of Sicily will have confirmed this new feeling but its origins were
English, bore centrally on Lawrence's political thought and were largely
the product of the First World War.

    Lawrence did not live long enough to enjoy his war record. He died
just at the moment when opposition to all wars had entrenched itself as a
fashion and when the heroics of those who had stood firm against war
fever in 1914 were attracting approval. Had he lived another four or five
years he would probably have become one of Julian Bell's war-
resisters.[48] Yet, although his part in it would remain for many years
unsung, the war profoundly affected the frame of mind in which
Lawrence contemplated individualism, aristocracy and the possibility
of a civilised democracy. This thinking is refracted rather than reflected
in the wartime novels, which are symbolic art forms sculpted, as Cynthia
Asquith nicely observed, by a man with a temperature of 103.[49] It is
rather in his private letters that Lawrence's suffering and mental shifts
are best chronicled. Not that those years enforced a consistent
hopelessness: for much of 1915, it may be recalled, Lawrence was
enthusiastic about his Rananim, a utopian colony to be created by
himself and his friends, and about proselytising for peace. Two
important contexts helped inspire this mood; but neither of them
appeared until Lawrence had spent a ghoulish half-year in the
desolation of his cottage at Chesham:

> Those five months since the war have been my time in the sepulchre.
> . . . I shall never forget those months in Bucks – five months & every
> moment dead, dead as a corpse in its grave clothes. . . .
>   Tomorrow Lady Ottoline is coming again & bringing Bertrand
> Russell – the Philosophic–Mathematics man . . . .   (*KL*, p. 28)[50]

These two links – the Garsington connection of Lady Ottoline Morrell
and, more important, the short-lived friendship with Russell – were to
provide a significant social and intellectual location for Lawrence.

    Garsington, with its post-Bloomsbury ambience, was perhaps more
of an aberration than a context. It was certainly not an acquaintance of
his choosing. To the extent that the Morrells' Oxfordshire home had
become a haven for those opposing the war, an overture to Lawrence

was not unnatural. But when Lady Ottoline wrote to Lawrence she had in mind her own ambitions as a cultural impresario more than Lawrence's stand over the war. Out of her approach there developed, nevertheless, an epistolary friendship which culminated in an offer to the Lawrences of a cottage at Garsington. Here was an opportunity for Lawrence to create the idealised community he had already been urging on his friends as 'a new Jerusalem', in Catherine Carswell's quip, 'within convenient distance of Oxford and Cambridge'.[51] He expounded the idea to Ottoline on 1 February 1915, feeling 'big with hope for the future':

> I want you to form the nucleus of a new community which shall start a new life amongst us – a life in which the only riches is integrity of character. So that each one may fulfil his own nature and deep desires to the utmost, but wherein tho', the ultimate satisfaction and joy is in the completeness of us all as one. . . . The present community consists, as far as it is a framed thing, in a myriad contrivances for preventing us from being cut down by the meanness in ourselves or in our neighbours. . . . I hold this the most sacred duty – the gathering together of a number of people who shall so agree to live by the *best* they know, that they shall be *free* to live by the best they know. . . . I do believe that there are enough decent people to make a start with. Let us get the people. (*CL*, p. 311)

The theme was to be recurrent over the next few years, especially after the suppression of *The Rainbow* in November 1915 and the introduction of military conscription in 1916 heightened Lawrence's sense of oppression. Yet it is hard to see how the world of the Morrells could have assimilated his strategy: indeed, the initial (and later) plans were based on finding a suitable site outside England for the colony. And the figures who comprised the core of Garsington society could hardly offer a congenial company for a commune. Lawrence himself, in the letter to Ottoline quoted above, finds time to attack Lytton Strachey. Later in the year he was to discover that Francis Birrell stimulated the same dreams of black beetles to which the famous encounter with Maynard Keynes had given rise (*Cl*, p. 311; *KL*, p. 39). Lady Ottoline, for her part, embodied in Lawrence's eyes the corrosive will satirised in Hermione Roddice; and, of course, after her role in *Women in Love* had infuriated her she began a programme of sustained malice against Lawrence. By 1917 enough had been said to make it plain that 'all the Ott. crowd' were against him. He had no patience with Gertler's clumsy attempts at diplomacy – 'like Mr Balfour discussing peace terms' – and the consignment of 'the whole Ottlerie' to the nether regions was the inevitable conclusion (*KL*, pp. 114, 143).[52]

Ottoline's lover, Bertrand Russell, looked far more promising as a soul mate. Russell had already turned away from his absorption in mathematics and had assumed a political stance on the left of Liberalism and tending leftwards, though he had by now turned forty.[53] His meeting with Lawrence at Greatham took place at his instigation *via* Lady Ottoline. What followed is well known: a discipleship astonishing in a man of Russell's critical calibre. 'He is amazing', ranted Russell, 'he sees through and through one. . . . He is infallible . . . he sees everything and is always right.'[54] The strange narrative then trundled forward – the agonising Cambridge visit with the sulky silences and Keynes in his pyjamas; the abortive attempt to collaborate with Russell on some political lectures during the autumn of 1915; the hopes, nevertheless, for some sort of '*Blutbrüderschaft*'; the gradual separation widening into a contemptuous rejection by Lawrence and a bitter denunciation by his erstwhile admirer. These events of 1915–16 are plainly significant for the surface texture of both biographies. They mark also, however, an important shift of focus in the way in which both men saw the political future.

Russell's view was expressed in the draft of *Principles of Social Reconstruction*, which Lawrence covered in scribbled criticism. The final product, moreover, has a clear Lawrencean imprint and becomes occasionally a manifesto for an expanded Rananim. 'The supreme principle, both in politics and private life' is thought sufficiently crystalline to be presented in one italicised statement: '*to promote all that is creative, and so diminish the impulses and desires that centre round possession*'. All the constitutional recommendations of the lectures are means to this single end, the maximisation of 'the joy of life, the quick affection, the creative insight, by which the world may grow young and beautiful and filled with vigour'.[55] This much at least (with the possible exception of 'vigour', which has a pronounced Russell flavour) had been imported from Greatham. Yet Lawrence disliked the book.[56] True, he maintained for the moment his affection for Russell personally and still hoped that they might work together later in the year; but in retrospect the hope seems wholly unreal. Some of the problems are obvious – Lawrence's swirling incoherence and his evasiveness when asked to set down his 'philosophy', for example. But from the point of view of their respective political theories there was a more fundamental lack of communication which stemmed from Russell's belief that Lawrence's political thought was socialist and psychologist. He was wrong on both counts.

'I wouldn't dream of discouraging his socialist revolution', Russell had written after the disastrous Cambridge visit.[57] This was not an unreasonable judgement. Less than a month earlier Lawrence had sent what was, for him, an unusually 'political' letter written in a vocabulary which implied a socialist position of some kind. 'There must be a revolution in the state', he had said. 'It shall begin by the nationalizing of all industries and means of communication, and of the land – in one fell blow. Then a man shall have his wages whether he is sick or well or old – if anything prevents his working, he shall have his wages just the same' (*CL*, p. 317).[58] The euphoria brought on by his finishing the rewriting of *The Rainbow* had more to do with these jejune ravings, however, than had any quasi-Marxist orientation. Lawrence may have pillaged his Georgeite past for some colourful political language, but little more need be read into it. His writings echo time and time again his suspicion and dislike of the 'state', and his disapproval predates his persecution by the British authorities during the war. In his first letter to Ottoline Morrell, for example, he declares the state 'a vulgar institution', 'an arrangement for myriads of people living together' rather than a positive social force (*CL*, p. 305). At just the time when he became involved with Russell, moreover, Lawrence's contempt for social equality was deepening into a political position. The single qualification of January 1915 – 'I am no democrat, save in politics' – is all but gone by July, when Russell received a very different delineation of the future from the 'socialist' missive of February. 'The deadly Hydra now', Lawrence told him, 'is the hydra of Equality. Liberty, Equality and Fraternity is the three-fanged serpent. You must have a government based on good, better and best' (*CL*, p. 354).[59] This is the mood which was to find literary expression in the writing of *Women in Love* over the following year:

We are all abstractly or mathematically equal, if you like. . . . But spiritually, there is pure difference and neither equality nor inequality counts. It is upon these two bits of knowledge that you must found a state. Your democracy is an absolute lie – your brotherhood of man is a pure falsity. . . . In the spirit, I am as separate as one star is from another, as different in quality and quantity. Establish a state on *that*. One man isn't any better than another, not because they are equal, but because they are intrinsically *other*. . . . I want every man to have his share in the world's goods, so that I am rid of his importunity, so that I can tell him: 'Now you've got what you want – you've got your fair share of the world's gear. Now you one-mouthed fool, mind yourself and don't obstruct me.'   (*WL*, p. 161)

There may be a commitment to distributism which socialists might applaud; but its *raison d'être* could hardly be less collectivist. Lawrence is seeking a confirmation of individual insularity, not the means of its abrogation.

Looking back on the Lawrence episode in his autobiography, Russell decided that one aspect of Lawrence's political thought which had attracted him was his 'thinking that politics could not be divorced from individual psychology'.[60] Again, this is a plausible appraisal of a writer who placed such manifest stress on subjectivism and the experiential. What Russell did not appreciate, however, was the degree to which psychology had no simple existence for Lawrence as an intellectual category. He saw it merely as a constituent of an amorphous view of the world in which philosophy, physiology and psychology interpenetrated. And, in so far as his political ideas were mediated in this way, it was the physiological, rather than the psychological, element which tended to be dominant. At the centre of Lawrence's thinking was certainly the individual; but he took the latter's physio/psychological make-up as his starting-point. What Russell believed to be undesirable incidental accretions – the blood language, for example, which Russell explained as an imposition from Vienna via Frieda[61] – remained at the core of Lawrence's speculations through forms of reasoning which Russell's training in deductive logic did not help him to appreciate. Lawrence's labelling of the spectre of Russell in a bathing-suit 'disembodied mind' went beyond a joke. He genuinely believed that Russell's understanding of 'mind' was foreshortened: he was 'so temporal, so immediate' (*CL*, p. 350).[62] In Russell, Lawrence sought some sense of the absolute and the infinite and found it wanting. If there was psychology in his politics, Lawrence conceived it in the way he later expressed it in *Psychoanalysis and the Unconscious* with its physical apparatus of thoracic centres and mood-moulding ganglia. At the beginning of his relationship with Russell he had seen that he did not possess the cerebral equipment which a full understanding of Russell's philosophy and mathematics would demand. Russell was slower to learn that his very possession of that equipment would put Lawrence's thinking beyond his reach. The 'finite and ready-defined self' (*CL*, p. 360)[63] which Russell presented to the world in 1915 was impermeable by the breadth of message which Lawrence believed himself to be uttering.

Russell was not unique in this disability. By the end of 1917 Lawrence was taking the view that there were no more than eight people in the world whose company he could tolerate for two hours without physical distress.[64] The failure of all his schemes in 1915 left him scrambled; 'he just s[at] and gibber[ed] with fury'.[65] Those whom he believed to have betrayed him were scrambled also into a common human mess, all 'world-builders à la Lansbury', all 'Garsington tea-party Bertie[s] (*KL*, pp. 131, 213). The Lawrence of *Aaron's Rod* and *Kangaroo* was already in embryo. No more '*Blutbrüderschaft*', just 'a sort of human bomb, black inside and primed'.[66]

Lawrence was still Lawrence after 1915; but he had traversed a considerable distance since the days of Hopkin, Dax, and Morley's *Life of Gladstone*. The socialism to which he once adhered had gone: its language was now past tense.[67] He had passed through a period of naïve populism, the Rananim period when everybody had been urged to 'begin to be free & happy with each other' and 'cease their analysis & introspection & individualism (*KL*, p. 62). Bottomley and Northcliffe, censorship and conscription, hounding and humiliation had then crushed all his social optimism. A loathing for equality of talents slid into a hatred of political democracy and humanity in the mass. The refusal of the latter to listen to him only confirmed its insignificance. 'I am most sick of this divinity of man business', he wrote to Kotelianski in a black moment at the beginning of 1916. 'People are *not important*: I insist on it. . . . Let them die, silly blighters, fools and twopenny knaves' (*KL*, p. 68).[68] In the past he might himself have been 'a nuisance and a fool'; but henceforth he would not bother his friends with his 'social passion and social insistence'.[69] Even his demotic vocabulary underwent a revolution. Bugs, beehives and beasts of the field began to inhabit his letters and the post-war fiction. Why should people be thought more important than horses and dogs? They are, after all, 'not *men*: they are insects'; 'like bugs they creep . . . and they are too many to crush. Oh, if one could but have a great box of insect powder, and shake it over them . . . and exterminate them' together with 'the whole beehive of ideals [which] has got all the modern bee-disease, and gone putrid, stinking'.[70]

What was elemental and permanent in the political thought which Lawrence took away with him from England needs to be distinguished, however, from the spontaneous scratchings of the tormented animal. The attacks on mankind are less a celebration of cruelty and violence than a reaction against its practice among and within states since 1914. Lawrence's idealised political community, in its various forms, was a refuge in a natural marsh of barbarism wherein 'the blood rises in our heel-prints' (*WP*, p. 25). The desirable polity is a Woodside, a soothing bower where 'we just live, nothing abnormal, nothing cruel and extravagant – just natural – like doves in a dove-cote' (*WP*, p. 129). Kangaroo says little more than this – behind the poetry of submission there is the same reassurance in the face of a cruel world:

> Life is cruel – and above all things man needs to be reassured and suggested into his new issues. And he needs to be relieved of the terrible responsibility of governing himself when he doesn't know what he wants, and has no aim towards which to govern himself. Man again needs a father – not a friend or a brother sufferer, a suffering Saviour. Man needs a quiet, gentle father who uses his authority in the name of living life, and who is absolutely stern against anti-life. I offer no creed. I offer myself, my heart of wisdom . . . .   (*K*, p. 126)

Violation was neither the purpose nor the means of Lawrence's politics. When it sometimes seems to be so in the post-1915 material it takes the form of a cat-swipe against his oppressors or, more usually, a refraction from the quirky individualism which Lawrence had been incubating since 1912–13.

In the period of Lawrence's maturity, English individualism was an etiolated doctrine of anti-statism which tended to derive from a wish, like Spencer's, to perpetuate qualities essential to survival in a competitive universe, or an attempt, like Auberon Herbert's or Hilaire Belloc's, to prevent the eradication of civic freedoms, or a hope, like Mallock's, that natural inequality might be maintained by social and political institutions. Lawrence's individualism began elsewhere, with his physio-psychological understanding of what the individual 'soul' comprised and of what was necessary to its life. This unit of social analysis was not co-extensive with the notion of 'personality' as conventionally conceived; it was a far more fluid impression which *The Rainbow* was intended to realise. In defence of an early draft of that novel, Lawrence told Edward Garnett that 'the old stable ego of the character' had to be rejected in favour of something more deliquescent. 'There is another ego', he argued, 'according to whose action the individual is unrecognizable, and passes through, as it were, allotropic states which it needs a deeper sense than any we've been used to exercise to discover are states of the same radically-unchanged element. . . . my diamond might be coal or soot . . . my theme is carbon' (*CL*, p. 282). In itself the idea was not the base for a political position, but it could become one when Lawrence entered the next phase of his life after 1915.

So when Lawrence pressed his hatred of the masses on Kotelianski in 1917 he had a theme to which he could revert. 'Henceforth', he wrote, 'I deal in single, sheer beings – nothing human, only the star-singleness of paradisal souls' (*KL*, p. 122).[71] These 'pure being[s]' (*R*, p. 320) with their 'proud individual singleness' (*WL*, p. 332)[72] are at the core of his individualism. They give it its eccentric character and are responsible for most of its structural difficulties.

Suppose, for example, one takes up *Aaron's Rod* as a presumed fruit of this thinking and tries to find within it a coherent political statement. It is not difficult to locate what looks like an individualist root in its conventional form:

'Why, I'll tell you the real truth,' said Lilly. 'I think every man is a sacred and holy individual, *never* to be violated. I think there is only one thing that I hate to the verge of madness and that is bullying. To see any living creature *bullied*, in any way, almost makes a murderer of me.' (*AR*, p. 328).

From this one may take it that the state is not allowed to apply compulsion to the individual except, presumably, over matters crucial to the state's competence *qua* state – the raising of revenue, legislating to counter the effects of disease or famine, and so on. The individual must be allowed – one elides into Lawrence's more personal account of individuality – the pleasures of 'alert enjoyment of being central, life-central in [his] own little circumambient world' (*AR*, p. 340).[73] The monopoly which must be granted to the citizen is one over his 'essential plasm', his 'invisible being' (*AR*, p. 198), so that he may hold in his own hands the possibility of 'self-effectuation' (*R*, p. 328).[74] Seen from the point of view of a 'single, sheer being' all this may be desirable; but the question arises, is it possible or desirable when placed in a social context? What happens when the plasm becomes plasma? What controls are to be instigated to prevent the violations Lawrence despises whilst maintaining inviolable the individual's control of his life centrality? What is the machinery of political management and what are the grounds on which consent is given or withdrawn? How is the political fleet, to vary the metaphor, to become more than what Lawrence had once called 'a ridiculous armada of tubs jostling in futility' (*R*, p. 174)?

A superficial answer may be found in Lawrence's penchant for certain forms of aristocracy or dictatorship. *Aaron's Rod* and *Kangaroo* present a language involving committal by inferiors to the care of superiors, a polity which might be brought about by the revolutionary cells of

Australian nationalism or by the sense of a (suddenly) enlightened
electorate who will vote for 'a proper and healthy and energetic slavery'
(*AR*, p. 327). What everyone wants in his deepest soul – the last page, this
– is 'the deep, fathomless submission to the heroic soul in a greater man'
(*AR*, p. 347). Citations of this sort are countless and easy; but they offer
little help. In the first place it might be argued, given the centre of interest
here, that this development owes little to Lawrence's English experience.
The problems that his dictators are to solve have an English origin but
the solution is Italian. Indeed, it is a joke with Lawrence that the best the
English could do by way of a dictator was Lloyd George. Secondly, the
solution is in any case false. It does not make the structural problems go
away but rather compounds them by inviting Lawrence to explain how
his political community is to work under the direction of an individual
or group of individuals and yet foster the virtues that are the ostensible
ground for its establishment. It is a square circle, a dictatorship which is
not only libertarian but which forces the individual to be free without
using force. In this respect, Tiverton's observation that Lawrence has a
streak of anarchism[75] is an *aperçu* worth developing. It has as much
relevance to Lawrence's utopian visions as his supposed 'fascism' and
adumbration of Auschwitz.

Or, put another way, it is equally irrelevant. For the point which is
most striking about Lawrence's political thought is not that it is anti-
statist or anti-democratic but that it is anti-structural. Anarchism and
dictatorship here fuse into a single expedient: they both offer ways of
theorising which minimise or altogether avoid discussion of how
political communities function, how they define and resolve conflicts
created by individuals, however paradisal, living in a community.
Unquestionably Lawrence amassed material on the basis of which he
could have presented a coherent political position. It would also have
been unusual in that it would have taken a series of physiological
assumptions in the direction of individualism rather than towards
collectivist genetics, which is what many of his contemporaries did. But
in fact his political thought led in no single direction. He showed himself
uninterested in providing a satisfactory account of the relationship
which should subsist between state and citizen. This was not an accident
of motivation, moreover: it was a predictable consequence of
Lawrence's understanding of ontology and epistemology. His politics
were non-Euclidean because such was the geometry of his universe. To a
degree perhaps unique among his generation, Lawrence could feel and
experience, and England was the source for most of those feelings and
experiences. Yet no context could be made responsible for what

Lawrence did with his data. The mental procedures which informed his politics also made it impossible for his politics to be communicated through the instrumentality of mere words, the static merchandise of the men he most despised.[76] His politics never reached paper because there was an important sense in which they coud not be 'thought' out or written about without doing violence to their message. Prescription, like so much else in Lawrence's thought, is subsidiary to affirmation. To seek it though textual analysis and deductive reasoning is a game as enjoyable and pointless as looking for a lecture in a psalm.

NOTES

1. 'In every phase she was so different. Yet she was always Ursula Brangwen. But what did it mean, Ursula Brangwen? She did not know what she was' (*R*, p. 437).
2. Martin Green, *The Von Richtofen Sisters* (London: Weidenfeld and Nicolson, 1974) p. 102.
3. A few months later Lawrence announced his sense of 'another world of reality'; he had 'lost' the old one (23 Sep 1917, *KL*, p. 123).
4. Letter dated 25 Dec 1915. Cf. Lawrence to Lady Ottoline Morrell ('Suffering'), 27 Dec 1915 (*CL*, pp. 404–5).
5. See Catherine Carswell, *The Savage Pilgrimage* (London: Secker, 1932) p. 59. Lawrence did admit, however, a 'logic of the soul' (*R*, p. 41).
6. In this latter-day sense Lawrence's understanding of intelligence is, *pace* Professor Leavis, peculiarly French. Cf. F. R. Leavis, 'Thought, Words and Creativity', *Thought, Words and Creativity: Art and Thought in Lawrence* (London: Chatto and Windus, 1976) pp. 15–33.
7. Cf. Ursula's question to Birkin: '"How can you have knowledge not in your head?" she asked.... "In the blood," he answered...' (*WL*, p. 92).
8. See Lawrence to Blanche Jennings, 25 June and (especially) 15 Dec 1908 (*CL*, pp. 18, 41): 'It doesn't matter how little you *know*, so long as you are capable of feeling much....' Ursulas college, it may be recalled, is 'a second-hand dealer's shop' (*R*, pp. 434–5).
9. Review of Eric Gill, *Art Nonsense and Other Essays*, quoted in 'W. Tiverton', *D. H. Lawrence and Human Existence* (London: Rockliff, 1951) p. 118.
10. Jessie Chambers to Helen Corke, n.d. (1933), in Helen Corke, *D. H. Lawrence: The Croydon Years* (Austin: University of Texas Press, 1965) p. 40.
11. The Liberal accretions of 1906 did return in general to their previous affiliations during the two general elections of 1910: see Neal Blewett, *The Peers, the Parties and the People: The General Elections of 1910* (London: Macmillan, 1972).
12. The Index to *The Times* contains over forty entries relating to the Coal Commission in the first half of 1919.

13. See Lady Cynthia Asquith, *Diaries 1915–18* (London: Hutchinson, 1968) p. 56 (20 July 1915). Cf. the delinquent coal duke in *The Rainbow* (*R*, p. 349).

14. For instance, Lawrence to Kotelianski, [?]11 March 1919: 'I daren't read the papers, I become at once ill' (*KL*, p. 164).

15. In *Kangaroo* the fall of Asquith's government takes place in the spring of 1917 (*K*, p. 250). Lloyd George had in fact become premier on 7 Dec 1916.

16. Cf. the reports of strikes in *Sons and Lovers* (*SL*, pp. 356, 478).

17. Green, *The Von Richthofen Sisters*, p. 156.

18. D. H. Lawrence, *England, My England* (Harmondsworth: Penguin, 1960) p. 15.

19. *K*, pp. 246, 250; Lawrence to Kotelianski, 10 Nov 1921 (*KL*, 229). Cf. *WP*, pp. 357–8.

20. Lawrence to Garnett, 3 July 1912. But cf. Green's view that during his walking-tour on the continent Lawrence had failed to 'shrug off his "English" personality' (*The Von Richthofen Sisters*, p. 118).

21. Witter Bynner, *Journey with Genius: Recollections and Reflections Concerning the D. H. Lawrences* (New York: John Day, 1951) p. 222. Cf. Lawrence to Carswell, n.d. (1922), quoted in Carswell, *The Savage Pilgrimage*, p. 182. Even before he left England, his strictures could be tired rather than venomous (cf. *AR*, p. 77).

22. Emile Delavenay, *D. H. Lawrence and Edward Carpenter: A Study in Edwardian Transition* (London: Heinemann, 1971).

23. Ibid., pp. 1–43.

24. Ibid., p. 5.

25. Ibid., p. 21.

26. The relevant early works are *Towards Democracy* (1883); *England's Ideal and Other Papers in Social Subjects* (1887); and *Civilization: Its Cause and Cure, and Other Essays* (1889). The agricultural theme is explored in a Fabian tract, *The Village and the Landlord* (1907) and in E. Carpenter, T. S. Dymond, D. C. Redder and the Fabian Society, *Socialism and Agriculture* (1908).

27. Quoted in Delavenay, *Lawrence and Carpenter*, p. 27.

28. Carpenter to Hopkin, 28 Mar 1916, quoted ibid., p. 31.

29. Ibid., pp. 39–40.

30. Carswell, *The Savage Pilgrimage*, p. 33n.

31. Harry T. Moore, *The Priest of Love: A Life of D. H. Lawrence* rev. edn (Harmondsworth: Penguin, 1976) p. 223. For Lawrence's 'Carlyliophobia', see Lawrence to Blanche Jennings, 4 May 1908 (*CL*, p. 8).

32. For instance, Lawrence to Blanche Jennings, 22 Dec 1908 and 6 Mar 1909 (*CL*, pp. 42, 51); Tiverton, *Lawrence and Human Existence*, p. 53.

33. See A. N. Lyons, *Robert Blatchford: The Sketch of a Personality* (London: Clarion, 1910). Blatchford is included in the list of writers for the *New Age* who 'either contributed frequently, or are sufficiently well-known to warrant mention' between 1907 and 1922: Wallace Martin, *The 'New Age' under Orage: Chapters in English Cultural History* (Manchester: Manchester University Press, 1967) p. 295. It is conceivable that Lawrence saw Blatchford's pamphlet *Land Nationalization* (1898) during his Eastwood period.

34. L. G. Chiozza Money, *Riches and Poverty*, 3rd edn (London: Methuen, 1906).

35. Israel Querido, *Toil of Men*, tr. F. S. Arnold (London: Methuen, 1909). Of the untranslated works, the closest in subject matter to Lawrence's writing of this period would seem to be *Menschenvee. Roman van het Land* (Haarlem, 1904).

36. Olive Schreiner, *Women and Labour* (London: T. Fisher Unwin, 1910). Helen Corke recalls that in June of that year she lent Lawrence Schreiner's *The Story of an African Farm*. See Corke, *In Our Infancy: An Autobiography* (Cambridge: Cambridge University Press, 1975) p. 184.

37. Lawrence to Blanche Jennings, 4 May and 1 Sep 1908 (*CL*, pp. 8–9, 27). Cf. the remarks on Ursula Brangwen's professors in *The Rainbow* (*R*, p. 436).

38. Moore, *The Priest of Love*, pp. 109–10.

39. A. W. Coats, 'John Elliotson Symes, Henry George and Academic Freedom in Nottingham during the 1880s', *Renaissance and Modern Studies*, VII (1963) 114, n. 1. I am very grateful to Colin Holmes for bringing this piece to my notice. Although Professor Coats's article is angled at an earlier controversy, his account of Symes's career valuably supplements the *Who Was Who?* entry (Symes died in 1921).

40. J. E. Symes, *A Textbook of Political Economy* (London: Rivington, 1888): Emile de Laveleye, *The Socialism of Today*, tr. G. H. Orpen (London: Field and Tuer, 1884) p. 307.

41. Coats, in *Renaissance and Modern Studies*, VII, 125–7. Symes probably encountered George through the offices of Stuart Headlam. For the latter, see Elwood P. Lawrence, *Henry George in the British Isles* (East Lansing: Michigan State University Press, 1957) p. 76, where Symes receives no mention.

42. It might be added that a college principal – 'such an old buck' – appears in this novel (*WP*, p. 135).

43. For the Liberal land initiative, see H. V. Emy, 'The Land Campaign: Lloyd George as a Social Reformer, 1909–14', in *Lloyd George: Twelve Essays*, ed. A. J. P. Taylor (London: Hamish Hamilton, 1971) pp. 35–68.

44. Green, *The Von Richthofen Sisters*, p. 124.

45. Tiverton, *Lawrence and Human Existence*, p. 52.

46. Lawrence to Hopkin, 24 Aug 1910. For an analysis of London politics in this period, see Paul Thompson, *Socialist, Liberals and Labour: The Struggle for London, 1885–1914* (London and Toronto, 1967).

47. Lawrence to Kotelianski, 11 Mar 1920. The Mond referred to was the son of Lloyd George's future Minister of Health, Alfred Mond, the first Lord Melchett. The two are conflated in Zytaruk's garbled summary (*KL*, p. 206n.) of Nehls's correct account (Nehls, II p. 596, n. 509). Cannan's *The Anatomy of Society* had appeared the previous year, during which, according to Aldington, its author had also been certified insane. See 'Cannan' in S. J. Kunitz and H. Haycraft, *Twentieth Century Authors: A Biographical Dictionary of Modern Literature* (New York, 1942) p. 244.

48. See *We Did Not Fight, 1914–18: Experiences of War Resisters*, ed. Julian Bell (London, 1935). The essay by Bertrand Russell, 'Some Psychological Difficulties of Pacifism in Wartime', makes no mention of Lawrence.

49. Cynthia Asquith, *Diaries 1915–18*, p. 424 (24 Mar 1918).
50. Lawrence to Kotelianski, 5 Feb 1915. The correspondence with Lady Ottoline had begun the previous month: see Lawrence to Lady Ottoline Morrell, 3 Jan 1915 (*CL*, pp. 315ff.).
51. Carswell, *The Savage Pilgrimage*, p. 33.
52. Lawrence to Kotelianski, 4 Apr 1917 and 2 July 1918. The only contact to have taken place between the Woolfs and Lawrence concerned the Zennor cottages which the Bloomsbury pair leased for a short time. See Quentin Bell, *Virginia Woolf: A Biography*, 2 vols (London: Hogarth Press, 1972) II, p. 65.
53. Russell was born in 1872, which made him thirteen years older than Lawrence, though this hardly validates Frieda Lawrence's recollection that at their first meeting in 1915 Lawrence was 'a raw twenty-six'. See *Frieda Lawrence: The Memoirs and Correspondence*, ed. E. W. Tedlock (1961) p. 137. Lawrence was in fact twenty-nine.
54. Violet Meynell's diary, quoted in Ronald C. Clark, *The Life of Bertrand Russell* (Harmondsworth: Penguin, 1978) p. 323.
55. Bertrand Russell, *The Principles of Social Reconstruction* (London, 1915) pp. 236, 204. For another example of the 'joy of life' motif, see pp. 134–5. It is also present in Russell's *Roads to Freedom* (London, 1918) pp. 145, 210.
56. 'I rather quarrelled with Russell's lectures' (Lawrence to Ottoline Morrell, [?]12 July 1915, *CL*, p. 353).
57. Quoted in Clark, *The Life of Bertrand Russell*, p. 323.
58. Lawrence to Russell, 12 Feb 1915. From the Georgeite point of view it is interesting that later in the letter he reverses the order of nationalisation and places land at the head of the list. Russell recommends land nationalisation in *Principles of Social Reconstruction* but *not* the abolition of rent (pp. 125–6).
59. Lawrence to Russell, 15 July 1915. Cf. *R*, p. 461.
60. Bertrand Russell, *Autobiography* (London, 1968) II, 20.
61. Ibid., p. 23.
62. Lawrence to Ottoline Morrell, [?]20 June 1915, *CL*, p. 350.
63. Lawrence to Cynthia Asquith, 16 Aug 1915, ibid., p. 360.
64. Cynthia Asquith, *Diaries 1915–18*, p. 357 (21 Oct 1917).
65. Ibid., p. 89 (17 Oct 1915).
66. 'No blood brotherhood. None of that' (*K*, p. 120). For Somers as a bomb, see *K*, p. 184.
67. '"*You're* a bit of a socialist though, aren't you?" persisted Levison, now turning to Lilly. "No," said Lilly, "I was"' (*AR*, p. 324).
68. Lawrence to Kotelianski, 15 Feb 1916. Cf. *R*, p. 250; *WL*, pp. 73, 192–3.
69. Lawrence to Carswell, n.d. (1918), quoted in Carswell, *The Savage Pilgrimage*, p. 109.
70. Horses and dogs are in Lawrence to Kotelianski, 12 June 1916 (*KL*, 80); for bugs see *KL*, p. 91 (4 Sep 1916). *WL*, p. 226, refers to 'vermin', and p. 289 to 'creeping democracy'. For the 'swarming' metaphor see *AR*, pp. 145, 326–7.
71. Lawrence to Kotelianski, 23 Sep 1917. 'Paradisal' had become a favourite adjective during the writing of *Women in Love* (*WL*, pp. 332, 357, 480).

72. The thing-in-itself is presumably distinct from the Kantian noumenon, which Lawrence elsewhere affects to despise.
73. Anna Brangwen had been, a few years earlier, 'an independent, forgetful little soul, loving from her own centre' (*R*, pp. 83–4).
74. It is interesting that Lawrence avoids the current Idealist expression 'self-realisation'.
75. Tiverton, *Lawrence and Human Existence*, p. 57.
76. 'Words' is, of course, the title of the concluding chapter of *Aaron's Rod*. For Lawrence the term is usually an allegation. Middleton Murry's *Still Life* is 'merely words, words, words' (Lawrence to Kotelianski, 15 Dec 1916, *KL*, p. 103). Cf. Somers's remark, 'if you don't know, it would only be words trying to tell' (*K*, p. 73). It was in *Women in Love*, however, that 'mere word-force' developed into a theme: see *WL*, pp. 91, 256, 327, 533.

6

The Sydney *Bulletin, Moby Dick* and the Allusiveness of *Kangaroo*

ANDREW PEEK

The virtual completion of *Kangaroo*, a novel of some 150,000 words, in the space of seven or eight weeks, whilst the novelist and his wife were staying in New South Wales, represents a *tour de force* in rapid composition; at the same time, bearing in mind the brevity of his stay and the highly limited contact he apparently had with Australians, we are inevitably encouraged to speculate about sources of information and imaginative stimulus utilised by Lawrence to supplement his own limited experiences in Australia.[1]

It has been interestingly suggested that reports in the *Sydney Morning Herald* of local disturbances in May 1921, the year prior to Lawrence's arrival, may have informed both the novelist's awareness of political feeling and unrest in contemporary Australia, and his imaginative use of them during the latter part of the novel.[2] *Kangaroo* itself makes reference to the Sydney *Sun*, the Sydney *Daily Telegraph* and, most important, the Sydney *Bulletin*, in whose pages the central figure of Somers finds much more than 'mere anecdotage. It was the sheer momentaneous life of the continent' (*K*, p. 300). A variety of quotations from the *Bulletin* are reproduced with the novel (*K*, pp. 297–9, 307, 354), in a different order from that in which they originally appeared, but otherwise unchanged except for correction of a spelling-error and minor changes, primarily in punctuation. Quite widely spread through the later part of the novel and consisting of eleven separate quotations in all, they create the impression of coming from a cross-section of numbers of the magazine: and it is interesting to learn that in fact they are all but one taken from six pages of *one* number of the *Bulletin* – the one for 22 June 1922 (pp. 16–22) – from the two regular sections entitled 'Society Section' and 'Aboriginalities'. The remaining quotation, referring to the behaviour of the Christianised Melanesians (*K*, p. 354), is taken from a longer note by a correspondent calling himself 'Friday Island', included in the 'Society Section' of the next but one issue of the *Bulletin* (for 6 July 1922). 'Friday Island's' note in the *Bulletin* is on the general subject of 'civilisation' as a 'thin veneer over a pre-historic impulse to sadism', a fact of some relevance to our reading of *Kangaroo*, since it is in the same chapter of the novel that refers us to this article (ch. 16) that we find the idea clearly and dramatically portrayed – in the murderous and explicitly sadistic revenge exacted by the Australian character Jack Callcott for the shooting of his leader, Kangaroo ('Having a woman's something, isn't it? But it's a flea-bite, nothing, compared to killing your man when your blood comes up' – *K*, p. 352). The note signed 'Globe' from the earlier number of the *Bulletin* about twenty bullocks following in each other's footsteps and stupidly drowning in the same waterhole (*K*, p. 307) sets Somers thinking about 'herd-unity, equality, domestication and civilization', thoughts which lead directly on to his lengthy conjectures in subsequent pages about the mob spirit, the urge to anarchy, and which are contrasted to his ideas about the marvellous communication of whale herds and the gesture of recoil – all details significantly framing the later stages of the novel. Thus, in the instances of the notes by 'Friday Island' and 'Globe', Lawrence's use of, and allusion to, the *Bulletin* relates closely to developments in his novel and may very well have partly prompted them.

This leads us on to more general inquiries about the extent to which elsewhere in *Kangaroo* we find such an apparently derivative type of allusiveness in operation, and about how far Lawrence was aware of using such a process; and, when, in the course of Somers's meditations about the instinctiveness of whales in chapter 16, we find an implicit allusion to the climax and conclusion of Herman Melville's *Moby Dick*, such questions become of considerable importance. In that chapter Somers compares the instinctive and unifying urge amongst men to revolt against old, irrelevant ideals with the 'whales which suddenly charge upon the ship which tortures them' (*K*, pp. 331–2). In the last of his brilliant, idiosyncratic essays on *Moby Dick*, Lawrence describes the *Pequod* as a 'symbol of this civilised world of ours'[3] and associates the White Whale with the forces of 'blood consciousness' and the gesture of instinctive, unreasoning recoil against the false idealism prevalent in Western culture since the Renaissance. Thus, when Somers, who clearly provides a thin disguise for the expression of Lawrence's current anxieties about the future of Western civilisation, fearfully foresees the masses in Australia (and throughout the West, as Lawrence's novel rather vaguely implies) like whales about to 'burst upon the vessel of civilization' (*K*, p. 332), we can recognise how events in chapter 134 of *Moby Dick* distinctively inform, and serve to increase the impact of, the analogy in chapter 16 of *Kangaroo*, even though it is the solitary figure of Moby Dick that turns back in recoil at the close of Melville's novel.

Apart from a note in Armin Arnold's *D. H. Lawrence and America* which observes that *Kangaroo* and *Moby Dick* both make reference to whales, and goes on to draw a casual and highly generalised connection between the two novels,[4] little has been made of Lawrence's evident allusion to events in Melville's novel; and yet it provides a likely clue to what lies behind probably the major artistic failure in *Kangaroo* – that is to say, the rendering of the titular figure of Ben Cooley or Kangaroo.

An Australian lawyer–politician and head of the nationalist and quasi-fascist Diggers movement, Kangaroo is intent upon persuading Somers, a writer and journalist recently arrived in Australia, to join his faction as its spokesman and as a 'power behind the throne' (*K*, p. 180) – a proposition by which the rather lonely and frustrated Somers is not untempted. Cast in a realistic mould, Kangaroo also has symbolic connotations, amongst which may be included his presentation as an unmistakably Promethean figure; and this is an aspect of the lawyer's character that Somers finds both striking and unacceptable. In chapters 6 and 7 in particular, Kangaroo's character compounds an ambivalent divinity and blasphemousness ('Why, the man is like a god', Somers tells himself, but later asks, 'What's the good, men trying to be gods?' – *K*, pp. 128, 234); the language used in Kangaroo's speeches is loaded with imagery of fire ('Seeds of fire. That's enough for me!' – *K*, p. 147); and, most significantly, he is impelled by the Promethean pride of self-consciousness, hallmark of the modern Promethean type, and thus exemplifies a trait viewed by Lawrence as a dangerous and debilitating characteristic of modern Western culture.[5] A lonely figure ('lonely as a nail in a post' – *K*, p. 117), an unbending monomaniac in the pursuit of his aims (following the 'absolute direction' of his soul, he remains 'fatal and fixed' - *K*, pp. 124, 117), Kangaroo comes to seem to Somers a drastically limited and essentially dehumanised man. Incapable of sustaining normative heterosexual relationships (as he himself admits in chapter 6), Kangaroo is increasingly seen as a sort of human machine, having only to 'turn on all the levers and forces of his clever, almost fiendishly subtle will, and he could triumph' (*K*, p. 124), and Somers eventually has little compunction in rejecting the Australian's offer and abandoning him immediately prior to his own departure from Australia *en route* for America, which marks the novel's close.

In each of the traits and characteristics noted above, Kangaroo corresponds to the character of Captain Ahab, another Promethean figure, solitary leader of his men, the effective deserter of his wife, a man 'left living on with half a heart' and caricatured as instrument and machine (see *Moby Dick*, ch. 41), also a paradoxical 'ungodly godlike' fusion (ch. 16). Ahab's undoubted energies are misdirected in the monomanic pursuit of the White Whale, who had taken off his leg near the Japanese coast, and in whom, as if by a bizarre but psychologically credible process of transference,

> all evil, to crazy Ahab, [was] visibly personified, and made practically assailable. . . . He piled upon the whale's white hump the sum of all the general rage and hate felt by his whole race from Adam down; and then, as if his chest had been a mortar, he burst his hot heart's shell upon it. (Ch. 41)

Whilst feeling compassion for Ahab's intentions, as the poignant mortar image indicates he should, the reader remains acutely aware of the grotesquely distorted motivation, and the cruel and ultimately self-destructive results of his pursuit of Moby Dick. Melville's novel, in other words, can be said to present a fable of the destructive plight of the fanatical idealist bent on exterminating the darker aspects of human existence, and, though he is a much less complex, and more overtly benevolent, type, precisely the same idea is being expressed through Lawrence's Kangaroo, another inflexible idealist. The Australian is an unquestioning believer in his own peculiarly insipid fusion of Christian and amatory love ('*Is* there any other inspirational force than the force of love? . . . There is no other' – *K*, p. 149), the value of the forces of reason and intellect to promote it ('I use [reason] at the service of love, like a sharp weapon' – *K*, p. 148), and a man who would take upon himself the role of a fatherly saviour of mankind from itself and all else wrong with the world:

> I offer myself, my heart of wisdom, strange warm cavern where the voice of the oracle steams in from the unknown; I offer my consciousness, which hears the voice; and I offer my mind and my will, for the battle against every obstacle to respond to the voice of life, and to shelter mankind from the madness and the evil of anti-life.
> (*K*, p. 126).

Somers, who becomes deeply and justly critical of Kangaroo, reminds us that we must not forget all that the Australian denies, what the English writer calls the 'dark God, the forever unrevealed. . . . The source of passions and strange motives' (*K*, p. 295). A contemporary review of the novel in *The Times Literary Supplement* perceptively identified Somers's 'dark god' with Melville's White Whale.[6] In this connection, it is relevant to juxtapose the moments of patent irony in both novels where their respective idealistic protagonists are destroyed through the agency of the life forces they seek to suppress and entirely fail to comprehend. The cornered whale is goaded into turning on Ahab and his ship, whilst Kangaroo is shot at a political rally in a manifestation of those passionate, violent, irrational feelings that are the antithesis of his mentally conceived love and idealising approach to life. The source of irony here is a common one: that in trying singlemindedly and inflexibly to rid humanity and the world of evil, one surrenders oneself to a cause which, because life is an infinitely complex mass of feelings, values and energies, will of necessity become life-destroying, rather than life-enhancing.[7]

On the face of it, Melville's mythopoeic whaling-captain and Lawrence's realistically portrayed lawyer–politician seem worlds apart, and there is a considerable contrast between the universality of Melville's fable about the danger of obsessive idealism and Lawrence's much more circumscribed view of idealism as signifying Christian love and preoccupation with the power of reason, will and intellect to the exclusion of other areas of religious and physical consciousness. The most significant discrepancy between Kangaroo and Ahab is, of course, measured in terms of artistic achievement and complexity: Ahab's idealistic streak upon which I have been concentrating is only one aspect of a rich and contradictory character which is dynamic, dramatic and profoundly engaging, whereas Kangaroo remains unconvincing, generally lifeless as a character, and is noisily verbose without managing to establish any genuine dramatic presence through the novel. In view of the often casual construction of *Kangaroo*, and the brilliant originality of such novels as *Sons and Lovers* and *The Rainbow*, this sort of derivative and sustained allusion to fable and character in another novelist's work may come as a surprise. But this is all surely very much to the point: Lawrence did not recognise how he was drawing upon Melville's figure and attributing to his own bathetic Kangaroo something of Ahab's imaginative stature.

Speaking more broadly about *Kangaroo*, the following picture emerges. It is a novel clearly begun out of Lawrence's experience prior to, and in, Australia (the descriptions of Australian scenery evidently draw on direct observation, and Kangaroo himself may be identified with close acquaintances, notably Kotelianski and Dr Eder), but with its impetus increasingly being maintained by less immediate factors, such as the charged evocation of old and bitter memories in the 'Nightmare' chapter, and the detailed use of journalistic and literary sources outlined above. Only in the final chapter, 'Adieu Australia', added, as Aldington tells us, after the Lawrences had arrived in America, do we observe a full return to the use of material with an immediately autobiographical basis, a characteristic that has tended to figure perhaps overprominently in our understanding of the genesis of *Kangaroo* and developments in it.

NOTES

1. Richard Aldington, in his Introduction to the Penguin edition of *Kangaroo*, convincingly argues that Lawrence's Australian novel 'was not even thought of before [his] arrival in Sydney (which starts the book) on May 26, 1922' (p. 7); and evidence in Earl and Achsah Brewster's *D. H. Lawrence: Reminiscences and Correspondence* (1934) indicates that it was finished (with the exception of the last chapter, added some time later) by 24 July 1922. Aldington notes that Lawrence 'met nobody socially' while in Australia (Introduction, p. 9).
2. Curtis Atkinson, 'Was There Fact in D. H. Lawrence's *Kangaroo*?', *Meanjin* (Melbourne), 29 (1965) 358–9.
3. D. H. Lawrence, *Studies in Classic American Literature* (Harmondsworth: Penguin, 1971) p. 168.
4. Armin Arnold, *D. H. Lawrence and America* (London: Linden Press, 1958) pp. 84–5.
5. Denis Donoghue's *Thieves of Fire* (London, 1973), a study of Prometheanism in literature, observes, 'the modern Promethean hero has given up his traditional role; he is no longer seen in public, exercising his will upon experience to the degree of destroying it. . . . The Promethean motive is now the pride of self-consciousness, and the play is performed in private, within the mind' (p. 96).
6. Repr. in *D. H. Lawrence: The Critical Heritage*, ed. R. P. Draper (London: Routledge and Kegan Paul, 1970) pp. 214–16.
7. Kangaroo might have been saved from death had Somers joined his cause and given him the will to pull through; however, Somers's abandonment of Kangaroo leaves the bullets to do their work, and serves to confirm the deadly power of the instinctive recoil from the forces of idealism.

7
A Spark beneath the Wheel: Lawrence and Evolutionary Thought

ROGER EBBATSON

Lawrence's art has its roots not only in the romanticism to which he stands as heir, but also in late-Victorian scientific rationalism. In particular he was affected by the idea of evolution, but simultaneously sought to redress its causal determinism with a more romantic apprehension of nature.[1] In a crucial scene of *The Rainbow* Dr Frankstone denies any 'special mystery' to life, whilst Ursula, gazing through the microscope, recognises a 'being infinite' in the heart of life (*R*, pp. 440–1). Lawrence imbibed the theory of evolution early: he read *The Origin of Species* and T. H. Huxley's *Man's Place in Nature* in 1907, and was familiar with Herbert Spencer's *First Principles* by 1909.[2] Jessie Chambers commented that this 'rationalistic teaching impressed Lawrence deeply. He came upon it at a time of spiritual fog, when the lights of orthodox religion and morality were proving wholly inadequate' (*ET*, p. 115). Reading in the literature of evolution proved seminal. What was it that Lawrence derived from this reading?

The Darwinian hypothesis that species were produced by development of varieties from common stock, and that new species emerged by a process of natural selection which was effected by the struggle for existence, marks Lawrence's early writing. Whilst modern biology sees natural selection in terms of differential reproduction, Darwin's language tended to stress that natural selection meant the death or survival of individuals whose variations were given. The image of nature as battleground is at the heart of mutability theory in *The Origin*, and recast in Lawrence's narratives: Gerald Crich is the supreme example of an organic being moving inexorably towards extinction, but there are many others, from the dead miner in 'Odour of Chrysanthemums' to the woman who rode away. Huxley's account of the struggle in nature is suggestive, since he stressed that sexual rivalry so prominent in the

90

Lawrencean world. Lawrence's men and women interact in a quasi-Darwinian way – it may be recalled how Darwin shows sexual selection operating through inter-male competition in animals. Huxley categorised organic beings into opponents (indirect opponents being rivals, direct opponents enemies) and helpers (*Man's Place in Nature*, p. 236). This type of biological analysis illuminates the rivalry over Lettie and Emily in *The White Peacock*, and the compensatory feeling of male brotherhood; the rivalry between Cecil Byrne and the dead Siegmund for Helena in *The Trespasser*, between Syson and Arthur Pilbeam in 'The Shades of Spring', and between Paul and Baxter Dawes in *Sons and Lovers*, to look no further.

As Huxley saw it, nature was in continuous ferment: 'spontaneous change is the rule, rest the exception – the anomaly to be accounted for. Living things have no inertia and tend to no equilibrium' (*Man's Place in Nature*, p. 256). This got translated, in Lawrence's theory of fiction, into a breakdown of traditional character typology. The role of the writer, Lawrence once remarked, was 'to stand right in the flux'. The writer's mind pervades the fiction and renders all characterisation new and tentative, so that Garnett needed to be warned, a propos *The Rainbow*, against looking for 'the old stable ego of the character'. Like the fiddle bow drawn across a sanded tray, characterisation would now take 'lines unknown' under the dominant exploratory consciousness of the author. The fictional character becomes no longer a set of attributes affixed to a proper name; by shedding his fossilised accretions of 'personality' the Lawrencean character moves towards authentic selfhood, as Aaron recognises: 'Now at last, after years of struggle, he seemed suddenly to have dropped his mask on the floor, and broken it. His authentic self-describing passport, his complete and satisfactory idea of himself suddenly became a rag of paper . . . he sat now maskless and invisible' (*AR*, p. 198).

Interpretation of the 'new life-prompting' leads the artist to discard form in favour of flux, as Paul Morel seeks to capture the 'shimmering protoplasm' in his painting, rejecting shape as 'a dead crust' (*SL*, p. 189). This piercing of the crust of reality into the central life flow is most fully accomplished in the sexuality which links human and non-human worlds within universal process. By discarding the shell of life, Paul and Clara, for instance, come to know that 'they were only grains in the tremendous heave that lifted every grass-blade its little height, and every tree, and living thing' (*SL*, pp. 430–1). The experiment of renewing the self is carried furthest in Birkin's reflections: 'How could he say "I" when he was something new and unknown, not himself at all? This I, this old formula of the age, was a dead letter' (*WL*, p. 459). Evolution of the self here demands the disintegration of 'identity', a process which Gerald cannot accept in his will-driven move towards death and extinction.

Lawrence's presentation of natural and human interdependence is a notable reflection of evolution theory, as instanced in Darwin's image of the tangled bank. Huxley showed how animals would eat plants, then later die and be 'returned into the inorganic world', making 'a constant circulation' from organic to inorganic (*Man's Place in Nature*, pp. 158–9). Lawrence characteristically rewrote this in 'Reflections on the Death of a Porcupine' (1925). 'The primary way, in our existence, to get vitality', he argued, 'is to absorb it from living creatures lower than ourselves.' There are different modes of absorption: 'devouring food is one way, love is often another. The best way is a pure relationship, which includes the *being* on each side, and which allows the transfer to take place in a living flow, enhancing the life in both beings' (*PhS*, p. 454). Clearly, Huxley's assertion of unity in nature had pierced the mental fog to which Jessie Chambers referred, and had proved heady reading for a young man brought up within the bounds of provincial Congregationalism. Lawrence already begins to translate Huxley into social terms in the essay 'Art and the Individual' which he prepared in the spring of 1908, concurrently with the second version of *The White Peacock*. Lawrence speaks of man's sympathy 'reverentially' recognising the 'vast scope of the laws of nature' and discovering 'something of intelligibility and consistent purpose working through the whole natural world and human consciousness'. When this happens, 'the religious interest is developed and the individual loses for a time the sense of his own and his day's importance, feels the wonder and terror of eternity with its incomprehensible purposes. This, I hold it, is still a most useful and fruitful state' (*PhII*, p. 222).

It is this sense of 'wonder and terror' that Paul experiences in 'Derelict'. Huxley gave Lawrence evidence of the feeling of incomprehension at the vastness of nature, but also of the interconnection of natural process in which 'the whole of the vast array of living forms' is 'constantly growing, increasing, decaying, and disappearing' (*Man's Place in Nature*, p. 167). The young writer presented this key concept quasi-socialistically in his essay, in the reference to a growing comprehension 'of the individual in the great social body whose interests are large beyond his personal feelings. He is a unit, working with others for a common welfare' (*PhII*, p. 222). Lawrence's preferred title for this essay was 'Art and Individual Development' – art, and all human activity, were to be viewed in evolutionary terms: 'We want, we are for ever trying to unite ourselves with the whole universe, to carry out some ultimate purpose – evolution, we call one phase of the carrying out' (*PhII*, p. 226).

In addition to evolutionary struggle, Lawrence's early work is permeated by the process of individuation, analysis of which culminates in *The Rainbow*. Lawrence's insight into this process derives substantially from Herbert Spencer, and *The Rainbow* and *Women in Love* are to some extent a fictional rendition of Spencer's principle of evolution and dissolution. Spencer believed there was a fundamental law of matter which he designated the law of persistence of force; the effect of this law was to bring about an advance from 'the homogeneous to the heterogeneous' (*First Principles*, p. 274). Evolution is defined as 'a change from a less coherent form to a more coherent form, consequent on the dissipation of motion and integration of matter' (p. 262). The process is thus 'a change from an indefinite, incoherent homogeneity' such as that characterising the earlier generations of Brangwens, to a 'definite coherent heterogeneity' exemplified by the later generations whom Lawrence studies. This movement is the result of 'the dissipation of motion and integration of matter' (p. 367). In the Hardy study of 1914 Lawrence expounds under the direct influence of Spencer. He observes that the more 'I am driven from admixture, the more I am singled out into utter individuality, the more this intrinsic me rejoices.' In its origin life was 'uniform, a great, unmoved, utterly homogeneous infinity, a great not-being', 'one motionless homogeneity'. Gradually this mass has stirred and resolved itself into many smaller, characteristic parts'; it has evolved 'from homogeneous tissue to organic tissue, on and on, from invertebrates to mammals, from mammals to man, from tribesman to me'; and 'there must always have been some reaction, infinitesimally faint, stirring somehow through the vast, homogeneous inertia' (*Hardy*, p. 44). The naked creative debt here is crucial: Lawrence was working simultaneously on the text of *The Rainbow*. Later, in 'The Two Principles' (1919), he examined this notion again. Although life moves on in 'creative singleness, its 'substance divides and subdivides into multiplicity'. In this way, when the egg divides 'a new stage of creation is reached, a new oneness of living being; but there appears also a new differentiation in intimate substance' (*PhII*, p. 229).

The cosmos, according to Spencer, is subject to the 'vast transformation' of evolution, which affects everything from the stars to the smallest organism. *First Principles* traces large movements of change. There is no stasis, since every object 'undergoes from instant to instant some alteration of state' (pp. 220–1). These alterations of state are due to what Spencer terms the 'continuous adjustment of internal

relations to external relations' (p. 50). The external forces have a
tendency to 'bring the matter of which living bodies consist into that
stable equilibrium shown by organic bodies; there are internal forces by
which this tendency is constantly antagonised; and the unceasing
changes which constitute Life, may be regarded as incidental to the
maintenance of the antagonism' (p. 60). It is manifest that 'co-existent
forces of attraction and repulsion imply certain laws of direction of all
movement' (p. 184): the antagonistic processes are evolution, 'the
integration of matter and concomitant dissipation of motion', and
dissolution, 'the absorption of motion and concomitant disintegration
of matter' (p. 228). Patterns of evolution and dissolution pervade
Lawrence's work, and attain definitive expression in *The Rainbow* and
Women in Love. Lawrence told Garnett that *The Rainbow* marked his
'transition stage' (*CL*, pp. 263-4), the product of 'deep feeling' trying to
'find its way out' (*CL*, p. 273). The concept of 'rhythmic form' which
Lawrence also announced to Garnett at this time clearly owes
something to Spencer, since the conception of the 'Wedding Ring'
sequence is prefigured in Spencer's argument, where the rise and fall of
organic life is described as 'a wave of that peculiar activity characterising
the species as a whole' (p. 209). Life as a succession of waves is central to
the presentation of the three generations of Brangwens, reflecting as
it does Spencer's thesis that life 'has not progressed uniformly, but in
immense undulations' (p. 210). The 'quick' Lawrencean novel transmutes
philosophical thought into kinetic art, as the novelist explained in 'The
Crown' (1915): 'This is art, this transferring to a slow flux the form that
was attained at the maximum of confluence between two quick waves'
(*PhII*, p. 412). Rhythmic form enables Lawrence in *The Rainbow* to vary
the timespan of the narrative from generalised states of long duration to
experiences of the intensely lived moment. The Victorian sense of
chronological time is displaced by waves of movement which are subtly
responsive to periodicity in human and natural life, a periodicity whose
final effect is to undermine 'objective' time schemes. In the corn-
harvesting scene between Will and Anna the rhythmic 'drift and ebb' of
labour draws the lovers closer in a momentary but timeless ecstasy
which is felt as more 'real' than everyday reality. Similarly, the
protagonist in 'The Man who Died' discerns, beneath the surface of
nature, 'the short, sharp wave of life' below. Material life, Lawrence
held, was a 'slow, big wave flowing back to the origin' (*PhII*, p. 412), and
it was in the flow and recoil of this wave that the Lawrencean new life
would be located.

With regard to social groups Spencer noted how, 'while each

individual is developing, the society of which he is an insignificant unit is developing too', the whole evolving towards what he calls 'increasing multiformity' (*First Principles*, p. 439). Man moves towards larger aggregates whilst paradoxically evolving as an individual. The 'degree of development' is registered by 'the degree in which the several parts constitute a co-operative assemblage'. This in turn leads to constant modifications of man's institutions (pp. 263, 256). Yet Spencer's vision culminates not in evolutionary grandeur but in dissolution, and the final pages of *First Principles* might be read in parallel with the closing scenes of *Women in Love*. Dissolution is 'apt to occur when social evolution has ended and decay has begun' and social evolution, like other forms, is dependent on energy 'which is gradually coming to an end' (*First Principles*, p. 416). Spencer asks, in words which presage the philosophy of Loerke and Gerald's icy disintegration, 'are we not manifestly progressing towards omnipresent death?' (p. 413). Spencer's final rhetoric foreshadows the implications of the closure of *Women in Love*: he sees evolution advancing towards 'complete quiescence' and terminating in 'universal death': 'a boundless space holding here and there extinct suns, fated to remain for ever without further change' (*First Principles*, pp. 423–4). In the Prologue to *Women in Love* Lawrence envisages mankind going through a process of 'decay and decomposition' and demands, 'what is the good of educating?', since 'Decay and decomposition will take their own way' (*PhII*, p. 98).

Spencerean evolution is part of Lawrence's imaginative being. The novelist deals repeatedly with the process of individuation, a wave-like process involving various antitheses – rural–industrial, passional–ideal, communal–individual, and so on. There is a pattern in the English novels of both a community evolving and of the individual involved in his own 'struggle into conscious being' within that community. Awakening consciousness separates the indvidual from work connected to the rhythms of nature and produces an effect of alienation, thrusting man into the 'advance-post of our time to blaze a path into the future', as the blurb for *The Rainbow* put it. The history of attaining selfhood in modern society is treated epically in *The Rainbow*, but the entire matter is adumbrated as early as *The White Peacock*, where George Saxton, the vigorous young farmer, is uprooted by the impact of culture as transmitted to him by Lettie. The essence of this first plot is Darwinian, each character enmeshed in a struggle to adapt to inevitable removal from the enclosed Nethermere valley; but even here the 'Scent of Blood' is pervasive, as it is in such early poems as 'Love on the Farm'.

Another text of some significance in the formation of Lawrence's response to nature was *The Riddle of the Universe* by Ernst Haeckel, which he had read by 1908.[3] Haeckel holds that life has a cellular basis. We must recognise in the cell 'the all-pervading "elementary organism" of whose social communities – the tissues – the body of every multicellular plant and animal, even that of man, is composed' (p. 6). Lawrence picks this up in 'Art and the Individual' when he refers to the 'individual in the great social body', who is a 'unit, working with others for a common welfare, like a cell in a complete body'. Lawrence also adopts Haeckel's distinction between the sensations of the individual cell which reveal themselves in 'the assertion of their individual independence', and the 'common sensation of the entire community of cells' – what he calls the 'mutually dependent "citizens" which constitute the community' (pp. 127–8). The image of the shifting patterns of individual and communal cells is dramatised in Lawrence's early work.

Haeckel's view is founded in his monistic philosophy: the universe is infinite and is composed of substance which 'fills infinite space, and is in eternal motion', a motion which sways between life and death, evolution and devolution. Monism, Haeckel explains, 'recognises one sole substance in the universe, which is at once "God and Nature"; body and spirit (or matter and energy) it holds to be inseparable' (pp. 11, 16). All mental and psychic phenomena are 'dependent on a definite material substratum' – the psychological processes are therefore subject to the law of substance (p. 74) – a postulate with which Ursula grapples, and which Lawrence came to reject. The task of the psychologist is the study of 'the long gradation by which man has slowly arisen through a vast series of lower animal conditions' (p. 88). Man may not be the end product of evolution; other worlds may produce higher beings who 'far transcend us earthly men in intelligence' (p. 303). This idea gained popular currency at the time, and Lawrence toys with it, notably in Mellors's delight in 'the extermination of the human species'. No species can achieve perfection, Haeckel holds, and all organisms are therefore subject to 'continuous adaptation' (p. 218). Haeckel postulates a universe whose nature is both unified and dual. The bases of the will are attraction and repulsion, and even the simplest molecules are animated by polarity and affinity (p. 184). The whole 'drama of nature' appears to consist in 'alternation of movement and repose' (p. 189). This prefigures Lawrence's dualistic thesis of the Will-to-Motion and the Will-to-Inertia in the Hardy study (*Hardy*).

The sum total of forces producing all phenomena is unchanging, and its source is the sun; Haeckel espouses sun worship (p. 229) in language close to Lawrence's frequent invocations to the sun. Then, towards the end of the book, Haeckel turns to ethics. Man has two sets of duties, to himself and to society. He is thus motivated by both egoism and altruism: egoism ensures his survival as an individual (cf. Paul's assertion of selfhood and release from his mother and other women), and altruism ensures the continuation of the species (pp. 285–6). Christianity, with its emphasis upon altruism, has led to isolation from nature and contempt for other organisms; the intimate sexual union is just as important, Haeckel argues, as the 'spiritual penetration of the two sexes' (p. 292). In the cathedral chapter of *The Rainbow*, Anna rejects Will's ecstatic response to the great enclosed space of Lincoln, feeling the freedom of the sky beyond and needing to reach open air. Similarly, Haeckel insists that truth dwells in 'the temple of nature' rather than in the 'gloom of the cloister'. The rationalist 'needs no special church, no narrow, enclosed portion of space' (*The Riddle of the Universe*, pp. 275, 281–2).

Haeckel's pantheist creed, founded in the cosmic law of his monism, his reintegration of matter and spirit, his cellular concept of the basis of organic and social life, and his unified vision of man and nature all made *The Riddle of the Universe* a significant text for the young Lawrence. What he came to reject of this tradition was its emphatic materialism. Haeckel's view of the formation of the universe was deeply mechanistic. He refers to the 'eternal birth and death of countless heavenly bodies' and goes on,

> While the embryo of a new world is being formed from a nebula in one corner of the vast stage of the universe, another has already condensed into a rotating sphere of liquid fire in some far distant spot; a third has already cast off rings at its equator, which round themselves into planets; a fourth has become a vast sun whose planets have formed a secondary retinue of moons, and so on.   (p. 304)

The process is pure causation, impelled by gravity and the law of substance. Lawrence replies in his introduction to Carter's *Dragon of the Apocalypse* in 1929, where he castigates the scientific authorities of his youth,

> Do you think you can put the universe apart, a dead lump here, a ball of gas there, a bit of fume somewhere else? How puerile it is, as if the universe were the back yard of some human chemical works! How gibbering man becomes, when he is really clever, and thinks he is giving the ultimate and final description of the universe!
>
> (*PhS*, p. 549)

But Lawrence reformulated the Haeckelian universe as early as *Sons and Lovers*. In the final scene, where Paul wanders in the dark countryside, he finds everywhere 'the vastness and terror of the immense night which is roused and stirred for a brief while by the day, but which returns, and will remain at last eternal'. Spencer had written that 'the Force which the Universe presents, falls into the same category with its Space and Time, as admitting of no limitation in thought' (*First Principles*, p. 443). This becomes transmuted into Paul's reflection, 'There was no Time, only Space.' The darkness is felt 'pressing him . . . into extinction, and yet, almost nothing, he could not be extinct'. Paul's imagination reaches out into the universe mediated to Lawrence by his evolutionary primers: 'Night, in which everything was lost, went reaching out, beyond stars and sun. Stars and sun, a few bright grains, went spinning round for terror.' Yet at the centre – and this marks the great Lawrencean assertion – stands the selfhood of Paul, 'infinitesimal' and 'yet not nothing' (*SL*, p. 510). The key to the universe in the Lawrencean version is not the laws of mass and energy, but the individual. In *Psychoanalysis and the Unconscious* he elaborated, 'Granted the whole cause-and-effect process of generation and evolution, still the individual is not explained.' 'Every individual creature has a soul, a specific individual nature the origin of which cannot be found in any cause-and-effect process whatever. Cause-and-effect will not explain even the individuality of a single dandelion' (*F*, p. 214). He added in *Fantasia of the Unconscious*, 'There never was any universe, any cosmos, of which the first reality was anything but living, incorporate individuals' (*F*, p. 150). The language of scientist and idealist alike is 'monkey-jargon': 'life, and life only, is the clue to the universe' (*F*, pp. 150–1). 'If we look for God', he observed in 'Democracy' (1920), 'let us look in the bush where he sings.' 'Every single living creature is a single creative unit' and the 'primal, spontaneous self in any creature has ascendance, truly, over the material laws of the universe; it uses these laws and converts them in the mystery of creation' (*PhS*, p. 525).

It is in the restatement of the 'mystery of creation' that Lawrence rejects his rationalistic teachers. As he was to write in 1929, 'After years of acceptance of the "laws" of evolution – rather desultory or "humble" acceptance – now I realize that my vital imagination makes great reservations'.[4] In the same light he claimed to have turned away from evolution (with a hit at Spencer): 'I don't believe in evolution, like a long string hooked on to a First Cause, and being slowly twisted in unbroken continuity through the ages. I prefer to believe in what the Aztecs called Suns: that is, Worlds successively created and destroyed'.[5] Life is not just 'a product of reactions in the material universe': 'Science supposes that once the first forces was [*sic*] in existence, and the first motion set up, the universe produced itself automatically, throwing off life as a by-product.' It is the explanation of the universe by rational empiricism which the mature Lawrence blames for the 'materialization and emptiness' of life (*PhII*, p. 229). The 'blood-consciousness' discerned in primitive races held the key to life, a key civilised man had mislaid:

> For oh, I know, in the dust where we have buried
> The silenced races and all their abominations,
> We have buried so much of the delicate magic of life.
> ('Cypresses', *CP*, p. 298)

The later Lawrence's reservations about evolution and its implications for mankind are recorded in the exasperated annotations Lawrence made in the early twenties to Ouspensky's *Tertium Organum*.[6] Lawrence's tart comments should not disguise the fact that he shared many ideas with Ouspensky, and that the book is a discussion of evolutionary theory of some moment to Lawrence's art at this time. Ouspensky argues that evolution should be discussed in relation to art. Through aesthetic creation 'men are creating a new world' which will be framed in the '*language of the future*'. 'Art anticipates a psychic evolution and divines its future forms' (p. 73). The artist is a seer, capable of 'conscious actions', but the aptitude for such acts resides only 'in some few persons whom it is possible to describe as MEN OF A HIGHER TYPE' (p. 79; cf. Birkin). Ouspensky sees evolution as a process going on in separate species in parallel, what he calls 'equivalent evolutions' which lead to the 'only real and important evolution for us – the evolution into superman' (p. 85). Evolution is dependent upon life, but the definition of this term is elusive. In the 'living organism, in the living cell, in the living protoplasm there is *something* indefinable, differentiating living matter from dead matter' (p. 103). This differentiation expressed itself in 'efforts of growth'. Science may only concern itself with outward 'events and circumstances': 'When it makes the attempt to get outside of its definite conditions (space, time, causation) . . . then it is transcending its own proper sphere' (p. 129). Empirical science will eventually be seen to deal with the 'unreal and illusory' (p. 177). Reality is glimpsed through the erotic, which arouses mankind to its '*principal function*, of which we know nothing' (p. 153), and through nature, in whose phenomena man senses a 'vivid emotionality' which transcends evolutionary struggle (p. 179). Nature has the power to awaken 'mystical moods', and, Ouspensky adds, 'The voice of sex embraces much of that same mystical sense of *nature*' (p. 275). Nature and sex are gateways through which man is delivered from a mechanistic universe. Those who perceive the living soul of the universe are a select few capable of further evolution. The future belongs '*not to man, but to superman*': 'A higher race is rapidly emerging among humanity, and it is emerging by reason of its quite remarkable understanding of the world and life' (p. 295). Evolutionists have applied their theory irrelevantly; not possessing the skill to see variety of form as constituting the unity of nature, they 'have recourse to the evolutionary idea, and regard this great variety of forms as an ascending ladder', whereas in reality it is 'different sides or parts of one whole which we do not know' (p. 298).

Lawrence bases his objections to this on Ouspensky's presentation of the psyche as choiceless. When Ouspensky argues that 'subservience to "pleasure–pain" must be governed by expedience' and that the pleasant is so because it is beneficial, Lawrence rebuts both him and the evolutionists: 'The most beautiful creatures brought about their own rarity by their beauty, and the struggle towards that beauty was not expedient not even strictly pleasurable – there is a deeper motive.'[7] Much of Lawrence's annotation seeks to refute Ouspensky's writings on animal perception and dimensional understanding; but, as Tedlock remarks, the most interesting aspect of Lawrence's treatment 'is his silence about Ouspensky's heralding of a new consciousness and a higher race of men'.[8]

Lawrence's claim to have rejected evolution was specious; he was affected by the theory at the deepest imaginative level. Birkin's Alpine meditations confirm this claim. 'Whatever the mystery which has brought forth man and the universe', Birkin acknowledges, 'it is a non-human mystery, it has its own great ends, man is not the criterion.' If man faltered, the 'eternal creative mystery' could dispose of him and 'replace him with a finer created being': 'Races came and went, species passed away, but ever new species arose, more lovely, or equally lovely, always surpassing wonder' (*WL*, p. 538). Birkin thinks like a man who has read Spencer and Haeckel, but the relatively unlettered Aaron Sisson, watching the Italian cypresses, comes to similar conclusions and regrets 'lost races, lost language, lost human ways of feeling and of knowing' (*AR*, p. 309). Lawrencean evolution therefore cuts both ways: it may be felt as loss of instinctive being or as hope of renewed life through the emergence of new orders. The core of evolution as espoused by Darwin, Huxley and Spencer is dynamic process, in which, as Engels observed, the concept of the individual is 'dissolved into something purely relative'. That sense of process is vital to Lawrence's artistic purpose, as he recognised in the Hardy study:

> It seems as though one of the conditions of life is, that life shall continually and progressively differentiate itself, almost as though this differentiation were a Purpose. Life starts crude and unspecified, a great Mass. And it proceeds to evolve out of that mass ever more distinct and definite particular forms, an ever-multiplying number of separate species and orders, as if it were working always to the production of the infinite number of perfect individuals, the individual so thorough that he should have nothing in common with any other individual. It is as if all coagulation must be loosened, as if the elements must work themselves free and pure from the compound.
>
> (*Hardy*, p. 43)

In the novel contemporaneous with this Spencerean reading of life, the coagulation of the early Brangwens is increasingly loosened until it produces, in Ursula, the individual so thorough that she has nothing in common with any other individual – she must await, at the close of the novel, the arrival of Birkin. The sense of progressive differentiation into heterogeneity shapes Lawrence's best work, as he confessed in 'Reflections on the Death of a Porcupine': 'Every cycle of existence is established upon the overcoming of the lower cycles of existence. The real question is, wherein does *fitness* lie?' Lawrence concedes that species must bow to the law of survival of the fittest, but he modifies determinism by insistence upon vitality as the determinant – a factor he derives from his concept of the 'fourth dimension', 'not to be reckoned with in terms of space and time'. In this essay Lawrence contrives to combine evolutionary causation with the mystical 'fourth dimension' of Ouspensky. Lawrence insists that 'any man, creature, or race moving towards blossoming will have to draw immense supplies of vitality from men, or creatures below, passionate strength'. Thus the 'torch of revelation is handed on' 'by every living thing, from the protococcus to a brave man or a beautiful woman': 'One cycle of perfection urges to kindle another cycle, as yet unknown' (*PhS*, pp. 452 ff.).

Lawrence speaks eloquently in the Hardy study of the 'vast, unexplored morality of life' and nature in 'its eternal incomprehensibility' (*Hardy*, p. 31). It is to the 'eternal incomprehensibility' of nature that Ursula turns after the confrontation with Dr Frankstone. It needs to be insisted, however, that the mystery inherent in the universe was admitted by the scientific writers whom the young Lawrence studied.

Huxley had noted that 'equilibrium of force' and 'permanency of form' were the characteristics of the inanimate. The scientist gives the name 'life' to those particles of matter which move in cycles and disturb the equilibrium. But how to define life? This *'spontaneity of action'* must be regarded as 'ultimate fact' (*Man's Place in Nature*, pp. 267–8). Lawrence arrived at a similar position. The universe, he held, had been created not out of matter alone but from 'some universal living self-conscious plasm': 'There is no utterly immaterial existence, no spirit. The distinction is between living plasm and inanimate matter' (*PhII*, p. 230). Empirical scientist and 'daimonic' novelist unite over the ultimate mystery. Like Gilbert Noon, Lawrence rejoices over 'inherent individual qualities in each separate organic growth' (*PhII*, p. 138). The ultimately unknowable nature of the universe is the first plank of Spencer's philosophy also. 'Ultimate Scientific Ideas', he wrote, 'are representatives of realities that cannot be comprehended' (*First Principles*, p. 48); they can only be known opaquely by science or religion. The existence of the universe is traced to a First Cause which is independent and infinite, but whose operations are hidden from men. The 'Power which the universe manifests to us is inscrutable', Spencer declared (p. 34). The onward impulsion of the First Cause is familiar to the reader of *The Dynasts*; as modern biology would express it, evolution is not teleological, directed by conscious purposeful urge, but teleonomic, moving automatically in the direction dictated by adaptation. In the poetry of the dying Lawrence the First Cause appears in a new guise:

> I am in the hands of the unknown God,
> he is breaking me down to his oblivion
> to send me forth on a new morning, a new man.
>   ('Shadows', *CP*, p. 727)

This phoenix-like impulse towards life derives from the reconciliation of evolutionary theory and nature mysticism which is Lawrence's peculiar hallmark. The synthesis, implicit in the romantic impulse towards merging with nature whilst minutely recording the detail of that natural world, is reached in Ursula's vision of the rainbow – an apocalyptic moment in high romantic style which yet arises naturally out of the evolutionary principle shaping the novel. Looking out on the industrial squalor of Beldover, Ursula knows 'that new, clean, naked bodies would issue to a new germination, to a new growth, rising to the light and the wind and the clean rain of heaven' (*R*, pp. 495–6). Lawrence's judgement in 'The Novel' (1925) aptly applies to his own masterpiece, in its dramatised actualisation of the evolutionary process: 'In the great novel, the felt but unknown flame stands behind all the characters, and in their words and gestures there is a flicker of the presence' (*PhII*, p. 419).

NOTES

1. Lawrence's debt to nature mysticism is explored in my study *Lawrence and the Nature Tradition* (Brighton: Harvester, 1980). Some duplication of material has been found necessary in order to articulate clearly Lawrence's relationship to evolutionary theory.
2. Herbert Spencer, *First Principles* (1862; London: Williams and Norgate, 1910); and T. H. Huxley, *Man's Place in Nature* (London, 1863; London: Dent, n.d.). (Page references are given in the text.) See Rose Marie Burwell, 'A Catalogue of D. H. Lawrence's Reading from Early Childhood', *D. H. Lawrence Review,* III (1970) 193–324, entries A72, A73, A225. The Lawrence figure in 'A Modern Lover' (1909), Cyril Mersham, has studied Darwin and Huxley. Spencer is admiringly referred to in Lawrence's paper of 1908, 'Art and the Individual' (*PhII*).
3. Ernst Haeckel, *The Riddle of the Universe* (1899), tr. J. McCabe (London: Watts, 1929). (Page references are given in the text.) See Burwell, 'Catalogue', *D. H. Lawrence Review,* III, entry A125.
4. D. H. Lawrence, *Selected Essays* (Harmondsworth: Penguin, 1960) p. 335.
5. D. H. Lawrence, *Mornings in Mexico* (Harmondsworth: Penguin, 1967) p. 12.
6. P. D. Ouspensky, *Tertium Organum*, tr. N. Bessaraboff and C. Bragdon (London: Routledge and Kegan Paul, 1949). (Page references are given in the text.)
7. E. W. Tedlock, Jr, 'D. H. Lawrence's Annotation of Ouspensky's *Tertium Organum*', *Texas Studies in Literature and Language*, II (1960) 206–18.
8. Ibid., p.208

8

'Blood-Consciousness' and the Pioneers of the Reflex and Ganglionic Systems[1]

CHRISTOPHER HEYWOOD

Studies of Lawrence's physiological thinking[2] have generally refrained from linking his ideas to developments in theoretical neurology in the nineteenth and early twentieth centuries. An exception occurs in Professor James C. Cowan's *Journey with Genius: D. H. Lawrence's American Journey*, where Lawrence's ideas are placed discerningly in the context of available anatomical knowledge.[3] Anatomical clarifications were, however, inseparable from major debates about function, and these are strongly reflected in all Lawrence's writing in this field. Lawrence saw his 'blood-consciousness' theory as a remedy to the inadequacies of psychoanalytic theory and practice, and various other cults of his period, but complicated the debate by nowhere revealing his sources. 'I am no scholar of any sort', he argued, but remained silent about scientific writers whom he may have had in mind when he added, 'But I am very grateful to scholars for their sound work' (*F*, p.11). The suggestion of this essay is that Lawrence made use of two major and originally rival theories on the function and structure of the involuntary nervous system, the one stemming from the work of Marie-François Xavier Bichat (1771–1802) and the other from the work of the Nottingham-born physiologist Marshall Hall (1790–1857). Hall's work on the reflex arc largely supplanted Bichat's 'ganglionic' theory by mid century, but Lawrence does not seem to have been aware of the synthesis of the two systems which stemmed from the work of Claude Bernard (1813–78).

Lawrence's reading habits point with fair certainty to his acquaintance with the work of both Bichat and Hall, the two principals contending for mastery of the theoretical debate in the first half of the nineteenth century.[4] Though neither is named in his writings, both were outlined and discussed in brief résumés which were available to

104

Lawrence, one in Eastwood and the other in Munich, during his formative years. Bichat and Hall were both forgotten names by the time Lawrence wrote, but the issues they raised were, and are, central to modern neurophysiological thought and experiment. The theory of ganglionic nervous control over involuntary bodily and muscular functioning stemmed from investigations by Galen and was developed in the seventeenth and eighteenth centuries. Its supreme expression in early modern times came from the hand of Bichat.[5] Conceived originally as a rival to the ganglionic theory, the 'reflex arc' mechanism of the spinal cord was first explained by Hall.[6] A copy of the biography by his widow, Charlotte Hall's *Memoirs of Marshall Hall*, was available to Lawrence in the library of the Mechanics' Institute at Eastwood.[7] A source for Lawrence's probable contact with Bichat was the translation of his best-known work, the *Recherches physiologiques sur la vie et la mort* (Paris 1801),[8] by Rudolf Boehm. An instructive Introduction accompanied this work, which appeared in 1912,[9] the year of Lawrence's entry into Max Weber's circle, the Kosmische Runde, in Munich.[10] The contention of this essay is that Lawrence knew the theoretical positions of both physiologists and that they contributed to the formation of his writing in two major periods.

Lawrence's physiological thinking passed through two main phases, one beginning in 1912, when the ideas of Bichat made their first appearance in his letters and writing, and another around 1926, when a cast of thought close to that of Hall became apparent. At the time of writing *The White Peacock* (1911), in the years 1906–10, Lawrence was acquainted with William James's *The Principles of Psychology* (1890),[11] and, as Professor Delavenay has shown, with Edward Carpenter's *The Art of Creation*.[12] Both these works carry physiological discussions which include reference to the two major branches of involuntary nervous activity, the reflex and the ganglionic, but omit reference to the work of Bichat and of Hall. Hall's explanation of spinal reflex functioning was first given in a paper read to the Royal Society and published in their *Transactions* for 1833.[13] The assumption that Lawrence was acquainted with the 'reflex arc' theory of Hall through Charlotte Hall's biography and its explanatory appendix, a reprinting of the anonymous review series in the *Lancet* during August 1846 (*Memoirs*, pp. 464–501), rests on Jessie Chambers's recollection that from an early age Lawrence was apparently 'acquainted with nearly everything in the little library' (*ET*, p. 93). In his book, Carpenter urged the notion of interdependence among three main parts of the nervous system: 'capacities of immense emotional agitation (the Sympathetic), capacities of swift reflex action and response (the cerebro-spinal), and the formation of powerful images (the cerebrum). These three elements cannot well be separated from each other.'[14] Carpenter here fore-shadowed Lawrence, since he saw these functions as inhering in the activities of 'all the great plexuses of the sympathetic Nerve-system'. Nevertheless, Lawrence's position for a decade and a half was remote from Carpenter's doctrine of balance. Ironically, Lawrence's position approximated more closely to that of Henry R. Binns, a correspondent from whom Carpenter sought advice about the puzzling theory of 'sympathetic' nervous functioning. Undoubtedly unknown to Lawrence, Binns concluded one of his two memoranda to Carpenter in these terms: 'The whole question is a very obscure one; physiology has tended to be in favour of the brain and against the Sympathetic System theories of the Bichat and Bernard these last twenty years: but . . . I think the evidence is in their favour.'[15] Carpenter's theory of triple functioning and the need for balance between three parts differs from the dualism of both Binns and Lawrence. The pressures of controversy in the background of Lawrence's early reading point to the difficulty of the field, and the obscurity attending any attempt at rigid definition. Nevertheless, the first of Lawrence's two major phases opened with a strong bias towards a position resembling that of Binns.

In Lawrence's thinking, any possibility of balance within a three-part system was rejected in 1912, when he adopted a stance closely allied to the tradition of Bichat. The role of Bichat's intermediary, Rudolf Boehm (1844–1926), clearly exceeded that of a passive translator. An inscription in his hand, 'to Henry Maudsley with the translator's best regards and respects', is preserved in a copy of his translation of the major work of a great English neurophysiologist, *The Physiology and Pathology of Mind* (1867), by Henry Maudsley (1835–1918).[16] Boehm's internationally distinguished career in pharmacology, his early studies in Munich and widely acclaimed studies in toxins and narcotics, suggest close links with Otto Gross, a principal figure in the Kosmische Runde; Bichat's doctrine of the cerebral origins of psychic aberrations would have been of interest to Gross.[17] Developed in *The Rainbow*, *Women in Love*, the essays on American literature[18] and the writings on the unconscious, Bichat's theory persistently reappears, coloured by numerous touches of thought evidently made available through Boehm's translation and introduction.[19] Boehm made no attempt to bring the light of modern criticism and experiment to bear on theories which had by 1912 become historical curiosities. Signs of Lawrence's dissatisfaction with the constraints of the Bichat system can be discerned from the early 1920s, but on his visit to Shropshire in 1924, as reported by Frederick Carter, he was still using the classic counters in Bichat's model of nervous activity, that is, a rigid contrast between the 'physical organic' and the 'nervous and cerebral psyche'.[20] These and other key phrases in Lawrence's physiological thought point to his dependence on early-nineteenth-century experimental theory in his persistent quest for certainty about nervous functioning and control.

Knowledge of the autonomic or 'sympathetic' functioning of the ganglia and plexuses attached to the nerves running parallel to the spinal column stemmed from anatomical researches by Galen and was extended after the mid seventeenth century by the work of Willis, du Petit and Whytt. But in the hands of Bichat these anatomical puzzles adopted strongly moralised, evolutionary and prophetic proportions. Experimental modifications to the work of Bichat depended on the emergence in the 1820s and 1830s of microscopes and methods capable of verifying or refuting his conjectures.[21] Generations of researchers and writers were, however, captivated by his bold, Cartesian art of simplification and his tirelessly pursued functional chains of thought. His title to being considered the father of modern physiology is upheld by many writers. Coleridge saw his links with German romanticism and the doctrine of Vitalism: 'Bichat . . . and the better disciples of the Nature-philosophy', he noted: '. . . the paramountcy of the Ganglionic in Sleep . . . the good side of this – i.e. ganglionic – system. As all Passions, and Feelings, so Love roots herein.'[22] Turning to the more substantial though less widely known work of Bichat on the common structure of tissues among seemingly unrelated bodily organs, George Eliot endowed her doctor hero Lydgate with a failed project for research springing from 'the fundamental knowledge of structure . . . at the beginning of the century', which, she explained, 'had been illuminated by the brief and glorious career of Bichat' (*Middlemarch*, ch. 15). By the end of the century, Bichat was a legend of the past: 'Je ne veux pas ici insister sur les doctrines', Raphael Blanchard conceded at the centenary celebrations,[23] deflecting attention from charges ranging from atheism[24] to imperfect experimental method. Bichat's theory of the power of the ganglia and plexuses to dominate cerebral functioning indirectly through the power exercised by their organ and agent, the heart, over the supply of blood to the brain, presented a considerable challenge to research. Demonstrations by later research from men such as Claude Bernard and Walter Holbrook Gaskell (1847–1914) yielded a radically different picture of closely linked cerebral, spinal and ganglionic systems with common structures and mechanisms. Their work was undertaken in the face of an orthodoxy stemming from Bichat, the magnitude of which is hinted in reminiscences which Gaskell included in his last work: 'Thus Bichat's teaching appeared to be based on the strongest possible foundations of fact, and the absolute independence of the animalic and organic nervous systems established.'[25]

In developing his system, Bichat assigned special values to several terms, notably 'organic', 'animal' (Gaskell's 'animalic') and 'sensation'. These special meanings reappear in Lawrence's work after 1912 and produce numerous difficulties of interpretation in his writing. Bichat envisaged an absolute division between the functions of the autonomic nervous system and its ganglia, and the functions of the cerebrum. To the latter he assigned the functions of sensation and the rational, voluntary, wakeful, exploratory, aesthetic and perfectible, but also destructive and predatory functions of man. Bichat termed the functions of the cerebrum 'animal'; the complement of the 'animal' system he termed 'organic', placing it under the control of the ganglia and plexuses of the 'sympathetic' nervous system. To this system he assigned the beneficent, synthesising, vegetative, creative and positive functions of restoring tissue destroyed by the depradations of the wakeful, predatory, 'animal' system. Within this paradigm, Bichat's aphoristic description of life as 'l'ensemble des forces qui résistent à la mort'[26] carried a specific dramatic meaning. The 'animal' side of man and its driving organ, the voluntary, will-dominated, active cerebrum, the seat of destructive, sensational and aesthetic nervous activity, drives the organism towards dissolution and death. In opposition, the 'organic' system, with its powers of restoration, construction and synthesis, resists the onrush of destruction. Death takes three forms: death of the heart, of the lungs and of the brain. Death of the cerebrum does not extinguish the activity of the heart, but death at the centre of the 'organic' system, the heart, results in death for the entire organism. In evolutionary terms, nature, the creation, is conceived as a fountain, the upsurge of 'organic' activity being perpetually countered by the downward torrent of 'animal', cerebral disintegration. In the human organism, the blood is the sole link between the two systems, carrying in itself the dual elements of creation and decay.

Lawrence's adherence to this imaginatively potent scheme of thought after 1912[27] stems, it seems, from the exposition of Bichat's thinking given by Boehm in his Introduction to the *Untersuchungen*. Lawrence's first expression of a belief in the potency of 'blood' and its dominance over the cerebrum appeared in the letter of 17 January 1913 to Ernest Collings:

My great religion is a belief in the blood, the flesh, as being wiser than the intellect. We can go wrong in our minds. But what our blood feels and believes and says, is always true. The intellect is only a bit and a bridle. What do I care about knowledge. All I want is to answer to my blood, direct, without fribbling intervention of mind, or moral, or what-not. (*CL*, p. 180)

In *Women in Love* (1920), Lawrence gave his most extended dramatisation of Bichat's cycle of thought. Traces of it appear in *Sons and Lovers* (1913), revised during Lawrence's first entry into the Munich circle, and it forms a sustaining idea in *The Rainbow* (1915). Analogies for the extended exploration of leading ideas through loosely organised scenes and symbols occur in the other arts of the period, *art nouveau*, *Jugendstil* and post-Wagnerian opera. In a penetrating description, Egon Wellesz characterised the tendency in music drama of the period:

The opera . . . lost its characteristic, self-conditioned form which had depended for its realisation on the composer's sense of dramatic structure, and assumed a form determined by his capricious interest in certain isolated moments of the action. This emphasis on the composer's personal taste meant also that the characters of the drama were no longer musically independent. They all spoke the same language . . . .[28]

The characters in *Women in Love* emerge in heightened moments of conflict and symbolic exploration. They are involved from the start in sustained arguments about the nature of voluntary and involuntary nervous control, the extension of cerebral functioning into the context of industry and education, and the alternatives offered by the functioning of the involuntary nervous system. Lawrence places his characters, their gestures, utterances and preoccupations within terms which are foreshadowed in the arguments of Bichat and his interpreter Boehm. Sensation, organic life, muscular activity, the will, the details of apparently haphazard animal imagery, the function of the blood as a link between the two systems, the inevitable onrush of death for the 'animal' system and the survival of the 'organic' – all adhere closely to the thinking of Bichat. Rupert Birkin's quest to emancipate his society and personality from control by the cerebral, sensational, predatory and destructive (in Bichat's sense) 'animal' functions is balanced against the inevitable dissolution of the industrialist Gerald Crich. Gerald's journey towards death is the logical expression of Bichat's notion of the deathward tendency of the 'animal' nature when it is insufficiently resisted by the action of the 'sympathetic', 'organic' nervous system. Ideally, the two systems are complementary, but, according to Bichat, death is the logical culmination of all nervous activity. Under the shadow of their father's death by cancer, the Criches of the younger generation, Gerald and Diana, undergo death of the brain and lungs respectively, but Birkin draws back and preserves the life of the heart. Expanded through a text which includes a wealth of anecdote and observation, Bichat's leading ideas provided a tightly jointed framework for a work which many commentators have taken as a personal improvisation.

By an argument which proved increasingly cumbersome to subsequent research and thinking, Bichat attributed parallel sensibility (irritability) and motion (contractility) to each of two mutually exclusive systems. The puzzling relationship of the two men in *Women in Love* stems from this principle. Birkin's proposal of a tie of blood with Crich re-enacts Bichat's principle of the control of cerebral activity through the power of the heart and ganglia to regulate the blood supply. The failure of the Birkin relationship and the death of Crich further dramatise Bichat's idea of the deathward journey of all cerebral activity. In Boehm's rendering, Bichat's ideas emerge thus:

As in the case of the sensibility and contractility of the 'organic' system, the sensibility and contractility of the 'animal' system are closely linked. (*Untersuchungen*, p. xxii)[29]

From this it may be assumed that the blood vessels are the sole agents for the influence of the heart on the life of the brain. (p. 25)

We can conclude from all this that the brain has no direct influence on the heart; on the contrary, it follows that the brain is directly subordinate to the heart as a consequence of the latter's powers of movement. (p. 106)

As noted above, the 'sympathetic' nervous system is totally independent of the cerebrum, and no nerve exists to which the term 'great Sympathetic' can properly be applied; rather, we are dealing with a branching series of nervous connections, each independently linked to a ganglionic centre which exists in a manner analogous to the brain, the centre of 'animal' life. (p. 108)

Boehm's text gives only part II of the *Recherches* – that is, Bichat's exploration of the three forms of death, which Lawrence dramatised in

Women in Love. A group of peculiarities in Bichat's thinking, discernible only in Boehm's Introduction, point to Lawrence's dependence on this source. Of this group, the salient elements are: that the child is born with a fully developed 'organic' system, but education is required for the development of the 'animal' system; that the appropriate occupations for the 'animal' functions are to be found in trade and industry, while the passions are the domain of the 'organic' system; that symmetry, expressed through the pairing of the organs of sense and the extremities, is the distinctive morphological mark of the 'animal' system, in contrast to the asymmetry, singularity and uniqueness of the components in the 'organic' system; that the expressions of cerebral activity and of the will and the 'animal' side included convulsive disorders, spasms of destructiveness, mania and epilepsy, as well as social activity, travel and exploration; and that the blood, the vital link between the two systems, carries in itself the material for the work of 'organic' reconstruction as well as the sludge and dross resulting from the work of 'animal' disintegration. Thus:

> The 'animal' functions are active immediately after birth, but require a slow process of education, applied first to the use of the sense organs and the voluntary muscles, and later to the development of the remaining spiritual powers . . . In the 'organic' life, the fœtus concentrates on the circulatory and digestive system . . . in contrast to the 'animal' life, the appropriate organs function perfectly from the outset and are not in need of training.   (p. xxiv)

> Through his 'animal' life, man is superior to other forms of life; trade and industry depend on its development; beauty and the breaking of the nervous circle in which beasts are imprisoned, is a property of the 'animal' life of man. Perfectibility, fulfilment, are possible only through the 'animal' life. The 'organic' life, in contrast, is as complete in the newborn infant as in the adult.
> The passions are the property of the 'organic' life. They are seated in the heart, the stomach, the lungs, etc. They influence the 'animal' life only indirectly, through the 'sympathies'.   (p. xix)

> The symptoms of apoplexy, epilepsy, catalepsy, narcosis, brain seizure, etc., emanating principally from the cerebrum, seem to me to emphasise the independence of the heart from the brain.   (p. 107)

> Dissolution (disassimilation), the process of elimination by exhalation and secretion . . . is opposed to assimilation. . . . As a result, the

blood constantly carries 'incremental' and 'excremental' substances, the latter in the form of sludge or dross, the former tending towards replacement.   (p. xvii)

Lawrence dramatised a parallel set of oppositions in *Women in Love*. The predatory, 'animal' side of man is represented by the Criches, the Roddices, and the Pompadour and Alpine group. Birkin and Ursula represent the singular, unique, solitary, asymmetrical, vegetation-oriented, 'organic' side of man. As in Wellesz's definition of operatic composition, all the characters are talking the language of the problem. Like figures within the arabesques of Klimt or the sinuous phrasing of Richard Strauss, they emerge in definition at moments of crisis, their gestures determined by the author's transparently veiled intellectual construction. At her moment of linkage with Loerke, who is symmetrically paired with Gerald Crich and who expresses through art the mechanised, mindless life of industrial society, Gudrun, their brightly costumed, aesthetic, sensational companion, falls prey to the convulsive onslaught of a lover whose brain decays in the process. The debt to Bichat's system is strong; nevertheless, the inherent difficulties of Bichat's thought lead to what may be described as aberrant readings of his system. Thus, Lawrence carries to an extreme the tendency to devalue cerebral activity, and in this phase of the action identifies it with mindlessness and the 'unconscious', a foil to the knowledge achieved by the ganglia, which represents true insight: Gudrun's persistently cerebral activity leads her to find 'in her subconsciousness' (*WL*, p. 550) that her impending affair with Loerke, the cerebral artist, wakeful, sensational, bat-like, rat-like, energetic, decadent, a 'mud-child', involves contact with another like herself, a creature of 'subconscious, sinister knowledge . . . a pure, unconnected will, stoical and momentaneous . . . the very stuff of the underworld of life' (*WL*, pp. 521–2). Loerke's position in the Bichat paradigm is unambiguous: a 'rat in the river of corruption', Birkin calls him, an animal with pointed, symmetrical features, eyes 'brown, full, like a rabbit's, or a troll's, or like the eyes of a lost being' (*WL*, pp. 522–3). Bichat's identification of 'animal' activity with black blood, and his emphasis on its power to stifle the 'organic' system, reappears in the 'black look of inorganic misery' which clouds Loerke's existence (*WL*, p. 516). The orthodox but archaic phrases of Bichat's system ring out in the evocation of Gudrun's despair: 'The world was finished now, for her. There was only the inner, individual darkness, sensation within the ego, the obscure religious mystery of ultimate reduction, the mystic frictional activities of diabolic reducing down, disintegrating the vital organic body of life' (*WL*, p. 550).

The positive aspect of Bichat's 'animal' system, the aesthetic impulse which Gudrun shares with her 'organic' sister, and which emerge in her animal sculptures, are cast off when Gudrun severs her tie with Ursula. The failure of Gerald's tie with Birkin heralds a similar disintegration, but Birkin draws back from further exploration and cerebral, imperial activity. Gerald, the 'wolf' (*WL*, p. 553), is the epitome of the industrial, cerebral man, and like Gudrun he is carried to the point where he becomes 'mindless' (*WL*, p. 515), in Bichat's terms an unconscious fragment of 'animal' existence. His jealously over Loerke 'withers my consciousness', he cries out, 'it burns the pith of my mind' (*WL*, p. 536). His attack on Gudrun is made with the 'animal' extremities, the symmetrical hands, after a last flicker of 'organic' life: 'a change came over his body, the hot, molten stream mounted involuntarily through his veins', but 'a fine recoil of disappointment . . . seemed gradually to be destroying his understanding' (*WL*, p. 555). A seemingly inexplicable eccentricity of Lawrence's phrasing, 'his consciousness was gone into his wrists, his hands' (*WL*, p. 561), has its origin in an aspect of Bichat's thought which was satirised by Magendie, according to which the 'animal' nature is located in the symmetrical extremities. A chain of symbolic incidents leads to this conclusion, each developing Bichat's conception of symmetry as the expression of the will, sensation, industrialism and art, and his identification of these activities as functions of man's 'animal' nature. Birkin is at first between two worlds, 'without any definite rhythm, any organic meaning' (*WL*, p. 104), close to the Criches and Roddices but drifting towards the 'organic' Ursula, whose 'spirit was active, her life like a shoot that is growing steadily, but which has not yet come above ground' (*WL*, p. 103). He ponders whether he took a drink by voluntary or involuntary means, 'by accident, or on purpose' (*WL*, p. 79) and foreshadows the debate of the sisters about whether Gerald's shooting-accident, in which his brother died, had 'an unconscious will behind it' (*WL*, p. 99). Gerald is driven towards a convulsive exercise of will and its inevitable consequence, death, but only after the failure of a cerebral, 'animal', sensational affair with the equally 'animal' Minette: 'black, electric comprehension . . . rapid vibrations ran through his blood and over his brain, he was no longer responsible. . . . Every one of his limbs was turgid with electric force, and his back was tense like a tiger's . . .' (*WL*, pp. 126–9). Birkin, in contrast, drifts without voluntary motivation, neutrally, towards Ursula, whose emblems are plants, shadow and 'soft dim magic' (*WL*, pp. 84–5). Gerald's response to Birkin corresponds to the body's assimilation of ganglionic nervous activity: 'It was as if Birkin's whole physical intelligence interpenetrated into Gerald's body, as if his fine, sublimated energy entered into the flesh of the fuller man, like some potency, casting a fine net, a poison, through the muscles into the very depth of Gerald's physical being' (*WL*, p. 349).

The union of Birkin and Ursula, 'the most intolerable accession into being, the marvellous fullness of immediate gratification, overwhelming, outflooding from the source of the deepest life-force, the darkest, deepest, strangest life-source of the human body, at the back and base of the loins' (*WL*, p. 396), becomes possible only after Birkin's rejection of Hermione Roddice. Hermione's association with education, aesthetic gratifiction, the will and muscular activity, and her destructive outburst aimed correctly (in Bichat's system) at Birkin's brain (ch. 8), identifies her as a member of the 'animal' group which Birkin must leave behind. Birkin's initiation into ganglionic consciousness undoubtedly owed something to Lawrence's long contact with Hindu physiological tradition; nevertheless, the exposition of the ganglionic system in James Pryses's *The Apocalypse Unsealed* (New York, 1910), his principal source of contact by the time of writing *Women in Love*, lacks the drama, the evolutionary thesis and the haunting verbal registers of Bichat and was, as Lawrence affirmed, a beginning only: 'it gave me the first clue'.[30] Birkin's transition towards the singularity and asymmetry of the 'organic' world of Bichat is expressed early: 'In the spirit, I am as separate as one star is from another' (*WL*, p. 161); it is perceptively seen by George Panichas, without reference to Bichat but in the context of the general acceptance of the doctrines of Vitalism after the later eighteenth century, as the 'ability to achieve the remarkable transition from personal to impersonal, from self to life, from the collective to the organic'.[31] A humorous illustration of the Bichat system occurs when Birkin and Ursula return the impulsively – that is, voluntarily – bought chair, evocative of symmetry and the 'animal' world of Bichat, to the 'quick, vital rat', the passing peasant type, as part of their progress towards living 'in the chinks they leave us' (*WL*, p. 450), as Birkin construes their correct function. In his rejection of Hermione, in phrase upon phrase, Birkin spells out in full the Bichat paradigm:

'Spontaneous!' he cried. 'You and spontaneity! You, the most deliberate thing that ever walked or crawled! You'd be verily deliberately spontaneous – that's you. Because you want to have everything in your own volition, your deliberate, voluntary consciousness. – You want it all in that loathsome little skull of yours, that ought to be cracked like a nut. For you'd be the same till it *is* cracked, like an insect in its skin. If one cracked your skull perhaps one might get a spontaneous, passionate woman out of you, with real sensuality. As it is, what you want is pornography – looking at yourself in mirrors, watching your naked animal actions in mirrors, so that you can have it all in your consciousness, and make it all mental . . . the great dark knowledge you cant't have in your head – the dark involuntary being. . . . In the blood . . . there you find yourself in a palpable body of darkness, a demon . . . .'   (*WL*, pp. 92–3)

Other symbolic incidents express the dominance exercised by the destructive, 'cerebral', predatory group over vegetation or the vegetarian animal species. Gerald's killing of a rabbit (ch. 18), his bloody brutalisation of a horse near the mechanised railway transport which bears his name (ch. 9), Gudrun's exercise of the will over the cattle (ch. 14) and the indecisive – that is, literally, involuntary – survival of Ursula and Birkin as isolated individuals, all speak the language of Bichat.

This frame of reference made its first appearance in *Sons and Lovers* (1913), revised after Lawrence's probable first encounter with Bichat's thinking, but ebbed away from *St Mawr* (1925) onwards, and is absent in *Lady Chatterley's Lover* (1928). The enigmatic 'drift towards death' noted by Lawrence in a letter (*CL*, p. 161) as the final destiny of Paul Morel,[35] is a tentative, early use of the Bichat signature: Paul has emerged from negative subservience and infantilism; the growth of voluntary active powers and his aesthetic sense brings him into contact with the destructive functions of cerebral, artistic, wakeful life. That way, Bichat argues, lies death; but here it is a 'drift', since Paul lacks the motivating, driving force of his dead brother William. In Will Brangwen the figure is repeated at greater length, foreshadowing the destructive cerebralism of Gerald: 'Sometimes he felt he was going mad with a sense of Absolute beauty, perceived by him through his senses . . . in the revelations of her body through his body, was the ultimate beauty, to know which was almost death in itself . . . ' (*R*, ch. 8). In *Fantasia of the Unconscious* (1922) and *Psychoanalysis and the Unconscious* (1923), Lawrence gave his most explicit rendering of Bichat's hypothesis. His appeal in these works to 'authorised science' and 'the nervous system' (*F*, pp. 28–30) rests on an assumption curiously counter to that of Gaskell. Lawrence addressed a world which had, as he saw it, forgotten the prophetic value of the ganglionic theory. In contrast, Gaskell strove to replace an orthodoxy stemming from Bichat with a theory including the spinal-reflex action, based on the research of Hall. Lawrence retraces Bichat's ground in most of his readings of physiological functions, but preserves a tendency towards aberrant readings of the type noted above. Lawrence's attribution of active powers to the ganglia, their dominance over the cerebrum, the endowing of the blood with powers of mediation and communication ('the blood has a unity and a consciousness of its own' – *F*, p. 166), the completeness of the 'sympathetic' system at birth ('from the lumbar ganglion . . . the milk is urged away down the infant bowels . . . towards excretion' – *F*, p. 36) and the dual functions of contractility and sensibility in each of two independent systems ('we have again a sympathetic centre poised in activity and knowledge, and a corresponding voluntary centre' – *F*, p. 137) repeat the main outlines of the Bichat system. Nevertheless, Lawrence's devaluing of the cerebrum to a 'switchboard' (*F*, p. 49) and the heterodox claim for 'knowledge' on the part of the ganglia, noted above, are aberrations from Bichat. Distortions may have stemmed from a variety of sources in experimental physiology after the work of Thomas Laycock (1812–76),[33] who leaned on the work of Marshall Hall; or, more probably, from Lawrence's acquaintance with the work of Hall himself, through the *Memoirs*. They are in general the inevitable consequence of Bichat's attribution of parallel powers of mobility and sensibility of two mutually exclusive systems within the single organism. In a persistent struggle to find meaning in this impasse, Lawrence leaned towards the ganglia as the principal sources of volition, knowledge and moral choice. Of Lawrence's various divergences from Bichat in the decade following 1912, none is more striking than the reference to the 'spinal cord' in *Twilight in Italy* (1916), written the year after Lawrence's first arrival in Munich: 'The will lies above the loins, as it were at the base of the spinal column, there is the living will, the living mind of the tiger, there is [*sic*] the slender loins. That is the node, there is the spinal cord.[34] In Bichat's thinking, the spinal cord is a neutral carrier of stimuli within the 'animal' system, but Lawrence here conflated the voluntary power of the sensory, 'animal' world of Bichat with spinal functioning as it emerged in the theory of Marshall Hall.

The *Memoirs* and the *Lancet* appendix give glimpses of the functions of procreation, digestion, respiration and circulation which Hall, in a lifetime of controversy, sought to remove from the theory of ganglionic domination. A veil of silence is drawn in these sources, however, over Hall's view of the initial act of procreation. In the paper 'Reflex Functions', Hall brings his argument to a close with a refutation of his contemporary, Jean-Louis Brachet (1789–1858), who had sought to explain this function within Bichat's terms:

M. Brachet . . . attempts to prove that some parts of the act and function of generation, in both sexes, besides the secretions, depend upon this [ganglionic or sympathetic] influence; whereas it is certain that they depend upon the lower portion of the medulla spinalis [spinal cord] and belong to the reflex functions. It is obvious, that, whilst the secretions may depend on the ganglionic system, the act of [sexual] excretion, and especially the action of the ejaculatory muscles, in an excited act of the reflex function, which has been fully proved to subsist in every portion of the divided medulla spinalis. . . . We know that some reptiles remain in coitu after the head is removed.[35]

Both this aspect of Hall's work and his opposition to the theory of Bichat are, however, discernible in occasional details and by implication from the sources available to Lawrence. The *Lancet* appendix explains: 'the separation by Bichat of the ganglionic nerves from the cerebro-spinal . . . was a mere classification based on morphology, rather than on experimental decomposition' (*Memoirs*, p. 493). In the *Lancet* appendix, the importance of an integrated, linked yet segmented chain of involuntary nervous activity is emphasised; its 'original, . . . diffusive . . . developmental' character, and its intertwining with voluntary activity, are repeatedly stressed: 'there is, perhaps, . . . no greater indication of [the Creator's] design than the extraordinary harmony which exists between the physical spinal motions occurring in an act of volition, and the voluntary movements themselves' (*Memoirs*, p. 473).

Lawrence's picture in *Lady Chatterley's Lover* of a society and its individuals in a state of shock adheres to the outlines of Hall's model of reflex functioning. The division of nervous activity into two realms is replaced by a unitary, segmented system, and the picture of society in torpor resembles the instances of hibernation which Hall explained by reference to spinal reflexes. The term 'blood' acquired a neutral value in Lawrence's last novel, approximating more to that developed by Hall, whose researches into circulation and campaign against indiscriminate blood-letting had led to his discovery of reflex functions. Thus, in *Lady Chatterley's Lover* the 'stupor of discontent' affecting post-war society is compared to a deep bruise: 'it would take many years for the lively blood of the generations to dissolve the vast black clot of bruised blood, deep inside their souls and bodies' (*LCL*, p. 52). Hall's experiments on animals by means of section of the spinal cord are echoed in the spinal injury to which Lawrence subjected Clifford Chatterley, who thus forfeits the nervous control required for locomotion and procreation.

Unlike Bichat, Hall located nervous control of the spasmodic disorders – epilepsy, apoplexy, and so on – in the spinal cord: 'all spasmodic diseases of the voluntary muscles', the *Lancet* appendix explains, 'are not, then, dependent on the voluntary motor system or upon the voluntary motor power, but on the spinal system' (*Memoirs*, p. 483). The reflex function ensured survival of the species, an activity in which Clifford is eclipsed by his employee, Mellors – 'the great object of the reflex function being the preservation of the individual from injury, and the perpetuation of the species' (p. 471). Lawrence's return to Eastwood yielded fruit in the form of a local anecdote as the foundation of his plot and a revival of memories of the great Victorian studies of failed matrimonial relationships: *Bleak House, Middlemarch, Two on a Tower*,[36] all of which are listed in the *Catalogue* of the Mechanics' Institute Library. His persistent difficulties with his reading public were the consequence of his lending vernacular and realistic expression to problems long accepted in bowdlerised or theoretical terms, in works available from the library itself. Thus, Mellors's encouragement to Connie Chatterley, 'Tha's got such a nice tail on thee . . . An' if tha shits and pisses, I'm glad' (*LCL*, p. 232), has its counterpart in the *Lancet* exposition of Hall's system: 'when the brain is injured . . . the reflex acts, the natural excitors of which remain, are performed the same as before; thus the bladder voids its contents, the rectum is emptied, and the foetus expelled from the uterus, perfectly, as far as the actions of the bladder, rectum and uterus are concerned' (*Memoirs*, p. 486).

Lawrence's acceptance of one aspect of spinal functioning entailed acceptance of others, notably its role in sensory experience. 'Sensation', a term persistently devalued under Bichat's influence in *Women in Love*, appears restored in *Lady Chatterley's Lover*. The third sexual encounter with Mellors precipitates a female orgasm, an item screened from view in the *Memoirs* and *Lancet* appendix alike, but implied, since other features of procreative nervous action are mentioned. Connie's 'disconnection . . . like a madness . . . it thrilled . . . till she felt she must jump into water and swim to get away from it; a mad restlessness' (*LCL*, p. 21) is stilled by the new experience: 'pure deepening whirlpools of sensation swirling deeper and deeper through all her tissue and consciousness, till she was one perfect concentric fluid of feeling, and she lay there crying in unconscious inarticulate cries' (*LCL*, p. 135). In another striking reversal of the Bichat paradigm, Hall annexed to the reflex system the field of convulsive disorders which loomed over Victorian social experience. The difficulty attributed to Michaelis by Lawrence, who sees in him 'the trembling excited sort of lover, whose crisis soon came, and was finished' (*LCL*, p. 30), is accounted for in spinal terms in the *Lancet* appendix: 'certain forms of impotence, dependent upon hasty, or imperfect, or entire loss of action of the vesciculae seminales and the ejaculatores, are caused by disordered states of the excitor and motor nerves engaged in the sexual function, or by disease of the spinal marrow' (*Memoirs*, p. 481). The distinction urged by Tommy Dukes between 'mental life' and 'real knowledge' is based on a distinction like Hall's and different from that of Bichat and his spokesman in *Women in Love*, Birkin. Like Hall, Dukes argues that mental life is generated by continuous activity involving the nervous system in all its branches; 'the mental life seems to flourish with its roots in spite . . . real knowledge comes out of the whole corpus of the consciousness; out of your belly and your penis as much as out of your brain and mind' (*LCL*, pp. 38–9). The awakening to mental and physical life of Connie Chatterley and of the man in 'The Man who Died' echoes the type of awakening based on spinal reflexes in hibernating animals noted in the *Memoirs* and the *Lancet* appendix. Through the work of Hall and others in the nineteenth century, Bichat's picture of two mutually exclusive forms of nervous activity was replaced by the unified, concentric system which Lawrence had clearly adopted by the time he wrote *Lady Chatterley's Lover*. His acceptance in this novel of the phrase 'stream of consciousness' marks a culmination in the transformation of his ideas. Originally coined by George Henry Lewes in his long and unnecessarily hostile commentary on the reflex theory of Hall ('the sensations of the alimentary canal generally pass unnoticed by us; but they form that stream of Consciousness'[37]) the phrase achieved its modern currency through the championship of Lewes's admirer William James.[38] Despite his quibble with Hall over the reading of the term 'sensation', Lewes built largely on foundations laid by the work of Hall. During his period of adherence to the ganglionic theory, Lawrence wrote, 'Stream of consciousness . . . immortal phrase of the immortal James. . . . Oh stream of hell which undermined my adolescence' (*F*, pp. 202–3). Like the term 'sensation', the phrase emerged in his last novel purged of sinister overtones and with a value similar to that assigned to it by Lewes: 'the quiver was going through the man's body, as the stream of consciousness again changed its direction, turning downwards' (*LCL*, p. 220).

Arguably, Lawrence owed his immersion in the thinking of Bichat to Otto Gross, who can be assumed to have had access to Boehm's text from 1912. The death of Gross in 1920 coincided with the culmination of Lawrence's adherence to Bichat's theory, in the publication of *Women in*

Love and the drafting of the works on the unconscious. The ensuing five years saw Lawrence at work on problems of leadership and cultural survival; conversations with W. E. Hopkin in the late summer of 1926 probably produced a return to early memories of Hall and of the novels in the Institute library. The library was by this date disbanded, but many items were known to and kept by Hopkin.[39] Hall's vision of a society transformed by knowledge of reflex functioning, his strong Methodist links, his love of Tuscany and the Nottinghamshire–Derbyshire countryside, and his invention of the modern method of artificial respiration which for long bore his name, are spelt out in the *Memoirs*; these themes lies at the root of Lawrence's last prose works. By whatever channels the work of these founders of modern theories of nervous action may have come to Lawrence's hands, they formed the basis of his thinking. His arguments and metaphors, it is suggested, emerge in sharp relief when the action and phrasing of his novels are traced against this background.

NOTES

1. In its original form this essay appeared as 'D. H. Lawrence's "Blood-consciousness" and the work of Xavier Bichat and Marshall Hall', *Etudes Anglaises*, 32, no. 4 (1979) 397–413. I thank the Research Fund of Sheffield University for grants enabling me to consult material cited here. In addition I thank the staff of the Bibliothèque d'Histoire de la Médecine, Paris, the Wellcome Institute, London, and the Wolfson Institute at the Maudsley Clinic, London, for assistance in tracing references and material.

2. Joseph Collins, *The Doctor Looks at Literature* (London, 1923) pp. 256–88; J. B. Coates, *Ten Modern Prophets* (London, 1944); Frederick J. Hoffman, 'Lawrence's Quarrel with Freud', in *The Achievement of D. H. Lawrence*, ed. by F. J. Hoffman and Harry T. Moore (Norman: University of Oklahoma Press, 1953) pp. 106–27; Leigh Trevis, 'D. H. Lawrence: The Blood-Conscious Artist', *American Imago*, 25 (1968) 163–90.

3. James C. Cowan, *Journey with Genius: D. H. Lawrence's American Journey* (London: Case Western Reserve University Press, 1970) pp 15–24.

4. I thank Dr Ruth Leys for enabling me to read her typescript article 'Background to the Reflex Controversy: William Allison and the Doctrine of Sympathy before Hall'.

5. Donal Shehan, 'Discovery of the Autonomic Nervous System', *Archives for Neurology and Psychiatry*, 35 (1936) 1081–113.

6. E. Clarke and C. D. O'Malley, *The Human Brain and Spinal Cord*

(Berkeley, Calif.: University of California Press, 1942) pp. 347–51; Sir Geoffrey Jefferson, 'Marshall Hall, the Grasp Reflex and the Diastaltic Spinal Cord', in *Science, Medicine and History. Essays in Honour of Charles Singer*, ed. E. Ashworth Underwood (London, 1953) pp. 303–20; Sir William Hale-White, *Great Physicians of the Nineteenth Century* (London, 1935) pp. 85–104; Max Neuburger, *Die historische Entwicklung der experimentellen Gehirn- und Rückenmarksphysiologie vor Flourens* (Stuttgart, 1897); Sir Humphrey Rolleston, *Centenary of the Nottingham Medico-Chirurgical Society* (Nottingham, 1928) pp. 15–19. I thank Dr Adrian Bower, of the Department of Human Anatomy at Sheffield University, for assistance in this reading.

7. Charlotte Hall, *Memoirs of Marshall Hall, MD, FRS.* (London, 1861); referred to here as *Memoirs*, with page references given in the text. This work appears as item 39 in the *Catalogue of the Library of the Eastwood and Greasley Mechanics' and Artizans' Institute* (Eastwood, 1895) p. 4 (Nottinghamshire County Library).

8. Referred to here as *Recherches*.

9. Xavier Bichat, *Physiologische Untersuchungen über den Tod*, ed. with an introduction by Rudolf Boehm (Leipzig, 1912); referred to here as *Untersuchungen*, with page references given in the text. This volume belongs to the Klassiker der Medizin series.

10. Martin Green, *The Von Richthofen Sisters* (London: Weidenfeld and Nicolson, 1974).

11. Rose Marie Burwell, 'A Catalogue of D. H. Lawrence's Reading from Early Childhood', *D. H. Lawrence Review*, (1970) 193–324.

12. Emile Delavenay, *D. H. Lawrence and Edward Carpenter: A Study in Edwardian Transition* (London: Heinemann 1971) pp. 118–63.

13. Marshall Hall, 'On the Reflex Functions of the Medulla Oblongata and the Medulla Spinalis', *Philosophical Transactions*, XXVI (1833) 635–65.

14. Edward Carpenter, *The Art of Creation* (London, 1904) p. 146.

15. Henry R. Binns, Letter of 4 Apr 1904, Carpenter MS 271.84, Sheffield City Libraries. I thank Professor Delavenay for this reference. The work of Claude Bernard (1813–78), the other physiologist referred to by Binns, appears to have been unknown to Lawrence. For Bernard's literary importance, see Reino Virtanen, *Claude Bernard and his Place in the History of Ideas* (Lincoln, Nebr.: University of Nebraska Press, 1960) pp. 117–28.

16. H. Maudsley, *Die Physiologie und Pathologie der Seele*, trans. Rudolf Boehm (Würzburg, 1870) in the Library of the Wolfson Institute, Maudsley Clinic, London.

17. For an obituary of Boehm by O. Gros (not Otto Gross), see 'Rudolf Boehm', *Deutsche medizinische Wochenschrift*, 52 (1926) 2000. See also Green, *The Von Richthofen Sisters*, pp. 62–73.

18. Another source of contact for Lawrence was Schopenhauer, whose doctrine of the blindness of the will (that is, the 'organic' impulses) and the powerlessness of the mental functions (the 'animal' or 'cerebral' system) in *The World as Will and Representation* owed much to Bichat, whom Schopenhauer frequently cites. I thank Dr Bruce Clarke for helpful suggestions in this context.

19.   Bichat's system was discredited in the 'Notes de l'éditeur' made by Françios Magendie (1785–1851) to the fourth edition of the *Recherches* (Paris, 1819), and disproved on experimental grounds by Magendie's pupil Claude Bernard.

20.   Frederick Carter, *D. H. Lawrence and the Body Mystical* (London, 1932) p. 26.

21.   Brian Bracegirdle, 'J. J. Lister and the Establishment of Histology', *Medical History*, 21 (1977) 187–91.

22.   The Notebooks of S. T. Coleridge, ed. Kathleen Coburn (London, 1973) III, 4409–10.

23.   Raphael Blanchard, *Centenaire de la mort de Bichat* (Paris, 1903) p. 13.

24.   T. Rennell, *Remarks on Scepticism . . . being an Answer to the Views of M. Bichat* (London, 1819); J. Bardinat, *Les Recherches physiologiques de Xav. Bichat sur la vie et la mort, réfutées dans leurs doctrines* (Paris, 1824).

25.   W. H. Gaskell, *The Involuntary Nervous System* (London, 1916) p. 12.

26.   Bichat, *Recherches*, p. 1.

27.   Lawrence made numerous references to 'blood' in his 'College Notebook' poems. See Warren Roberts, *A Bibliography of D. H. Lawrence* (London: Rupert Hart-Davis, 1963) pp. 344–5, item E317. The suggestion cannot be ruled out that the Bichat system was known to him in some form before the appearance of the *Untersuchungen*. The crystallising of his ideas after 1912 suggests that a first-hand reading of Bichat would have fallen on fertile ground. I thank Dr Holly Laird for her reference to this material.

28.   Egon Wellesz, *Essays on Opera* (London, n.d.) p. 120.

29.   'Animalische Sensibilität und Kontraktilität sowie organische Sensibilität und Kontraktilität sind eng aneinander gebunden.'

30.   Cited in Thomas H. Miles, 'Birkin's Electro-Mystical Body of Reality: D. H. Lawrence's use of Kundalini', *D. H. Lawrence Review*, IX (1976) 194–212.

31.   George A. Panichas, *Adventure in Consciousness* (The Hague: Mouton, 1964) p. 4. Criticism of Lawrence's work generally gains in clarity when it is placed against the background of his physiological thought. Thus, the view of David Cavitch – 'Birkin more ardently and openly seeks Gerald's love as his romance with Ursula proves successful and vivifying to him. Lawrence hoped to show through Birkin that the free, unified man will express his sensual affections, his unconscious feelings, in every relationship with things and persons. Gerald perversely dies' – approximates to a recognition that ganglionic functioning, considered by Carpenter and others to be predominant among women, acts as a vital principle to the two men, but is ineffectual in the case of the predominantly cerebral Gerald Crich. David Cavitch, 'On *Women in Love*', in *D. H. Lawrence. A Collection of Criticism*, ed. Leo Hamalian (New York: McGraw-Hill, 1973) pp. 63–4.

32.   See Harry T. Moore, *The Life and Work of D. H. Lawrence* (London: Allen and Unwin, 1963) p. 83.

33.   Richard Hunter and Ida MacAlpine, *Three Hundred Years of Psychiatry* (London: Oxford University Press, 1963) pp. 1079–84.

34. D. H. Lawrence, *Twilight in Italy* (London: Jonathan Cape, 1926; first published 1916) p. 49.
35. Hall, in *Philosophical Transactions*, XXVI, 660–1.
36. J. R. Ebbatson, 'Thomas Hardy and Lady Chatterley', *Ariel*, 8 (1977) 85–95.
37. George Henry Lewes, *The Physiology of Common Life* (London, 1859–60) II, 280. See also pp. 151–272 (ch. 9: 'The Spinal Chord and its Functions').
38. William James, *Principles of Psychology* (London: Macmillan, 1890) I, 234–401 (chs 9–10).
39. L. Paulin, 'Old Libraries of Nottinghamshire' (1950, typescript in Nottingham County Library) p. 28.

9

Lawrence and Expressionism

HENRY SCHVEY

Although it is not unusual to see the name of D. H. Lawrence coupled in some way with Impressionism, Fauvism, Cubism, or Futurism (movements which Lawrence knew and wrote about), there have been very few attempts to connect his work with German Expressionist literature or art. The reasons for this are indeed substantial: Lawrence was apparently unfamiliar with the movement, and never mentions the term 'Expressionism' or any of its leading exponents in his writings. Indeed, as Breon Mitchell writes in his essay 'Expressionism in English Drama and Prose Literature', the impact of Expressionism 'on the English novel was practically nil. . . . Expressionism in prose literature was not even recognized by English critics, let alone emulated by English novelists. . . . English critics first began to discuss Expressionism around 1924, that is, at about the same time as it was dying out in Germany' – concluding that 'the thematic material used by the Expressionists held little attraction for English writers'.[1]

Since Lawrence was obviously not influenced by the movement, and if the case for linking Lawrence with Expressionism is such a weak one, an obvious question is, why bother to undertake it at all? The most recent attempt to do so, Max Wildi's article 'The Birth of Expressionism in D. H. Lawrence', written in 1937, is handicapped by its extremely vague interpretation of 'Expressionism' to cover 'all anti-realist as well as anti-idealist movements, irrespective of national and personal origin, reaching from Strindberg in the north to Marinetti in the south and covering many "isms", of which the original "Expressionism" . . . is but one of many forms'.[2]

The present essay will attempt to indicate Lawrence's affinities with Expressionism in a more precise way: first, by citing the presence of various Expressionist characteristics in Lawrence's literary work; second, by comparing Lawrence's chief obsession, the relationship between the sexes, with its treatment by the Austrian Expressionist

124

painter and playwright Oskar Kokoschka; third, by considering some of Lawrence's own paintings within the context of Expressionist art.

In discussing the presence of Expressionist characteristics in Lawrence's literary work I shall confine myself to the two companion novels *The Rainbow* and *Women in Love* (originally conceived as a single work, *The Sisters*), not only for reasons of concision and because these works are generally considered to be Lawrence's finest contributions to the novel, but because it was while he was working on them (1913–16) that he decisively broke with the realistic style which characterises such earlier works as *The White Peacock* (1911) and *Sons and Lovers* (1912). As he wrote in a letter to Edward Garnett in January 1914, 'I have no longer the joy in creating vivid scenes, that I had in *Sons and Lovers*' (*CL*, p. 263). This interest in the representation of the visible world is superseded by a desire to depict something else, another mode of reality. As he wrote in another letter, 'One must put away all ordinary common sense, I think, and work only from the invisible world. The visible world is not true. The invisible world is true and real.'[3]

In abandoning the world of the visible for the invisible, Lawrence echoes such prominent Expressionists as Kasimir Edschmid, who wrote, 'Die Welt ist da. Es wäre sinnlos, sie zu wiederholen', or Paul Klee, whose *Schöpferische Konfession* begins with the words, 'Kunst gibt nicht das Sichtbare wieder, sondern macht sichtbar.'[4] As Ulrich Weisstein has stated, what the Expressionists wished to render visible were 'soul states and the violent emotions welling up from the subconscious'.[5] In its search for the essential man, the core of experience, Expressionist literature does away with personality in the traditional sense and instead offers archetypes – elemental conflicts between man and woman, father and son, as in the plays of Kokoschka, Sorge and Hasenclever, and the early music dramas of Schoenberg; or man directly and mystically confronted by eternity as in the plays of Barlach. Such an art, then, is ultimately to be seen as a form of religious communication and is marked above all by its concentration and intensity.

At the same time as the Expressionists were forging their most radical experiments in the arts, Lawrence was working on *The Rainbow* and *Women in Love*, in which he projected the 'powerful, spontaneous, often explosive life of the universe, deforming in the process the conventional shape of things in an attempt to give them an essential one'.[6] In arguing, as he did, that 'my novels must be written from the depths of my religious experience' (*CL*, p. 273), Lawrence fashioned characters based not on traditional notions of personality but on, as he put it, 'blood-consciousness'; arguing that 'it is necessary for us to realize that there is this other great half of our life active in the darkness, the blood-relationship' (*CL*, p. 393).

Although it would be an oversimplification to suggest that Lawrence's characters are reduced to nameless types in the style of Expressionist drama, he too, in his attempt to penetrate below the surface of his characters' consciousness to the blood relationships underneath, dispensed with surface 'personality' in order to uncover the archetypal self. Instead of personality in his novels he strives to 'create a new life, a new common life, a new complete life from the roots that are within us' (*CL*, p.395).

The most famous statement about Lawrence's conception of character comes in a letter to Edward Garnett written in 1914, while he was working on *The Rainbow*. It bears quoting again in the present context:

> I don't so much care about what the woman *feels* – in the ordinary usage of the word. That presumes an *ego* to feel with. I only care about what the woman *is* – what she IS – inhumanly, physiologically, materially . . . instead of what she feels according to the human conception. . . . You musn't look in my novel for the old stable *ego* – of the character. There is another *ego*, according to whose action the individual is unrecognizable, and passes through, as it were, allotropic states which it needs a deeper sense than any we've been used to exercise, to discover are states of the same single radically unchanged element. (Like as diamond and coal are the same pure element of carbon. The ordinary novel would trace the history of the diamond – but I say, 'Diamond, what! This is carbon.' And my diamond might be coal or soot, and my theme is carbon.)   (*CL*, p. 282)

As for many of the Expressionists, Lawrence's concern with elemental man is most clearly revealed in his treatment of the relationship between the sexes, the central theme of much of his work, and about which he wrote that 'The whole crux of life now lies in the relation between man and woman, between Adam and Eve. In this relation we live or die' (*CL*, p. 484).

Like the Expressionists, Lawrence depicts the relationship between the sexes in mystical or visionary terms, often using a quasi-biblical language filled with repetition and exclamation to underline the ecstatic tone. This style, with its 'pulsing, frictional to-and-fro, which works up to culmination' as Lawrence put it (*PhII*, p. 276), allows the author to move from what is done or said to that which is unconsciously felt. A scene between Tom and Lydia Brangwen in *The Rainbow* may serve as an example:

> They had passed through the doorway into the further space where movement was so big, that it contained bonds and constraints and labours, and still was complete liberty. She was the doorway to him, he to her. At last they had thrown open the doors, each to the other, and had stood in the doorways facing each other, whilst the light flooded out from behind on to each of their faces, it was the transfiguration, the glorification, the admission.
>   And always the light of the transfiguration burned on in their hearts. He went his way, as before, she went her way, to the rest of the world there seemed no change. But to the two of them, there was the perpetual wonder of the transfiguration.   (*R*, pp. 95–6)

Following this moment of unity, the rainbow image is evoked for the first time in the novel, and the Brangwens and their little daughter Anna seem completely divested of any social reality and have been raised to the level of archetypes of man, woman and child:

> Anna's soul was put at peace between them. She looked from one to the other, and she saw them established to her safety, and she was free. She played between the pillar of fire and the pillar of cloud in confidence, having the assurance on her right hand and the assurance on her left. She was no longer called upon to uphold with her childish might the broken end of the arch. Her father and her mother now met to the span of the heavens, and she, the child, was free to play in the space beneath, between.   (*R*, p. 97)

Thus far, I have briefly indicated various characteristics which Lawrence shares with his German Expressionist contemporaries: the break with realism, the concern with the elemental in man resulting in the creation of archetypes, and the conception of art as visionary or religious experience whose style is marked by intensity and concentration. To these one might add the interest in the primitive, evidenced by several of Lawrence's own paintings, as well as the discussion of a piece of African sculpture in *Women in Love*, in which Birkin maintains, in contrast to Gerald, who denies it the status of art, that it 'conveys a complete truth. It contains the whole truth of that state. It is so sensual as to be final, supreme (*WL*, p. 87).

Lawrence did not, however, share the Expressionist tendency toward pure formalism, whether in language, colour or sound. An important influence was exercised here by Wilhelm Worringer's *Abstraktion und Einfühlung*, a work which has been termed 'the aesthetic Bible of Expressionism',[7] and which strongly influenced the Anglo-Saxon variant of Expressionism, Vorticism, through Worringer's disciple, T. E Hulme.

In contrast to his Expressionist tendency towards abstraction, Lawrence deprecated the search for what he called 'Significant Form', calling it 'the magic jargon of invocation, nothing else (*Hardy*, p. 145). Since for Lawrence the artist '*can* only create what he really religiously *feels* is truth, religious truth really *felt*, in the blood and the bones' (*Hardy*, p. 140), art that is concerned with pure form divorced from the life of man is 'just shadows, minds mountebanking and playing charades on canvas. . . . But of course it is all games inside the cemetery' (*Hardy*, p. 149).

In his illuminating criticism of Cézanne, he argues that the painter's genius consists not in paving the way towards abstraction but in the discovery of the essential 'appleyness' of the apple, a more not less true-to-life representation of reality than so-called realists such as Daumier and Courbet were capable of. Thus Lawrence views Cézanne as a spiritual brother in search of the unseen essence of the material world, and to extend his explorations further into the realm of abstraction, as did the Cubists, is a distortion rather than the logical fulfilment of his true genius.

In the character of the sculptor Loerke in *Women in Love*, Lawrence vents his hostility towards formalism in art. For Loerke, 'a rat in the river of corruption', there is no relation between art and life, since art only has to do with itself. Like the Futurists and Vorticists Loerke also venerates the machine, arguing that we should 'make our places of industry our art' and that 'art should *interpret* industry, as art once interpreted religion' (*WL*, p. 518). In the novel, Ursula expresses Lawrence's opposition to this view of the separation between life and art. In his letters, Lawrence praises Futurism for its 'purging of old forms and sentimentalities', while condemning its 'cure or escape', which is intellectual and dead rather than instinctive and vital (*CL*, pp. 279–80). In writing about the painter Duncan Grant he said,

Tell him not to make silly experiments in the futuristic line. . . . Most puerile is this clabbing geometric figures behind one another, just to prove that the artist is being abstract, that he is not attempting representation of the object. The way to express the abstract-whole is to reduce the object to a unit, a term, and then out of these terms and units to make a whole statement. . . . It is an Absolute we are all after, a statement of the whole scheme – the issue, the progress through time – and the return – making unchangeable eternity. (*CL*, p. 308)

In one of his most successful paintings, *Flight back into Paradise*, Lawrence depicts the woman liberating herself from the bondage of the machine. This theme also appears in both novels under consideration, especially *Women in Love*, where Gerald Crich, who is frequently referred to as 'God of the machine', is symbolically associated with ice, cold, spiritual hollowness and finally death. His end, by freezing to death in the snow-covered mountains of Switzerland, forms the climax of the novel, and is prefigured by the description of him in the opening chapter: 'In his clear northern flesh and his fair hair was a glisten like sunshine refracted through crystals of ice. And he looked so new, unbroached, pure as an arctic thing' (*WL*, p. 61).

Through the fate of Gerald, Lawrence projects his apocalyptic message concerning the modern fixation on the machine as Godhead. By contrast, Birkin, the novelist's *alter ego*, is torn between unqualified pessimism and despair over the present, and the hope of a sharp, revolutionary break with the past. Thus the assertion that the 'thematic material used by the Expressionists held little attraction for English writers. . . . A sharp break with tradition, the complete restructuring of the social and political order, and violent *Aufbruch* even on the personal level simply were not ideas appealing to literary England',[8] must be qualified with regard to Lawrence in *Women in Love*. How else can we account for Birkin's repeated insistence that 'I would die like a shot to know that the earth would really be cleaned of all people. . . . Man is a mistake, he must go' (*WL*, p. 188), and 'You've got very badly to want to get rid of the old before anything new will appear – even in the self. . . . When we really want to go for something better, we shall smash the old . . .' (*WL*, pp. 105–6)?

Having indicated some of the main connections between Lawrence and Expressionism, I should now like to make an explicit comparison between Lawrence's treatment of the theme of the relationship between the sexes and a similar theme in the work of Oskar Kokoschka, whose paintings have often been linked with Expressionism (despite Kokoschka's reluctance to bind himself to any movement), and whose early plays have often been called the first Expressionist dramas.

Perhaps the clearest indication of Lawrence's views on the sexes, the theme which dominates so much of his work, is to be found in his *Study of Thomas Hardy*, written in 1914 while Lawrence was working on *The Rainbow*. In the essay Lawrence reveals his ideal of a perfect union between man and woman, a state expressed with crude beauty by Tom Brangwen in *The Rainbow* when he says, 'it seems to me as a married couple makes one Angel' (*R*, p. 138). In such an ideal union, individuality is perfectly blended with togetherness, forming what Birkin in *Women in Love* calls a 'mutual unison in separateness'. However, in reality such unison is impossible, and the result for Lawrence is that 'Until eternity, there shall be this separateness, this interaction of man upon woman, male upon female, this suffering, this delight, this imperfection' (*Hardy*, p. 55).

Because 'there is never to be found a perfect balance or accord of the two Wills, but always one triumphs over the other', all human aspiration is an attempt 'to recover balance, to symbolize that which is missing' (*Hardy*, p. 59). Interaction between the sexes is for Lawrence dominated by images of missed communication or domination of one partner by another; 'it is as if life were a double cycle, of men and woman, facing opposite ways, revolving upon each other, man reaching forward with outstretched hand, woman reaching forward with outstretched hand, and neither able to move till their hands have grasped each other', which, being impossible, results in their passing on again, away from each other, 'travelling opposite ways to the same infinite goal (*Hardy*, p. 61).

Something of this striving for union is conveyed in the corn-harvesting scene in *The Rainbow*, where Lawrence depicts Anna and Will putting up sheaves in a visionary moonlit landscape which emphasises the universality of the action:

> They worked together, coming and going, in a rhythm, which carried their feet and their bodies in tune. She stooped, she lifted the burden of sheaves, she turned her face to the dimness where he was, and went with her burden over the stubble. She hesitated, set down her sheaves, there was a swish and hiss of mingling oats, he was drawing near, and she must turn again. . . .
>
> And always, she was gone before he came. As he came, she drew away, as he drew away, she came. Were they never to meet? Gradually a low, deep-sounding will in him vibrated to her, tried to set her in accord, tried to bring her gradually to him, to a meeting, till they should be together, till they should meet as the sheaves that swished together.   (*R*, pp. 122–3).

This image of the sexes as both attracted and repelled, eternally separated yet trying to make contact, is the thematic core of the four highly visual plays Kokoschka wrote between 1909 and 1918. It is, however, perhaps most beautifully realised in the double portrait of the art historians Hans and Erica Tietze of 1909 (Figure 1). In this painting, Lawrence's image of the outstretched hands which do not meet, or the movement of the sheaves in the harvest scene, is embodied in the hands of the man and woman, which are at the point of making contact but do not touch.

In Lawrence's novels and essays, relations between the sexes and the state of sublimely balanced tension are seldom sustained for long. More often we find a more violent sexual struggle depicted, as in the battle to the death between Gudrun and Gerald, culminating in Gerald's death at the end of *Women in Love*, or in the chapter 'Anna Victrix' in *The Rainbow*, where Anna Brangwen dances out the nullification of her husband:

> They fought an unknown battle, unconsciously. Still they were in love with each other, the passion was there. But the passion was consumed in a battle. And the deep, fierce, unnamed battle went on. Everything glowed intensely about them, the world had put off its cloths and was awful, ·with new, primal nakedness.   (*R*, p. 168)

The same battle of love–hate is enacted in each of Kokoschka's early plays. As Eurydike asks the dying Orpheus at the conclusion of Kokoschka's autobiographical play about his obsessive love for Alma Mahler, *Orpheus und Eurydike*, 'Ob es Hass ist, solche Liebe?'

For both Kokoschka and Lawrence the struggle for sexual supremacy is frequently depicted as a kind of perpetual vampirism. In Kokoschka's first play, *Mörder Hoffnung der Frauen* (1909) there is the following dialogue:

MANN   Ich frass dein Blut, ich verzehre Deinen tropfenden Leib.
FRAU   Du Vampyr, frisst an meinem Blut, Du schwächst mich.[9]

In *The Rainbow* we have the following: 'he was pulling her down as a leopard clings to a wild cow and exhausts her and pulls her down. . . . He wanted her in his power. He wanted to devour her at leisure, to have her' (*R*, p. 185).

In Lawrence's novels and in the plays and paintings of Kokoschka, the sexual drama is played out against cosmic background of solar and lunar forces representing the power of the man and woman respectively. In *Mörder Hoffnung der Frauen* the Woman threatens the Man by saying,

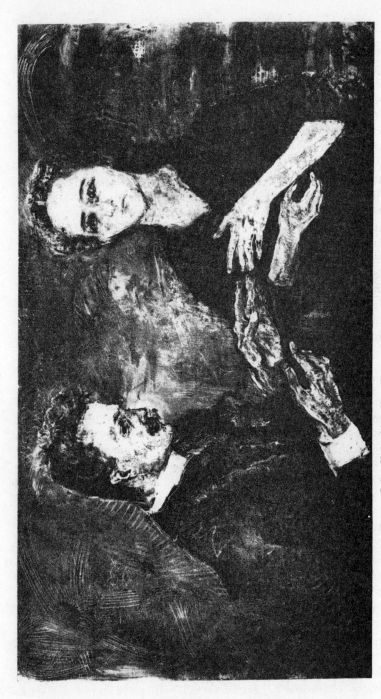

FIGURE 1   Oskar Kokoshka. *Hans Tietze and Erica Tietze-Conrat*, 1909 (courtesy of the Museum of Modern Art, New York: Abby Aldrich Rockefeller Fund)

'mit meinem Atem erflackert die blonde Scheibe der Sonne', and, if we look closely at the background of the Tietze double portrait, we see an exploding sun scratched in (with the back of the brush!) behind the figure of the man, a crescent moon behind the woman. Similarly, in *Women in Love*, in the scene where Birkin throws stones at the reflection of the moon in a still pond, Lawrence uses the metaphors of sun and moon as metaphors for the relationship between Ursula and Birkin:

And his shadow on the border of the pond was watching for a few moments, then he stooped and groped on the ground. Then again there was a burst of sound, and a burst of brilliant light, the moon had exploded on the water, and was flying asunder in flakes of white and dangerous fire. Rapidly, like white birds, the fires all broken rose across the pond, fleeing in clamorous confusion, battling with the flock of dark waves that were forcing their way in. The furthest waves of light, fleeing out, seemed to be clamouring against the shore for escape, the waves of darkness came in heavily, running under towards the centre. But at the centre, the heart of all, was still a vivid, incandescent quivering of a white moon not quite destroyed, a white body of fire writhing and striving and not even now broken open, not yet violated. It seemed to be drawing itself together with strange, violent pangs, in blind effort. It was getting stronger, it was reasserting itself, the inviolable moon. And the rays were hastening in in thin lines of light, to return to the strengthened moon, that shock upon the water in triumphant reassumption. (*WL*, p. 323)

Related to this solar–lunar dichotomy is the fact that both Lawrence and Kokoschka saw the sexual struggle as being made up of opposing, yet complementary, forces in which the male represents what Lawrence called the will-to-motion and the female the will-to-inertia. About these forces (which, as he clearly specified, were not to be seen as positive and negative) Lawrence wrote that they 'cause the whole of life, from the ebb and flow of a wave, to the stable equilibrium of the whole universe, from birth and being and knowledge to death and decay and forgetfulness' (*Hardy*, p. 60). This opposition of wills can be detected in the placement of the figures in the Tietze portrait, with the male figure intently concentrating on the meeting hands and the female seemingly oblivious and self-absorbed. However, it is even more in evidence in what is perhaps Kokoschka's best-known work, *Die Windsbraut*, painted in the same year (1914) as *The Rainbow* and the *Study of Thomas Hardy* were published (Figure 2). Here the two lovers

FIGURE 2   Oskar Kokoschka, *Die Windsbraut*, 1914 (courtesy of Öffentliche Kunstsammlung, Kunstmuseum Basel)

(the artist and his mistress, Alma Mahler) are depicted lying on a huge conch shell, adrift in a tempest-tossed sea. It is clear that Kokoschka has demonstrated the opposition between the sexes in his treatment of the two lovers. The woman, whose body is painted in soft, milky hues, lies asleep, oblivious to the raging storm, while the man is awake and anxious, his body seemingly stripped of its covering of skin so that tendons and muscles lie bare. For Lawrence, analogously, woman is immortal, immutable and stable, while man 'is a raging activity . . . stirred into thought by dissatisfaction', yet requiring the stability of woman for his completion (*Hardy*, p. 58).

Thus far, in attempting to demonstrate various characteristics of Lawrence's literary Expressionism, I have neglected one aspect of his art which further aligns him with his Expressionist contemporaries – namely, his paintings.

Although Lawrence wrote and thought about art throughout his career (both Paul Morel, the protagonist of *Sons and Lovers* and Cyril Beardsall in *The White Peacock* are artists) and drew and painted (mainly copying older works) throughout his life, he only began taking up painting seriously in 1926, at the age of forty. His first and only exhibition, which opened in 1929 and was successful, was raided by the police and closed three weeks after opening.

It would be absurd to suggest that Lawrence was a great – or even a good – painter, and unlike Kokoschka's dramas, which are worthy of serious attention in their own right, the paintings of Lawrence would probably not warrant discussion were he not a great novelist. None the less, it would be a mistake to ignore them here, particularly as they do contribute to a fuller understanding of Lawrence's Expressionism.

Although errors in proportion and anatomical distortion may be the result of simple mistakes rather than what Heinrich Wölfflin described as the Expressionist's 'purposeful negation of correctness',[10] it is obvious that there is a tremendous intensity which gives interest to many of the canvases, and that colour is, as with the Expressionist painters, determined by the emotional effect desired, or, as van Gogh observed 'instead of trying to reproduce exactly what I have before my eyes, I use colour more arbitrarily so as to express myself more forcefully'.[11]

This is demonstrable in several of Lawrence's copies of earlier masterpieces. In his copy of Giotto's *Joachim and the Shepherds*, for example, he changed the bone-white hill in the background to green, and in his version of Piero di Cosimo's *Death of Procris* he deliberately chose to make the blood a lurid red, totally out of place in terms of the original. When his error was indicated to him, Lawrence justified his use of colour in a way that is most revealing, since it is not only very Lawrencean, but also highly Expressionistic:

> I delighted so in painting that bloodstream. I could not resist the urge to make it real red-red, only I couldn't get it bloody enough, the warm, slightly steaming, liquid red blood. I wanted to experience the lust of killing in that picture. . . . I often feel I could kill and enjoy it.[12]

In some of the paintings where the anatomical uncertainty is not too obtrusive, such as *The Feast of the Radishes*, *Red Willow Trees*, *Resurrection* and *Dance Sketch*, the intensity of the colours (somewhat reminiscent of Nolde) and the pulsating rhythms (suggestive of Kirchner) provide a clear insight into Lawrence's concern with the vital essence of things, which is the hallmark of the Expressionist artist. Even Herbert Read in calling Lawrence 'an extreme example of that type of artist who seeks a direct correspondence between feeling and representation, to the neglect of the more sophisticated values of proportion and harmony', admitted that 'in spite of his literary approach and technical inadequacy . . . every picture *lives*'.[13]

In this perception, of course, we find revealed the core of Lawrence's philosophy, both as painter and novelist, for his was not an emotionally detached search for Significant Form, but rather, as it was for the Expressionists, 'religious truth really *felt*, in the blood and the bones' (*Hardy*, p. 140).

NOTES

The author would like to acknowledge the assistance of the Netherlands Institute for Advanced Study, Wassenaar, where he was a Fellow during the 1980–1 academic year.

1.   Breon Mitchell, 'Expressionism in an English Drama and Prose Literature', in *Expressionism as an International Phenomenon*, ed. Ulrich Weisstein (Paris: Didier; Budapest: Akademiai Kiado, 1973) p. 183.
2.   Max Wildi, 'The Birth of Expressionism in the Work of D. H. Lawrence', *English Studies*, 19 (1937) 241–52.
3.   Quoted ibid., p. 252.
4.   Quoted in *Expressionism as an International Phenomenon*, p. 23.
5.   Ibid.
6.   Wildi, in *English Studies*, 19, p. 252.
7.   *Expressionism as an International Phenomenon*, p. 36.
8.   Mitchell, ibid., p. 183.
9.   Oskar Kokoschka, *Dichtungen und Dramen* (Hamburg: Christians, 1973) p. 41. For Kokoschka's illustration portraying 'the flayed body of a dying or dead man with twisted limbs in the arms of a pale woman with brutal hands and bared teeth . . . a strange version of the Pietà as well as an evocation of that monster who kills through her love', see 'The Symbolist Legacy in the Works of Kokoschka', in *Homage to Kokoschka. Prints and Drawings Lent by Reinhold, Count Bethusy-Huc* (London: Victoria and Albert Museum, 1976) pp. 18–22; also, Henry I. Schvey, *Oskar Kokoschka: The Painter as Playwright* (Detroit: Wayne State University Press, 1982), *passim*.
10. Quoted in Peter Selz, *German Expressionist Painting* (Berkeley: University of California Press, 1974) p. 15.
11. Quoted in *Expressionism as an International Phenomenon*, p. 40.
12. Quoted in *The Paintings of D. H. Lawrence*, ed. Mervyn Levy (London: Adams and MacKay, 1964) p. 63.
13. Herbert Read, 'Lawrence as Painter', ibid., pp. 63–4.

10

Lawrence, Otto Weininger and 'Rather Raw Philosophy'
EMILE DELAVENAY

Significant similarities as well as important divergences between the ideas of D. H. Lawrence and those of Otto Weininger were first noted by Janko Lavrin, whose penetrating analysis 'Sex and Eros (on Rozanov, Weininger, and D. H. Lawrence)' did not, however, attempt to seek mutual influences.[1] The two books and personality of the Viennese prodigy, who committed suicide at the age of twenty-three, 'enjoyed immense prestige' in the early years of the century.[2] Of twenty-eight editions of his *Geschlecht und Character* between 1903 and 1947, twelve appeared between May 1903 and May 1910. He was thought of either as a brilliant disciple of Freud, or as a contradictor of psychoanalysis. He was, in the German-speaking world, a master of 'modernism'[3]. In England he was best known through the 1906 translation *Sex and Character*,[4] a book revealing 'a prodigious sum of culture and learning' but also described by Le Rider as 'a dreadful pandemonium teeming with the worst forms of fanaticism: anti-feminism, anti-semitism, a passion for irrationalist metaphysics'.

My early interest in a possible flow of ideas from Weininger to Lawrence was discouraged by the dismissal of the thought by Havelock Ellis when I discussed it with him. But David Garnett when questioned told me that 'we', meaning his generation, 'all had read Weininger'.[5] Robert Nichols and Cecil Gray recorded Philip Heseltine's keen interest in the Austrian at the time he and Lawrence indulged in long 'philosophical' fantasies at Garsington and later in Cornwall.[6] Neither Ernest Seillière[7] nor Martin Green,[8] in their studies of Lawrence's points of contact with German thought, has mentioned Weininger. When I completed my work on Lawrence's formative years I was able to draw attention to what looked like borrowings from *Sex and Character* in the 1914 *Study of Thomas Hardy*.

The recent publication of Jacques Le Rider's brilliant book on
Weininger and of a French translation (*Des fins ultimes*) of Weininger's
posthumous *Über die letzten Dinge*[9] revives the subject: the question
arises of the possible formative influence of the latter work upon
Lawrence's 'philosophy', especially as formulated in that other near-
pandemonium, the *Study of Thomas Hardy*.

The idea of a booklet on Hardy had arisen from a publisher's
suggestion (*Letters*, II, 193). It soon became a vehicle for a
superabundance of ideas, symbols and metaphors which had occupied
his mind since the end of 1912. I am showing elsewhere[10] that chapters 7
and 8 of the 'Hardy' papers were in part, among other things, the essay
on the Futurists Lawrence had in mind in June 1914, incorporating
ideas found in his letters of the previous spring. He admitted that this
book was 'queer stuff' and seemed to be 'about anything else in the
world' but Hardy, calling it 'a sort of Confessions of my Heart' (*Letters*,
II, 212, 220, 235). So much was it a transitional work, failing to integrate
its themes and symbols into a fully coherent philosophy, that he again
and again undertook its revision, first in 'The Crown' and later in the
mystery manuscript 'Goats and Compasses', which Heseltine alone
seems to have read.

The letters of 1913 and the *Hardy* text suggest that ideas absorbed in
early 1913 underwent a process similar to that by which his reading of
the Futurists left traces in his correspondence before finding its way into
the literary philosophical mixed bag which the intended booklet on
Hardy grew into. Of particular interest are the letters to Henry Savage
about his friend the poet Richard Middleton, who had taken his own life
in 1911. As was the case with Marinetti and his friends, we are faced here
with a combined assimilation of ideas and passionate rejection of certain
attitudes and reassertion of personal views arising from Lawrence's own
human experience.

Sex and Character is an expanded thesis in philosophy presented to the
University of Vienna; at least its first part claims scientific value,
compatible with the state of biology and psychology at the time. It soon
becomes a treatise of logic, ethics and aesthetics, as well as a virulent
attack on women and Judaism. It will help if I summarise here its main
subjects.

The main argument stems from a theory of *bisexualism*, then shared
by Weininger with Freud and Fliess: living beings cannot be described
bluntly as of one sex or the other (p. 9). Male and female 'plasmas' are

distributed in each one of us in varying proportions. An individual may be three quarters male and a quarter female. He will know true sexual union only when he finds his *complement*, three quarters female and a quarter male, thus achieving the sum of 'a complete male and a complete female'. It follows that 'love children' are 'the finest, strongest, and most vigorous of human beings' (p. 43), fertilisation having 'the best results when it occurs between parents with the maximum sexual affinity' (p. 36) an idea, incidentally, found in Lawrence's letters (*Letters*, I, 429).

From bisexuality it follows that *sexual inversion* has biological causes, and cannot be regarded as 'pathological' or as 'an acquired vice'. There is 'no ethical difference' between homosexual and heterosexual desire. (Rumours had been rife in Vienna of Weininger's homosexuality, and he had once tried chemical experiments aiming at curing homosexuals.)

A *woman's* demand for *emancipation* is proportional 'to the amount of maleness in her' (p. 64); women interested in intellectual matters are sexually intermediate forms. Woman, in so far as she is predominantly female, is the greatest enemy of her own emancipation.

From the lengthy philosophical-*cum*-cultural dissertations in the second part of *Sex and Character*, only the main themes are of interest here. Foremost among them is that of the supreme value of *consciousness*, an essentially male characteristic: 'the male lives consciously, the female lives unconsciously' (p. 102). Only a man can be the supremely conscious being, the *genius*, who has 'equal parts of himself and his opposite' in him, and possesses an 'extremely comprehensive consciousness'; there is in him 'not only the universality of men, but of all nature' (p. 111). He is the man 'with the strongest demand for *timelessness*, with the greatest desire for value' (p. 136). His is 'a kind of higher masculinity', and woman 'cannot be possessed of genius'.

Long demonstrations aim at showing the 'soullessness' of woman, who is non-moral, not immoral. Womanhood divides into two types, *mother* and *prostitute*; analogies are sought between motherhood and sexuality. Woman is sexual, not erotic; her love is but a means to an end, procreation. It is 'fundamentally immoral' to idealise her as a *Madonna*: 'Love is murder. The sexual impulse destroys the body and mind of the woman, and the psychological eroticism destroys her psychical existence' (p. 249). Woman represents universal sexuality, is interested mainly in pairing and matchmaking. 'Man is form, woman is matter' (p. 293), and man 'not only *forms himself but woman also*' (p. 295). Man alone can achieve individuality, become a 'monad'; 'the meaning of woman is to be meaningless', whereas man is 'the image of God, the absolute something' (p. 297).

The penultimate chapter is devoted to a full-scale attack on *Judaism*, with several references to Houston Chamberlain, whom Weininger had known in Vienna. The Jewish writer is at pains to show that some 'pure Aryans' share the faults he finds in Judaism; in spite of this he shows a biologically based racial bias against the Chinese, negroes and Jews, while stating that his hostility is directed against 'a tendendy of the mind'. And this tendency Jews share with women. 'Judaism is *saturated with femininity*, with precisely those qualities the essence of which I have shown to be in strongest opposition to the male nature' (p. 306). The Jew 'is fully at one with his father' (p. 310), he is 'at the opposite pole from *aristocrats*, with whom the preservations of the limits between individuals is the leading idea' (p. 311). He lacks true mysticism, and his monotheism 'is not a religion of reason, but a belief of old women founded on fear' (p. 314). 'Christ was *the man who conquered in Himself Judaism*, the greatest negation, and created Christianity . . .the strongest affirmation and the most direct opposite of Judaism' (pp. 327–8).

A recent convert to Protestantism whose sincerity cannot be questioned, Weininger is then ready for his final recommendations. Woman must renounce coitus. 'There should be neither sexuality nor love, for both make woman the means to an end' (p. 329). 'Man must free himself of sex, for in that way, and that way alone, can he free woman.' And this strange book ends on a Nietzschean note with an idea not uncommon at the turn of the century, the hope for the advent of some sort of bisexual *superman*: truth will not prevail until the two become one, until from man and woman a third self, neither man nor woman, is evolved (p. 345). Both Edward Carpenter and Lawrence, in their separate times, toyed with the same idea.[11]

Weininger's friend Moritz Rappaport published in 1903 the posthumous volume *Über die letzten Dinge* (*On the Last Things*), of which a revised and expurgated second edition (1907) was reprinted several times – notably in 1912, when Lawrence first went to Germany. It contains a long essay on Ibsen's *Peer Gynt*, followed by 'Aphorisms', essays on characterology, one on the unidirectionality of time, twenty pages of notebook jottings under the heading 'Metaphysics', an 'Essay on Culture in relation to Faith, Fear and Science', and so on including many tributes to Wagner. This volume can be considered to answer to the definition of 'rather raw philosophy' by which Lawrence, writing to Savage, describes some of his favourite reading (*Letters*, II, 114). I propose to show that it can be included under that heading in his reading of 1913.

Having established that Lawrence had read all Carpenter's works,[12] I assumed that he first knew of Weininger's existence and his theory of bisexualism through significant quotations made by Carpenter – in particular, ten lines printed as a preamble to *The Intermediate Sex*. But Lawrence, whose only written mention of Carpenter is to be found in a September 1915 letter to their mutual friend William Hopkin, broke his silence on Weininger only once, towards the very end of his life, in his review of Rozanov's *Fallen Leaves*,[13] and, even then, not without some degree of reticence:

> Anyone who understands in the least Rozanov's state of soul, . . . must sympathize deeply with his real suffering and his real struggle to get back a positive self, a feeling self. . . . How much, and how little, he succeeded we may judge from this book: and from his harping on the beauty of procreation and fecundity: *and from his strange and self-revealing statements concerning Weininger.* Rozanov is modern, terribly modern. And if he does not put the fear of God in us, he puts a real fear of destiny, or of doom; and of 'civilisation' which does not come from within, but which is poured over the mind by 'education'.   (*Ph*, pp. 391–2; emphasis added)

George Zytaruk has shown[14] the deep influence exercised by Rozanov's views on procreation and fecundity on Lawrence's later work: views, of course, directly opposed to Weininger's, in spite of the fascination the Austrian aroused in the Russian. I have found only one mention of Weininger in the section of *Fallen Leaves* translated into English, but it needs quoting in full:

> From every page of Weininger's there is heard a shout: 'I love men!'
>   'Well, you're a sodomite then', and with that you may shut the book.
>   The book is all interwoven of *volo* and *scio*: his *scio* is profound, at any rate where it *concerns the survey of nature*. With a woman's eye he has caught the thousands of details hitherto unnoticed: he has even noticed that 'giving suck to a child excites woman'. (Hence the constant overfeeding of babies by their mothers and nurses, and the consequent gastric complaints of babies, with 'which you simply can do nothing'.)
>   'Oh, you female! As though you *yourself* gave suck to a baby, or wished to do so!'
>   'Woman is boundlessly grateful to man for copulation: and when

the man's semen flows into her, it is the culminating point of her existence.' He says this more than once, and keeps on reiterating it in his book. You can point your finger at him saying: 'Don't betray the secret, you female! Try to hide your dreams!!'

He speaks of *all women*, as if they were all his rivals, just with the same irritation. But women are more generous. Each one of them having her true husband, makes no claim whatever to the street males, but leaves to Weininger's share quite a large number of trousers.

His jealousy of women (for men) made him hate 'women rivals'. And along with this he is full of the most profound moral nostalgia: and thereby he has revealed the deep moral nature of woman, which he, in his jealousy, denies. He embraced Christianity: as women generally (Saint Olga, Saint Clotilda, Saint Bertha) were the first to embrace Christianity. Jews, on the contrary, he hates: again for the reason, that they are his rivals ('the feminine nature of Jews is my idée fixe').[15]

Lawrence thought that Rozanov's attitude to the Jews was 'extraordinary' and showed 'uncanny penetration'. In fact *Fallen Leaves* abounds in traditional Russian anti-semitism, a mixture of hatred, jealousy and fascination. Lawrence, however, fails to clarify, by quotation or comment, in what respect he found Rozanov's passage 'self-revealing'. Could there have been, as late as 1929, something deeply personal behind this reticence? Was fear of the British censor a sufficient explanation?

He was more outspoken in a 1913 letter to Savage about Middleton[16] which contains his first known written reference to homosexuality: 'I should like to know why nearly every man that approaches greatness tends to homosexuality, whether he admits it or not: so that he loves the *body* of a man better than the body of a woman – as I believe the Greeks did, sculptors and all, by far' (*Letters*, II, 115).

'Whether he admits it or not' calls to mind two significant passages. Ursula (*R*, p. 407) never told her most intimate friend about her past lesbian attachment to Winifred Inger: 'That was a sort of secret sideshow to her life, never to be opened. She did not even think of it. It was a door she had not the strength to open.' And Birkin, in the Prologue to *Women in Love* Lawrence chose to suppress, also kept a door closed:

This was the one and only secret he kept to himself, this secret of his passionate and sudden, spasmodic affinity for men he saw. He kept this secret even from himself. He knew what he felt, but he always kept the knowledge at bay. His a priori were: '*I should not* feel like this', and

'It is the ultimate mark of my own deficiency, that I feel like this.' Therefore, though he admitted everything, he never really faced the question. He never accepted the desire, and received it as part of himself. He always tried to keep it expelled from him. (*PhII*, p. 107)

Lawrence shows sympathy with Rozanov's 'struggle to get back a positive self, a feeling self'. Was this not Birkin's struggle? But Rozanov, while he saw his way to redemption, was 'always acting up, trying to *act* feelings because you haven't really got any. . . . Just to *make* yourself have feelings, when you have none. This was very Russian, and is very modern. A great deal of the world is like it today' (*Ph*, p. 389). Lawrence's 1929 diagnosis of the modern sickness had not changed since he conceived *Women in Love*. Does it suggest an awareness of Weininger's ideas and personality nowhere explicitly found in his writings, but wholly consistent with his comments on Middleton?

Lawrence could have had easy access to *Sex and Character* at any time after 1906. But had he read the posthumous *Über die letzten Dinge*? He and Frieda were lent Alfred Weber's flat, the upper story of a house at Icking, from 2 June 1912 until 5 August. They spent occasional days at Munich, visiting the Jaffes, who knew the circle of artists and writers at Schwabing known as the 'Cosmics'. Lawrence's German was at that time rudimentary. They again stayed at Irschenhausen in the Jaffes' house from 15 April to 15 June 1913, and from 9 August to 15 September. His letters to Savage run from July 1913 to June 1914. By then his German was probably fluent enough for him to read books and reviews, with or without Frieda's help, and he would certainly have browsed in the literature which the Jaffes left around their country house. I make this statement notwithstanding Marianne Jaffe von Eckart's assertion, many years later, that there would not normally be books in Alfred Weber's flat.[17] To my knowledge the question was not put to her about her parents' country house.

Lawrence could also have become aware of Weininger's European reputation in Italy, through Italian translations of *Sex and Character* (in 1912) and *Über die letzten Dinge* (in 1914), and through essays by Giovanni Papini and Giulio Augusto Levi. Papini's review of *Sex and Character*[18] was provocative enough for a reader as convinced as Lawrence was of the redeeming virtue of a woman's love, and it might have revived his interest in a writer whose main interests ran close to his own.

As Jacques Le Rider notes, Weininger 'synthesised all the intellectual currents of his time: Nietzscheanism, Wagnerism and anti-semitism connect him with the very first of the post-1870 "moderns".... *Sex and Character* is also one of the earliest manifestos of the Expressionists.'[19] Le Rider lists an impressive number of famous men, from Kafka and Musil to Wittgenstein, Berdiaev and Rozanov, via Schoenberg and Spengler, who admit a debt to the Austrian. The thought therefore occurs that any convergence between Lawrence's ideas and Weininger's might be accounted for by their common immersion in the stream of German and Austrian thought and art from Schopenhauer, Nietzsche and Wagner through Houston Chamberlain to the Munich 'Cosmics'. But it is remarkable to what extent, over the period which extends from the final work on *Sons and Lovers* to the completion of *Women in Love*, Lawrence concentrated on subjects shared with Weininger: love and woman's claim to emancipation (the 'Hardy' papers and *The Rainbow*), the relation of genius to time and eternity (*Hardy*, 'The Crown'), Madonna worship and the idealisation of woman ('The Crown', 'The Novel'), Judaism as predominantly female (*Hardy*), the significance of the change from a 'female' to a 'male' religion, the nature of genius and of a potential 'superman'. This mere catalogue should not obliterate their basic divergence over woman: whereas Weininger sees her as an obstacle to the efflorescence of genius and to his contact with the cosmos, Lawrence, at least in the 1913–15 period, seeks through her contact with the cosmic life force and sees in the co-operation of the sexes the means to achieve 'supreme art'.

Beyond these general considerations, a fragment from Weininger's diary challenges us to a close study of textual similarities between *Über die letzten Dinge* and Lawrence's writings of 1913–14. It suggests a much more direct influence than had so far been held conceivable. In a late travel diary Weininger notes,

> Light is the symbol of consciousness.... Night (sleep) corresponds to the unconscious. ... Light does not smoke; all fire smokes (black, antimoral; absolute Nothingness; diamond as the opposite, representative of the Something, completely transparent; transparency as a moral symbol; significance of the opposition in psychology: coal–diamond.)[20]

Could Lawrence's metaphor-hungry imagination have failed to register the vivid opposition 'coal–diamond', and the insistence on its psychological significance, if he had read this? The much-quoted passage of his letter to Garnett on the 'old stable ego of the character', with its indirect suggestion of the working of the unconscious, owed something to his recent reading of Marinetti. Probably Weininger suggested the metaphor of the allotropic states of the ego:

> There is another ego, according to whose action the individual is unrecognizable, and passes through, as it were, allotropic states which it needs a deeper sense than any we've been used to exercise, to discover are states of the same radically unchanged element. (Like as diamond and coal are the same pure single element of carbon. The ordinary novel would trace the history of the diamond – but I say 'diamond, what! This is carbon.' And my diamond might be coal or soot, and my theme is carbon.)   (*Letters*, II, 183)

Allotropes, the unconscious, coal and diamond as metaphor of psychological variations, even the smoke or soot – can this be a mere meeting of minds?

Another letter (19 Jan 1914, *Letters*, II, 137–8) reveals the gradual formulation of what became the idea of the allotropic states of the ego. It is here combined with the notion of the 'angel' in each human being, which often remains unuttered in the 'unbegotten hero' (*Ph*, pp. 429ff.)[21] For Lawrence, Greek sculpture reveals something of the eternal stillness that lies under all movement, under all life, like a source, incorruptible and inexhaustible. Compare Weininger: 'The still stars represent the angel who is in man' (*Des fins ultimes*, p. 104). So to speak, the diamond hidden in the carbon? In his letter of January 1914 Lawrence goes on,

> As a rule one sees only the intertwining of change and a distortion of half-made combinations, of half-resolved movements. But there is behind every women who walks, and who eats a meal, a Venus of Melos, still, unseeing, unchanging, and inexhaustible. And there is a glimpse of it everywhere, in somebody, at some moment – a glimpse of the eternal and unchangeable that they are. And some people are intrinsically beautiful – most are pathetic, because so rarely they are their own true beauty. And some people are intrinsically . . . fearful-strange forms half-uttered. And all a man can do is to struggle to be true to his own pure type. And some men are intrinsically monkeys, or dogs – but they are few, and we must forget them, once they are muzzled.   (*Letters*, II, p. 138)

Not only does man's struggle to 'be true to his own true type' conform to

Weininger's Nietzschean idea of man's struggle towards genius, but in the section 'Metaphysics' of *Über die letzten Dinge*, a few pages before the 'coal–diamond' contrast, he strove to formulate a 'universal symbolism' founded on an animal psychology. The dog is for him 'the symbol of a criminal', of the loss of personal value; the horse (rather like St Mawr?) symbolises 'aristocratic genius'; finally, 'we call some people pigs, camels, monkeys, cows, donkeys or dogs' (*Des fins ultimes*, pp. 174, 181). Man, especially genius, is a 'microcosm' in whom 'all things in the world are present' (p. 166) and a monkey is a caricature of the microcosm (p. 181).

The letters to Savage abound in instances of the two minds operating on the same thought with the same metaphors. Savage had edited Richard Middleton's posthumous poems, many of them haunted by a sense of failure with women he either loved or thought he loved: and his volume of essays *Monologues*,[22] with a (for the time) courageous apologia for suicide a propos both of John Davidson's death and of Housman's *Shropshire Lad*. Poets, Middleton asserted, did not kill themselves for a plate of soup but because of 'the bitterness of the unhonoured prophet' (*Monologues*, p. 68). The then-taboo theme of homosexuality ran through some of the essays, especially in connection with A. E. Housman's poetry. The essay 'Dreaming as an Art' suggests familiarity with Freud's *Interpretation of Dreams*: 'It is quite possible to regard our dreams as a kind of dramatic commentary on our waking life, or as an expression of the emotions which the intellect has forced us to suppress in that life' (p. 39).[23]

Of the two essays which incensed Frieda and Lawrence, 'The New Sex' is comparatively anodyne, but 'Why Women Fail in Art' is offensively reminiscent of Weininger's worst onslaughts. Artists are driven by a 'desire for self-expression', but the author doubts whether 'in this sense of the word women have any self to express' (p. 127). They 'exhaust their creative energies in trying to invent themselves'; they 'do not exist at all' and can only exceptionally 'claim an individual character' (pp. 127–8). More than Oscar Wilde, whom he quotes ('A sphinx without a secret'), Middleton echoes *Sex and Character*, quoting no sources: it would not have been consonant with the light touch of the popular essayist to name unknown Austrians, Freud or Weininger, around 1909.

Frieda and Lawrence reacted with fury. And Lawrence rode his 1913 hobby horse. A woman has to find from a man complete satisfaction, 'physical at least as much as . . . psychic, sex as much as soul': 'So she goes for man, or men, after her own fashion, and so is called a Sphinx, and her riddle is that the man wasn't able to satisfy her – riddle enough for him' (*Letters*, II, 94–5).

One of Middleton's poems,[24] 'To Althea, who Loves Me Not', while not specifically disapproved of, was characteristic. Althea will sooner or later yield to 'a king to whom belongs / The mastery in all things passionate', thus 'crown[ing] the victor stooping for [her] sake': she will then learn

> That you, whom God might covet when desired,
> Are something less than human when possessed.

The poet speaks of her 'mean, ignoble mind', exclaiming,

> What's this she-thing to me, who can create
> A thousand better puppets in a day
> Puppets with soul, better to love or hate.

The literary source of the sentiment seems probable: 'from genius itself, woman is debarred' (*Sex and Character*, p. 113), whereas genius is 'the really divine spark of mankind' (p. 171).

For Lawrence also, the artist has more life in him than other people, but he also needs physical and psychic satisfaction: 'He must get his bodily and spiritual want satisfied in one and the same draught. So he must endlessly go for women, and for love. And I reckon an artist is only an ordinary man with a greater potentiality – same strength, same make up, only more force'. Therefore Middleton (and so, presumably, Weininger?) was 'wrongly directed': 'He hated his flesh and blood. His life went on apart from his own flesh and blood – something like a monk who mortifies the flesh. . . . [Poets] go on the loose in cruelty against themselves, admitting that they are pandering to, and despising, the lower self' (*Letters*, II, 95). So Middleton 'stamped' his own flesh and blood 'out of life'.

The theme of self-hatred becomes dominant in the letters to Savage, and is applied with pertinence and insight to the 'modern' in general. Weininger, as it happens, divided men into two types, the self-lover and the self-hater. In another paper he toyed with a dichotomy into sadist and masochist, the second being very similar to his 'self-hater', who hates 'his empirical ego' (lower self, or body), but loves his 'intelligible ego' (*Des fins ultimes*, p. 60). He is unable to love anything but eternity, and so 'cannot love a concrete woman': 'in the extreme case, the sex act, for instance, is for him totally impossible' (p. 62).

Lawrence, who would answer Weininger's definition of the masochist if not the self-hater, seeks a fusion of 'one's physical and mental self' which should enable a man 'to produce good art'. Middleton's trouble was his failure to achieve this fusion; he was 'hindered' by 'some dross': 'And so again he hated himself. Perhaps if he could have found a woman to love, and who loved him, . . . he would have been pure. He was always impure. I can't explain the word impure, because I don't know what it means' (*Letters*, II, 115). By the autumn of 1914 he was able to attempt a clarification of his meaning: 'could I then, being my perfect self, be selfish? A selfish person is an impure person, one who wants that which is not himself. Selfishness implies admixture, grossness, unclarity of being' (*Ph*, p. 432) – a thought recalling Weininger on *Peer Gynt*:

> Ibsen knows that alone the possession of an 'I' in the higher sense brings man to recognize in another the 'Thou', since the fundamental condition of all altruism is that self-respect presupposes respect for others. Thus individualism is diametrically opposed to egotism. That is why he presents Peer Gynt as heartless and egocentric. (*Des fins ultimes*, pp. 39–40)

Where Weininger denied woman a self, a character, Lawrence recognised in her an individual, even when he dismissed as futile her demand for the suffrage (*Ph*, pp. 404ff).

He had given Middleton's impurity a name. The following, from his letter of 31 October 1913, just precedes his reference to greatness and homosexuality, already quoted:

> That heavier, more enduring part which was not a lyric poet but a man with dramatic capabilities, needed fertilizing by some love. And it never was fertilized. So he destroyed it, because perhaps it had already begun to corrupt. I believe he would have loved a man more than a woman: even physically: like the ancients did. I believe it is because most women don't leave scope to the man's imagination, – but I don't know. (*Letters*, II, 115)

Weininger was obsessed by the idea of the *Doppelgänger*: 'There is no man who could spend his life in a room surrounded by mirrors' (*Sex and Character*, p. 210); the very word 'double' would raise 'a deep dread in the mind of any man'. His self-haters are afraid of their double, and pretend that they 'can love only someone unlike themselves. . . . Compelled as they are to hate that which resembles them, they *attempt* to satisfy their need for love by taking as objects people unlike themselves; by definition they do not succeed' (*Des fins ultimes*, pp. 59–60). Fortuitously or not, Lawrence again works on the same ideas very much with the same phraseology:

> I believe a man projects his own image on another man, like on a mirror. But from a woman he wants himself re-born, re-constructed. . . . And one is kept by all tradition and instinct from loving men, or a man. . . . And one doesn't believe in one's own power to find and form the woman in whom one can be free – and one shoots oneself, if one is vital and feels powerfully and down to the core.   (*Letters*, II, 115)

'Man is form, woman is matter', 'man not only forms himself, but woman also' (*Sex and Character*, pp. 293, 295): was Lawrence describing Weininger's suicide as well as Middleton's, using the former's very phraseology? At all events he generalises on suicide as an effect of the modern sickness:

> Most poets die of sex – Keats, Shelley, Burns. . . . But study Burns a bit, or Verlaine, to grasp Middleton – and Baudelaire. They've all – not Burns – Baudelaire, Verlaine and Flaubert – got about them, the feeling that their own flesh is unclean, corrupt. And their art is the art of self-hate and self-murder.   (*Letters*, II, 101)

Flaubert 'hated himself', felt 'nothing but disgust' for his body. Possession of a woman 'left a residue in him, which went corrupt. The old artist burned up this residue to Almighty God. What is offered to God in all time is largely unsatisfied sex' (*Letters*, II, 101).

Here he has found the idea which, elaborated and to some extent clarified in the *Study of Thomas Hardy*, will be the point of departure for a discussion of 'female' and 'male' religions. As for Flaubert, having no God, he felt unclean. Like Weininger and Nietzsche, Lawrence feels that 'God must exist for me to exist; I am only as far as I am God. . . . Faith in God is, finally, only perfect belief in oneself. . . . The Ego does not diminish but grow when it has authentic faith' (*De fins ultimes*, pp. 196–7). And Lawrence on Verlaine, Baudelaire and Flaubert: 'They denied love, and lived by hate – hate is the obverse of love, the recoil of unsatisfied love. They *wanted* to love themselves in the flesh – their intellectual dogma said so. "We are God, all that there is of him"' (*Letters*, II, 101).

Had Lawrence and Frieda heard from their Munich friends echoes of

Weininger's sensational suicide ten years before, and of Strindberg's laying a wreath on his grave? Lawrence hated Strindberg (*Letters*, I, 509). His aversion was profound for those who gloried in 'the suicide of the Egoist', the 'Strindberg set' (*Letters*, II, 247). In November 1913 he went on, 'To understand Middleton you must understand the whole suicidal tendency that has overspread Europe since 1880 – half Sweden commits suicide – a great deal of Germany and France – it is the Northern races – Madam [*sic*] Bovary is Flaubert suiciding his soul' (*Letters*, II, 101).

A few weeks earlier he had referred (*Letters*, II, 34–5) to Novalis, comparing Savage's poetry to that of this 'sensuous mystic', who, according to Weininger, was a 'very great genius' and had first 'called attention . . . to the association between sexual desire and cruelty (*Sex and Character*, p. 248; *Des fins ultimes*, p. 72) – a discovery Lawrence had made by November 1912: 'It is sex lust fermented makes atrocity' (*Letters*, I, 469).

One of his last letters to Savage introduces Whitman. Again the themes are genius, the cosmos, woman and unsatisfiedness. For Weininger genius is a microcosmos, whose system is the same as the system of the world. Lawrence writes,

> [Whitman] is too self-conscious to be what he says he is: he's not Walt Whitman, I, the joyous American, he is Walt Whitman, the Cosmos, trying to fit a cosmos inside his own skin: a man rongé with unsatisfiedness not at all pouring his seed into American brides to make stalwart American sons, but pouring his seed into the space, into the idea of humanity. . . . *To make an idea of the flesh and blood is* wrong.   (*Letters*, II, 129; emphasis added)

Similarly Weininger had denounced Dante's 'transference of his own ideal to the person of a concrete woman' (*Sex and Character*, p. 249) and found in the Madonna worship of great artists 'a destruction of woman. . . , a replacement of actuality by a symbol' (p. 250). And for Lawrence Whitman's poetry

> is neither art nor religion nor truth. Just a self-revelation of a man who could not live, and so had to write himself. . . . He never gave his individual self into the fight. . . . He never fought with another person. . . . [He] did not take a person: he took that generalized thing, a Woman, an Athlete, a Youth. And this is wrong, wrong, wrong. He should take Gretchen, or one Henry Wilton.   (*Letters*, II, 130)

He was to renew in 'The Novel' his attack on the falsehood of Dante's Beatrice and Petrarch's Laura. When in 1913 he sketches out these ideas in private correspondence, he is not shy of referring to homosexuality in connection either with Whitman or with Middleton.

The raw material contained in those letters to Savage was to be elaborated into a would-be comprehensive system of 'philosophy', first in the *Study of Thomas Hardy*. In this work Lawrence is concerned with love and sex, with religion as an expression of human desire, with the full achievement of the self, with the relation of individual to social morality and of 'natural law' to conventional social codes; leaving aside for the present purpose his theory of artistic evolution, in part inspired by Boccioni, this leads to his idea of a 'supreme art' to spring from the harmony and conjunction of male and female.

Basic to the general argument is the idea, which he knew from Carpenter's works, and which Frieda may have reinforced thanks to her smattering of psychoanalysis, of bisexualism, on which *Sex and Character* is founded. Not only does Lawrence take it for granted but he extends it. While the 'male stream' and the 'female stream' are manifested 'in the flesh', the physical, or sex, is not the only 'indication of the great male and female duality and unity'. The spirit is also male and female. Like the flower of the poppy, which is both, 'the consciousness . . . is of both' (*Ph*, p. 443). Here is the main difference between Weininger's system and Lawrence's, and it is as if in the *Hardy* study the Englishman were engaged in an argument with the Austrian, starting from common premises but upholding the cause, not of woman, but of communion of the sexes.

From the notion of the bisexuality of the spirit Lawrence goes on to apply it to religion: the soul seeks its 'complement in the spirit like the body in the flesh': 'The religious effort is to conceive, to symbolize that which the human soul, or the soul of the race, lacks. . . . It is the portrayal of that complement to the real life which is known only as a desire' (*Ph*, p. 447). As in individuals, so in 'races': with some of them the female element, with others the male, predominates. And so with religions. A predominantly female race will form a male idea of God, because 'the attributes of God will reveal that which man lacked and yearned for in his living' (*Ph*, p. 446). Writing to Savage about the self-hating moderns, who denied God, he had written, 'If you read David's Psalms, you will see that God is to him like a great woman he adores.' With variations the idea is expanded in the *Study of Thomas Hardy*: 'For centuries, the Jew knew God as David had perceived Him, as Solomon had known Him. It was the God of the body, the rudimentary God of physical functions (*Ph*, p. 450). Allowing for a personal reading of the Psalms, this echoes Weininger's view that 'Judaism is saturated with femininity' (*Sex and Character*, p. 306), the Decalogue demanding of 'obedient followers, submission to the will of an exterior influence, with the reward of earthly well-being' (p. 313). 'The Jew lived on in physical contact with God. Each of his physical functions he shared with God, he kept his body always like the body of a bride ready to serve the bridegroom. He had become the servant of his God, the female, passive' (*Ph*, p. 450). This God of a female race is the Father, and also the Law; he is One, 'owing to the complete Monism of the female, which is essentially static'. Lawrence has absorbed Weininger's view of Judaism, monist because 'saturated with femininity', the family playing a larger role than with other people since Judaism is 'feminine and maternal in its origins' (Weininger having read Bachofen!).

In opposition to this monist concept 'It were a male conception to see God with a manifold Being, even though he be One God' (*Ph*, p. 451). Lawrence is here at one with Weininger and his mentor Houston Chamberlain, whose Aryan God was manifold. And with both of them he sees Christ, the Son, rising 'from the suppressed male spirit of Judea' with a new commandment, 'Thou shalt love my neighbour as thyself', and repudiating woman: '"Who is my mother?" He lived the male life utterly apart from woman' (*Ph*, p. 452). 'With Christ ended the Monism of the Jew. God, the One God, became a Trinity, three-fold' (*Ph*, p. 453).

In his attempted synthesis Lawrence combines this idea with the notion of 'aristocrat'. Weininger saw the Jew 'at the opposite pole from aristocrats, with whom the preservation of the limits between individuals is the leading area' (*Sex and Character*, p. 311); for Lawrence the aristocrat is 'separate', isolated, detached (*Ph*, pp. 487, 435, etc.). Recognition of the existence of my neighbour, separation of the individual from the group – that is the break with Judaism and the age of the Law: 'Such is the cry of anguish of Christianity: that man is separate from his brother' (*Ph*, p. 452); 'Man must be born again "Unto knowledge of his own separate existence as in Woman he is conscious of his own incorporate existence"' (*Ph*, p. 453).

The Age of the Son is thus that of Love, but deviates into love of one's neighbour and rejection of the flesh: 'In the Father we are one flesh, in Christ we are crucified, and rise again, and are One with Him in spirit' (*Ph*, p. 465). When, only 'after the Renaissance', Christianity 'began to exist, there triumphed the love of the Mystic Marriage, of the death of the body'. And so Northern humanity 'has sought the female apart from woman'. On this opposition of the Law and Love Lawrence builds, adapted from Boccioni, an aesthetic theory of the successive ages of art. He castigates 'the great Northern confusion', the 'desire to have the spirit mate with the flesh, the flesh with the spirit' (*Ph*, p. 473). He sees the Holy Ghost as the Reconciler, an idea he develops later in 'The Crown', and he finally formulates his somewhat obscure theory of a 'supreme art' which 'knows the struggle between the two conflicting laws, and knows the final reconciliation, where both are equal, two in one, complete' (*Ph*, p. 515).

While the conclusions are radically opposed to Weininger's idea of the exclusively male nature of genius, a passage from *Über die letzten Dinge* may have triggered the whole argument on Love and the Law. The two types, self-lover and self-hater, in the essay on Ibsen, are said to 'broaden out into the ideas of father and son' (*Des fins ultimes*, p. 62). 'Only the self-lover is capable of being a father in the strict sense', while the self-hater 'is not even able to love the creatures of his mind' (pp. 60–1). The self-lover is described as feminine, prone to 'love life'. The self-hater sees in love an effort to transcend the self; he is addicted to negation as a means of seeking 'that which is truly worthy of love. . . . He succeeds only in loving eternity. He cannot love a concrete woman'. A synthesis is thus achieved between Jew and self-lover, Christian and self-hater:

> Let us think of the role played in the New Testament by the 'father' idea. The Jews had not conceived that their God might be the father of mankind. For them he was the Lord, and they were his servants. . . . But Jesus Christ was not one of those who loved themselves and their subjective self. . . . He who feels he is a son can only hate himself.
>
> (p. 62)

On the strength of what precedes, the debt of the Lawrence of 1913–14 to Weininger in the formulation of his own *Weltanschauung* would seem considerable. Their common exposure to the Nietzschean and 'Cosmic' stream of thought does not alone account for the similarities of ideas and formulations which we have detected. And there are other analogies, perhaps less characteristic, but worth noting, of which here are a few instances:

> All disease has psychic causes, . . . is a psychic element which has become unconscious and has 'entered the body.'
>
> (*Des fins ultimes*, pp. 110–11)

I am quite certain that when I have been ill, it has been sheer distress
and nerve strain which have let go on my lungs.

                    (Irschenhausen, 15 Sep 1913, *Letters*, II, 73)

There is no such thing as chance. – If there is chance, there is no
God.   (*Des fins ultimes*, p. 88)

It is no accident that Shelley got drowned – he was always trying to
drown himself – it was his last mood.   (*Letters*, II, 115)

And Birkin, in *Women in Love*, refuses to believe in chance or
accident.   (*WL*, ch. 2)

Weininger denies evolution, and finds the Jews readily beguiled by
Darwinism (*Sex and Character*, pp. 314, 315, 317). Lawrence (*Ph*, p. 485)
challenges the concept of evolution of Darwin, Spencer and Huxley. In a
letter written in July 1917 (*CL.*, p. 518) he altogether denies evolution.
'Timelessness', the ability of the self to attain 'eternity', preoccupied
both. Lawrence saw it achieved through the sexual union of body and
spirit of 'true complements', or in artistic creation, which he conceived
for the future as a result of true sexual union. For Weininger, the
individual could triumph over time by concentrating in one instant 'the
universality of his "I" and of the world' and genius was 'the only
timeless man' (*Des fins ultimes*, p. 86; *Sex and Character*, p. 136).

His letters to Savage and others, his interpretation of Hardy's
characters, show Lawrence concerned with 'the struggle to get back to a
positive self': his own, Birkin's and Rozanov's struggle, and the battle in
which Middleton and Weininger failed. All the 'moderns' whom he
mentions are seen by him as self-haters, some of them as homosexuals.
Rozanov's comments on Weininger's homosexual tendencies were not
news to him in 1929. His insistence on woman's positive, rehabilitating
role in his 1913 letters is significant. It seems inconceivable, considering
those letters, the Prologue to *Women in Love*, the review of *Fallen Leaves*,
that he had not given early thought to the Weininger case. And also
inconceivable, considering the internal evidence, that he had not read
Über die letzten Dinge by 1913.
   The contents of his letters, whole sections of the *Study of Thomas
Hardy*, the review of Rozanov's book fit together like pieces of a puzzle
in the light of the works and fate of Weininger and of Middleton, casting

new light on Lawrence's personal struggle for a positive self, and on Frieda's role in this struggle at the time; perhaps, also, on his failure to refer to Edward Carpenter and to Weininger as writers who had meant something to him. They had not only supplied him with ideas. Their personal problems were probably very close to his own, and therefore their influence of a too intimate nature for him to wish, or feel it safe, to name them.

Those who put their faith only in external evidence may not follow me in my conviction that *Über die letzten Dinge* was, for a time, if not a bedside book, at least one eagerly read by him in his search for a 'raw philosophy' which he might refine. The community of Lawrence scholars observed pained silence when I showed that Lawrence had read Houston Chamberlain, at a time when, according to H. G. Wells, everyone did, at the beginning of the First World War. So I should like to end on a challenge to the prisoners of external evidence.

This is what Lawrence wrote to Ernest Collings, his engraver friend, in January 1913:

> Böcklin – *or somebody like him* – daren't sit in a café except with his back to the wall. I daren't sit in the world without a woman behind me. And you give me that feeling a bit: as if you were uneasy of what is behind you. Excuse me if I am wrong. But a woman I love sort of *keeps me in direct communication with the unknown*, in which otherwise I am a bit lost. (*Letters*, I, 503; emphasis added)

In the absence of any text (I am still searching) which Lawrence might have read, mentioning Böcklin's peculiarity, I turn to Weininger. He greatly admired the Swiss painter, whom he names three times: once in *Sex and Character*, to introduce the idea of the microcosmic genius in harmony with the cosmos;[25] twice in *Uber die letzten Dinge* – in an essay on 'seekers and priests', as a 'priest' type who 'stoops to sensuality' and is close to nature (*Des fins ultimes*, p. 126), and in a footnote to 'Science and Civilisation', where he discusses the 'fear of oneself', 'the fear of the empirical ego'. This he associates with 'absolute phenomenalism', 'according to which perception is real, so that I am not sure that *a wall I have just looked at* continues to exist once I have *my back to it*'. This view creates a risk, the 'elimination of the continuity of the ego, which objectively corresponds to the continuity of the world'. 'If I wonder *whether the wall still exists when my back is turned*, it seems that . . . the existence of the world, of the transcendental object, is reduced to a sign, and thus rendered unreal and valueless' (pp. 199–200, emphasis added).

Weininger's general theme is the relation of subject to object, of the ego to the cosmos. He who fears his concrete ego fears that his 'non-temporal self may be reduced to a point of time'. And here is the footnote: 'The reduction of the ego to an atom of time, its loneliness in time (rather than its connection to all eternity) is symbolised with absolute genius by the unicorn in Böcklin's famous painting *Schweigen im Walde*' (p. 199).

My rash hypothesis, which I would withdraw at the sight of other evidence, is this: Lawrence writes, 'Böcklin – *or somebody like him*'. What did that mean? Wasn't he sure that he meant the painter? Was he alluding to somebody, possibly Böcklin, who was 'a bit lost', needed to be kept 'in direct communication with the unknown' and required 'a connection to eternity'? Was he in fact referring to a garbled memory of something he had read in German, about an ego collapsing and reduced to a mere atom of time, and associating Böcklin's name with the idea of a wall behind somebody's back?

We may never know, but the thought is tempting, and provides a pleasant footnote to my analysis of Lawrence's large debt to Weininger.

NOTES

1. Janko Lavrin, 'Sex and Eros' (on Rozanov, Weininger, and D. H. Lawrence)', *European Quarterly* (London), I, no. 2 (Aug 1934) 88–96.
2. Jacques Le Rider, *Le Cas Otto Weininger, Racines de l'antiféminisme et de l'antisémitisme* (Paris: Presses Universitaires de France, 1982).
3. Ibid. p. 21.
4. Otto Weininger, *Sex and Character*, authorised translation from the 6th German ed (1904) (London: Heinemann; New York: Putnam, 1906). Page references are given in the text. This translation is considerably shorter than the current German edition and is noticeably bowdlerised. See Otto Weininger, *Geschlecht und Character* (Vienna and Leipzig: Wilhelm Braumüller,1903; Matthes and Seitz, 1980).
5. Emile Delavenay, *D. H. Lawrence: l'homme et la genèse de son oeuvre (1885–1919)* (Paris: Klincksieck, 1969) p. 383.
6. Ibid., pp. 383–4.
7. Ernest Seillière, *David Herbert Lawrence et les récentes idéologies allemandes* (Paris: Boivin, 1936).
8. Martin Green, *The Von Richthofen Sisters* (London: Weidenfield and Nicolson, 1974).
9. Otto Weininger, *Des fins ultimes* (Lausanne: L'Age d'Homme, 1981). Page references to this translation of *Über die letzten Dinge* are given in the text.
10. Emile Delavenay, 'D. H. Lawrence and the Futurists' (forthcoming).

11. Emile Delavenay, *D. H. Lawrence and Edward Carpenter* (London: Heinemann, 1971).
12. Ibid., *passim*.
13. V. V. Rozanov, *Fallen Leaves* (Bundle One), tr. S. S. Kotelianski with foreword by James Stephens (London: Mandrake Press, 1929). Reviewed by D. H. Lawrence in *Everyman*, 23 Jan 1930.
14. George J. Zytaruk, *D. H. Lawrence's Response to Russian Literature* (London, 1971).
15. Rozanov, *Fallen Leaves*, pp. 13–14. Neither of the passages quoted by Rozanov is to be found in the English translation of *Sex and Character*, which lacks most of the notes.
16. Richard Middleton (1882–1911), poet and essayist, who commited suicide in Belgium at the age of twenty-nine.
17. Letter from Marianne Jaffe von Eckart to Hanna Jahnke-Lee , 19 Jan 1979.
18. Giovanni Papini, 'Un nemico della donna', *La Stampa* (Turin), 21 Dec 1912.
19. Le Rider, *Le Cas Otto Weininger*, p. 221.
20. From Otto Weininger, *Über die letzten Dinge,* p. 139. The French translation, *Des fins ultimes*, is garbled at this point (p. 183), through the omission of a line. I am indebted to Jacques Le Rider for the full text from *Über die letzten Dinge*.
21. 'Work, the Angel and the Unbegotten Hero', ch. 5 of the *Study of Thomas Hardy*, in *Phoenix*. The theme of work and civilisation also developed in this chapter is not unlike a discussion in Weininger's *Über die letzten Dinge* (*Des fins ultimes*, pp. 213–14).
22. Richard Middleton, *Monologues* (London and Leipzig: T. Fisher Unwin, 1913) essays mostly reprinted from *Vanity Fair* and *The Academy*. Page references are given in the text.
23. Middleton's awareness of recent German thought appears explicitly in a clear-sighted passage from 'The Biography of a Superman' in his *The Ghost Ship and Other Stories* London: T. Fisher Unwin, 1912) p.229: 'He had drawn from the mental confusion of the darker German philosophers an image of the perfect man – an image differing only in inessentials from the idol worshipped by the Imperialists as "efficiency".'
24. Richard Middleton, *Poems and Songs*, and *Poems and Songs, Second Series* (London: T. Fisher Unwin, 1912). 'To Althea, who Loves Me Not', appears in *Second Series*, pp. 67–8.
25. This mention of Böcklin appears towards the end of the chapter 'Talent and Genius' but is omitted from the English version of *Sex and Character*. I am indebted to Jacques Le Rider for the information.

11

Reverberations: 'Snapdragon'

ANNEMARIE HEYWOOD

In 1914 D. H. Lawrence wrote to Edward Garnett, who had suggested that he was 'a Frenchman and a Cockney': 'Primarily, I am a passionately religious man', and explained that he saw himself as 'religious' in the sense that 'all the time, underneath, there is something deep evolving itself out in me. And it is *hard* to express a new thing, in sincerity . . . my Cockneyism and commonness are only when the deep feeling doesn't find its way out, and a sort of jeer comes instead, and sentimentality, and purplism'. (*CL*, p. 273). His task as an artist, Lawrence knew, was to block these forms of vulgarity and to become passive, vatic or, as he phrased it in 'Thought', 'a man in his wholeness wholly attending'.

The problem of a poet whose essential vocation is to inhibit interference from conscious and habitual mental processes is one of finding plausible occasions for the 'something deep evolving itself out' to manifest in its own mode. Put in the terminology of Freud, whose gift to the world was precisely a technique for recognising the unconscious, he must contrive manifest occasions for the fixing of latent contents. This essay does not pursue 'Freudian' discoveries; my aim is rather to catch the fugitive process. Ionesco alludes to this enterprise where he says,

> To discover the fundamental problem common to all mankind, I must ask myself what my fundamental problem is, what my most ineradicable fear is. I am certain then to find the problems and fears of literally everyone. That is the true road into my own darkness, which I try to bring to the light of day. . . . A work of art is the expression of an incommunicable reality that one tries to communicate – and which sometimes can be communicated. That is its paradox and its truth.[1]

For one reader at least, Lawrence's poem 'Snapdragon' communicates

158

in this way, and does so by, in the words of Northrop Frye, drawing us 'to a point at which we seem to see . . . a number of converging patterns of significance'.[2] When I. A. Richards discusses the man with the wooden leg in *The Philosophy of Rhetoric*, he is looking at a similar apperceptive trick:

> It is literal in one set of respects, metaphoric in another. A word may be *simultaneously* both literal and metaphoric, just as it may simultaneously support many different metaphors, may serve to focus into one meaning many different meanings. The point is of some importance, since so much misinterpretation comes from supposing that if a word works one way it cannot simultaneously work in another, and have simultaneously another meaning.[3]

I am not then suggesting that the poem draws on several patterns of significance to achieve an effect of mature and complex allusiveness. On the contrary. It is really quite a simple poem, and not the most pleasing or accomplished. But it haunts; and haunts because it strikes a chord which reverberates in several organised dimensions of experience. It is possible to experience it thus, or thus, or thus, like a *Gestalt* puzzle. And the various meanings, or poetic truths, are not all, and not necessarily, mutually enriching.

A poem which reverberates in several apperceptive configurations at once produces, as Empson observes in his analysis of 'Marvell's Garden', a sense of 'various interlocking hierarchies (knowing that you know you know, reconciling the remaining unconscious with the increasing consciousness, uniting in various degrees perception and creation, the one and the many)'.[4] Empson is right, I think, to see in Marvell's poem a striving for harmony under the control of consciousness. Lawrence, on the other hand, strove in the first place to surrender consciousness, to still it in order to attend to 'the something deep evolving itself out'. To invert the Empson formula, his most achieved poems reconcile the remaining conscious with the increasing unconsciousness. But the procedure remains the same, one of 'uniting in various degrees perception and creation' – or rather, as I propose to see it for the purposes of this essay, perception and emotion, ethical impulse and creation. It is the aim of this essay to explore this process.

As we peel apart the conceptual filters through which we apprehend a poem such as this, we find that the first (say) three are mutually enriching and enhancing, but that the last one subverts the whole picture: the ground of the elaborated figure becomes manifest as a poetic truth in its own right. Lawrence said it in 'A Young Wife':

> At the foot of each glowing thing
> A night lies looking up.
>
> (*CP*, p. 215)

Lawrence's own conscious control may well have ceased with level 3. He rendered an anecdote, charged with a potent emotional complex, and structured into a certain polemical drift. At level 4 all this elaboration turns out to have been a mere pretext for rendering perceptible the 'deep evolving . . . out' of the 'underneath'. It is the implications of what becomes visible at this, the latent archetypal, level that this essay is mainly intent on pursuing by looking at (a) the poem's formal (prosodic and syntatic) structure; (b) the anagogical symbols embedded in it and their analogues elsewhere; and (c), briefly, their subsequent development.

I am aware that such a permissive approach to the experiencing and understanding of a poem – an approach which does not inhibit apprehensions within its texture of gleams of a larger coherence, unknown to the poet though this may have been – may seem to many literary scholars quite inexcusably lax and arbitrary. And the danger certainly exists that the reader may simply use a poem as a vehicle for a reverie of his own. But is it really a danger? In a sense much poetry is indeed nothing if not a controlled invitation to dream. And anyone who has at all immersed himself in the observation of symbol behaviour will know that the occurrence and patterning of symbolic images is by no means fortuitous and subjective, but can in fact be seen as the phenomenology of that very evolving-out the observation of which Lawrence saw as his life's work. Symbols, to put it another way, might be looked at as the analogical trigger system of the unconscious, in the same way that mathematics is the digital trigger system of the conscious mind.[5] Symbols are types of truth. Silberer tells us that what matters and endures is not the meanings of these types (which are various and mutable) but the symbols themselves.[6] In most cases the analogies I shall employ are drawn from the anagogical vocabulary of alchemy, which, in its spiritual application, is metamythology or, in the words of Silberer, the mythological science of the titanic impulses and their education. Alchemical imagery is therefore highly appropriate to the re-cognition of mythopoeic imagery in art and dreams.

I   PERCEPTION

On the face of it, Lawrence presents us with an anecdote, a metonymic incident. The poem crystallises the nature of a nascent relationship in a playful transaction, a game in a sunny garden. The man is becoming increasingly aware of the woman's physical presence as she walks in front of him between flower borders. She squats down and initiates the game by squeezing open a crimson snapdragon's lion mouth (I believe the flower's German name, *Löwenmäulchen*, also lies submerged among the triggers in this poem; it becomes important at the symbolic level); her gesture is teasing, suggestive, provocative. Threatened by her boldness, the man retaliates: in his hand the flower is throttled and torn. By means of the flower both have signalled their readiness for sexual love and displayed the character of their desire without recourse to words – 'delicate, creative desire sending forth its fine vibrations in search of the true pole of magnetic rest in another human being – how it is thwarted . . . by . . . ideas and ideals and conventions.'[7] In 'Snapdragon' direct communication is established, not only between the two actors in the metonymic scene but also between poet and reader.

As always, Lawrence contacts the reader through an image which is made hypnotically real through iterative suggestion. By this means he sets up a sensory focus of contemplation which blocks interference from exterior sources – such as the reader's own stock of 'ideas and ideals and conventions' – and enforces a '*coming to the senses*'. We are *made to see* a phenomenologically stated inner experience – call it desire – which by this means opens itself to deeper questioning.

II EMOTION

'Snapdragon' does much more than poetically state desire; it interrogates its character. The poem carries charges, charges which remain baffling perhaps because we tend to register them conventionally – in the modes that Lawrence describes as 'sentimentality and purplism'. These charges are found to lie embedded in adjectives (e.g. 'blind', 'hot', 'sweet'), but chiefly – and this may account for their compelling force – in verbs and verb forms, especially the past participle (e.g. 'swollen', 'throttled', 'choked') adjectivally used and suggestive of the body's kinesthetic experience of itself.

In her searching, intelligent and attuned account of Lawrence's poetry, *Acts of Attention*, Sandra Gilbert acknowledges the importance of this poem and finds expressed in it 'the love and hate', or 'the death and sex polarity', 'sex and cruelty', 'the electric charge of sadism and masochism'.[8] There is a danger in such formulations (which Gilbert avoids by leaving it there) of psychologising the poetic anecdote. Insights into a fantasised psyche, conclusions about Lawrence's sexual proclivities, are not warranted. For Lawrence is writing about the primary libido as such, not about the quirks of his own appetite. This point – which we do well, I think, always to keep in mind – is made emphatically in the famous 'allotropic states' letter to Garnett:

> I don't so much care about what the woman *feels*. I only care about what the women *is* – what she IS – inhumanly, physiologically, materially – according to the use of the word: but for me, what she *is* as a phenomenon (or as representing some greater, inhuman will), instead of what she feels according to the human conception.
>
> (*CL*, p. 282)

He is interested in emotion as 'allotropic states' because, he declares ringingly, 'My theme is carbon.'[9] The compelling emotional shock waves released in this poem, then, by means of metaphorical elaborations of the metonymic base episode – the shocks of swooning, panic, desire, destructiveness, triumph – are allotropic phases of *libido as such* arcing inhumanly between its cathectic poles. The perceptual elaboration of these phases into emotions – 'sentimentality and purplism' – is a secondary work Lawrence tried to avoid, and of which his reader is wise to be watchful.

III ETHICAL IMPULSE

There also seems to be a normative, polemical impulse to this poem. Lawrence, the self-appointed Savonarola of sexual ethics, is making a point about the war of the sexes and the correct apportioning of initiative. All this strikes me as tedious and dogmatic, an intrusion from the prescriptive intellect. The lesson about the proper management of seduction is, significantly enough, articulated through the overt grammatical structure of the poem: the bold woman tries it on; there is a kind of breathless shock; then she is put in her place; male ascendancy is competitively asserted and proved victorious; the woman finds her submissive function and rejoices in it; an asserted ecstasy 'proves' the redemptive function of the the dominant male who risks 'death' in order to defy 'not-to-be'. This polemic strikes one as both too assertive and brittle. It loses touch with the energy charges it is organising. I hope to show that the reason for its brittleness may be sought in the fact that it is contradicted by the symbolic import of the metaphors chosen, and by the deep bias of Lawrence's character pattern as reflected in them. He recognised, of course, the moralising tendency in himself, and its tediousness, and chastises it in Birkin, of whom he writes, in chapter 11 of *Women in Love*, 'There was his wonderful, desirable life-rapidity, . . . and there was at the same time this ridiculous, mean effacement into a Salvator Mundi of a Sunday-school teacher, a prig of the stiffest kind' (*WL*, p. 190).

IV CREATION

The poem, then, offers an evocation of the heavy charges of preconscious emotion playing between a woman and a man, which compound mutual desire and define its scope. But it does more. In the process of elaboration it generates an almost hallucinatory pattern of key symbols in balanced configurations. I shall discuss the symbols themselves below as (i) framing symbols (sun and moon, cup and sword) and (ii) agents (bird, snake and dragon–lion), and shall interest myself in the male–female polarities which the poem so clearly is playing with.

(*a*) One clue to the latent structure is given by the prosodic format of the poem. Gilbert offers the following account:

> As in 'Love on the Farm' . . . he . . . contented himself with a crude attempt to fit his rhythms to his mood. To do this, he worked out a verse structure in which a basic, six-line, rhymed stanza in roughly iambic pentameter formed a kind of ground bass against which stanzas of varying lengths, metres, and rhyme patterns could be played. The basic stanzas contained most of the essentials of the narrative, while the varying stanzas contained the poet's flights of fancy, the symbolic or expressionistic material.[10]

She appears to find no significance in the hourglass structure of the poem as a whole. In fact, the introductory 'narrative' section leads into a section of tighter, roughly trimetric lines which focus on the woman's brown hand holding the flower, and develop the symbols of the cup and the brooding bird. This in turn leads into the heart of the poem, the italicised central lyric of dimetric lines in a pulsing, grammatically unstructured, rhymed, verbless gnomic spell:

> This bird, this rich
> *Sumptuous central grain*
> This mutable witch
> This one refrain
> This laugh in the flight
> *This clot of night*
> This field of delight
> (emphasis added)

This expands again into another section of roughly trimetric iambs restating the triumph of the woman's brown bird-likened hand settling 'to drown / The nest in a heat of love', before expanding once again into the opening pattern of pentameters for the 'narrative' reversal, the triumph of the pale male hand which introduces the symbols of the 'sword' ('Like a weapon my hand was white and keen') and snake ('For my hand like a snake watched hers, that could not fly') and the defiant invocation of the red harvest moon in the final stanza.[11]

The lines I have italicised show that the hourglass structure is indeed eloquent. It is poised around a 'central grain', a 'clot', or a stop like the transition from systole to diastole. I feel quite strongly that this is not the kind of artful contrivance which aims at a concrete allegory, but arises from a mimetic compulsion, a close attentiveness, an adhesion somehow, to the vast organic surge (as breath or pulse) which, at this level, the poem might be felt to monitor.

(*b*) Gilbert also dismisses as 'irrelevant flights of fancy'[12] the archetypal material which lies hidden in this pattern and which I believe constitutes the ground meaning, the 'something deep evolving itself out', the 'night looking up', announced in the verbless central lyric. These symbols – dragon-lion, bird, serpent – the dynamism of their constellation and their relation to the symbols of sun and cup in the opening, and moon and sword in the closing stanzas, I now propose to consider in some detail.

In discussing the symbol configurations I find myself in a position similar to that of Lawrence in letting the deep 'find its way out'. It seems impossible to grasp in conceptual pincers: the only way to let this level speak to us is through echoes and mirrors.[13] The aim of the exercise should not be seen as explanatory or interpretative, but rather as comparative, analogical, a meditation on correspondences. Symbols cannot be verbally translated into cognate concepts in any case; they should be left to resonate in the reader's prepared mind with that degree of specificity which they alone possess. What I *am* concerned with here is, first, to establish that such a degree of specificity does indeed operate here, and, secondly, to offer suggestions as to the area of human experience in which resonance is invited.

Symbolically the poem declares itself by setting up, within the first three lines, a ritual space, a *temenos*:

> her garden, where
> The mellow sunlight stood as in a cup
> Between the old grey walls.

The first two stanzas suggest a ritual involving two persons. One might see them as subject and object, agent and reagent, dancer and watcher, or indeed in other ways. The suggestions of a dance-within-the-space are strong; they are conveyed in, for example, the *swing* of her white dress / That *rocked* in a *lilt* along', 'the *poise* / Of her feet as they *flew for a space*, then *paused to press* / The grass deep down with the royal burden of her',[14] and 'the *tread* of her'. The complementary role is sketched in 'I did not dare / To raise my face, I did not dare look up', 'I followed, followed', and 'I watched'. They are initiand's functions. The dominant symbol of the grail cup, which expands psychedelically to encompass his heart, his throat, the flower, and the whole 'morning world' in turn, asserts of course a corresponding function. The garden space and hourglass articulation of time frame the ritual suggested through the action of the poem. Read within this organisational frame, the episode in the garden is enacted entirely within inner space or – if the formula is preferred – within the psyche. The two agents, woman and man, and the patient between them are internal potencies and no longer Lawrence and his lady love, whether she be Louisa Burrows or Frieda. Jung has done much to advance our perceptions of such transactions as ritual phases in the 'individuation' process, and his interpretations of archetypal symbols and transactions are found suggestive and revealing by many. It is my own belief that there is in his brilliant and illuminating account still something biased and reductive, that it offers a splendid analytic tool rather than explanation and answer. With this reservation, I shall use terms which he has made familiar and which are therefore more lucid than neologisms or the more precise language of the obscure sources which Jung synthesised.

(i) *Framing symbols*. Before turning to the agents, however, I propose to consider the framing symbols of cup and sword, sun and moon. It will be noted that the word 'sword' nowhere appears in the poem. It is, however, sufficiently implied by the lines 'like a weapon my hand was white and keen' and 'my heart leaped up in longing to plunge its stark / fervour within the pool of her twilight'. It is further implied, as its symbolic complement, by the very presence of the cup. As Silberer says: 'It is necessary . . . to think independently of the words used and regard them only in their context.'[15]

Jung and von Franz in *The Grail Legend* offer the following definitions of these symbols. The grail cup, introduced in the second line, is the 'vessel of the sun', the Feminine as Virgin Mother, 'that which receives, contains, supports'. The sword is that which 'serves to separate or, metaphorically, to "differentiate", so it can also stand for the mind, especially the intellect or understanding intelligence, of whose "incisive" quality we speak'.[16] It is, they further suggest,

> *a symbol of the divinity concealed in man*, an inner psychic god-image which transforms itself in and through itself. . . . The sword is also thought of, in the texts of the alchemists, as similar in nature to their 'divine water' and to the 'stone'. Their Mercurius serves for instance as a permeating spirit, *'penetrabilior ancipii gladio'* ('sharper than a two-edged sword'). The sword signifies that life-urge which leads to the recognition of the Self.   (p. 89)[17]

Joseph Campbell both enlarges and focuses the symbolism of the cup: 'The Castle of the Grail, like the bowl of the baptismal font, of the sanctuary of the winged serpent, is the place – the *vas*, the *temenos* – of regeneration and as such a sanctuary in which sexual symbolism is both appropriate and inevitable.'[18] As for the sword, I think a passage from Carter's notes on Lawrence throws a keen light on what it symbolises (amusingly enough, he does not use the word either): 'What, then, is it, this continence of power, hardgripped, with the lightning in it? What is its shape or name? Genius? Daemon? Spirit? It is that which makes and seeks danger, going gently until the raging instant to burst explosive and terrific. Something that we call male.'[19]

The cup of the first half of the poem then might, I propose, be felt as the ground in which being realises itself as becoming. In the trimetric section it accordingly receives its proper sacramental liquid – sun/wine/blood – and is hovered over by a brown bird, a cuckoo who is 'like a dove'. We take note that Lawrence is discouraging a pious reading, but for all that he does not defuse the potency of the hovering pentecostal bird: indeed, he invites recognition. The cuckoo itself, moreover – the brown speckled 'reiver' chosen, one feels, as a cheeky alternative – has, according to Jane Harrison, a cognate potency: 'Upon the thunder-axe is perched a bird. . . It is the bird of spring, with heavy flight and mottled plumage, the cuckoo. . . The idea, *the coming of a life-spirit from the sky*, is the same whatever bird be the vehicle' (emphasis added).[20]

In the final section the cup becomes the dark pool under the red harvest moon. And in the lines

> And my heart leaped up in longing to plunge its stark
> Fervour within the pool of her twilight

we recognise the sacramental union of fire and water which, as Joseph Campbell reminds us, lies embedded in the Holy Saturday ritual of the blessing of the new fire: 'The female water spiritually fructified with the male fire of the Holy Ghost is the Christian counterpart of the water of transformation known to all systems of mythological imagery.'[21]

The poem thus symbolically enacts a spring or Easter ritual, a sacramental transformation, of which the Christian variant is merely the most familiar. It is when we turn to the symbolic agents – bird and serpent – and the symbolic patient – dragon–lion – that the specific transaction within the archetypal scenario begins to exfoliate and show its drift and its relevance to the artisitic vocation of the poet.

(ii) *The agents.* At the anecdotal level there are two agents, a queenly female and a male initiand. A third potency is introduced in the snapdragon, which becomes the ritual focus. To begin with, the man identifies closely with the snapdragon, and indeed with the 'morning world': their unity forms the cup. The experience is one of engorgement, flooding by a spectrum of sun/wine/blood. The woman's brooding hand makes this happen within the man's solar world. A 'sumptuous central grain', a 'clot of night' is invoked. In the second phase the man's pale hand 'like a weapon' overpowers the snapdragon, crushing it, and thus 'defeats' the bird. The sunlit garden cup turns into 'the pool of her twilight', the brooding bird is displaced by a suggested sword. Dusk, death and triumph prevail, as sunlight, life and peace did in the first half. (Compare the Tarot images of sun and moon in Figures 1 and 2.) The triumph emphasised is not that by either bird or snake over the dragon–lion, but the defeat of bird by serpent: 'For my hand like a snake

FIGURE 1

FIGURE 2

watched hers, that could not fly'.[22] It is, unmistakably, a triumph of joy, Dionysiac: 'Then I laughed in the dark of my heart, I did exult', 'their joy that underlies / Defeat in such a battle', 'And I do not care . . . if the joy . . . ha[s] risen red on my night'.

The dragon (snapdragon) or green lion (*Löwenmäulchen*) is, in alchemical symbolism, rhythmic life itself, chthonic, chaotic, dangerous, potent, unthinking, seeking only its own fulfilment, but able, as images of the alchemical perfection declare, to be totally transmuted. Arcanum XI of the Tarot (Figure 3) depicts the very action which is playfully rehearsed by the two agents in Lawrence's poem. The puzzling ambiguity of the action depicted is not resolved by analogies, such as the beautiful image from the *Rosarium philosophorum* (Figure 4), or the following sayings, from the Gospel of Thomas, and a sermon by Meister Eckhart respectively, which touch on the same operation:

FIGURE 3   FIGURE 4

Jesus said, blessed is the lion which the man eats and the lion will become man; and cursed is the man whom the lion eats and the lion will become man.[23]

The highest component of man is blood. . . . If the blood conquers the flesh, man is humble, patient, chaste, and has all the virtues, but if the flesh rules the blood, then the man is haughty, irritable, unchaste, and has all the vices.[24]

I am almost certain that Lawrence did not know the Tarot, and he did not need to. The image cropped up spontaneously as a 'real-life' anecdote and gathered allusiveness in 'evolving itself out'. Jung has found a similar spontaneity in the archetypal behaviour of dreams and 'active imagination', and Silberer observes that in the anagogic art of the alchemists 'the mythical and the individual images meet in the most vivid way, without destroying each other'.[25]

But the real triumph lies in the confrontation of the bird by the snake. The various mythological meanings attached to bird and snake are listed in Cirlot's *Dictionary*, where they may be explored. Very briefly, the serpent is energy itself – magnetic, or vital energy, and is properly associated with the chthonic, female sanctities. The bird, pertaining to the element of air, expresses soaring energies of thought, spirit, soul, imagination. In Vedantic and Germanic traditions it is solar, and male. Moreover, Cirlot observes, 'The bird has a formidable antagonist in the snake or serpent. According to Zimmer, it is only in the West that this carries a moral implication; in India, the natural elements only are contrasted – the solar force as opposed to the fluid energy of the terrestrial oceans'.[26] The confrontation of bird and snake or their cognate alternatives – most commonly 'the ever-dying, ever-living lunar bull consumed through all time by the lion-headed solar eagle'[27] – is an archetypal theme, as Figures 5–7 illustrate. The 'biting' here, incidentally, should perhaps be understood less as hurt or aggression than as 'the imprint or seal of the spirit upon the flesh',[28] and is in that respect similar to 'piercing', anagogically understood.

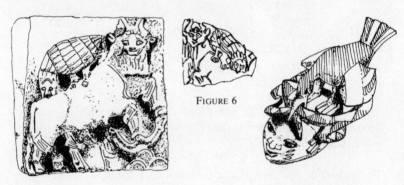

FIGURE 6

FIGURE 5

FIGURE 7

'The functions of the mythological symbols', Campbell suggests, 'are four: mystic, cosmological, sociological, and psychological'.[29] The 'biting' of the female snake/bull by the male bird/lion embodies a phase of maturation which has analogies on all these planes. In individual psychology it represents 'growing-up': socialisation, the displacement of dreaming and oceanic love by self-reflective knowing, active doing and conscious choice.[30] In cultural history it seems to mark the supersession of matriarchies and earth cults by patriarchies and 'personality gods'. Empson's 'reconciling the remaining unconscious with the increasing consciousness', symbolically transcribed, might well bear the smiling face of Typhon in the Greek vase painting reproduced in Figure 8.

In Lawrence's case, and at this stage in his life, such a poetic ritual has a peculiar poignancy and rightness. But the remarkable fact is that his ritual reverses the polarities illustrated above: the serpent out-

FIGURE 8

FIGURE 9

manoeuvres the bird, the moon conquers the sun. This reversal is in line with what I suggested above in connection with Empson's reading of Marvell: that in Lawrence the central effort is to sacrifice consciousness to the unconscious. In the poem the paradoxical ritual is successful, and makes possible the *hieros gamos*, the sacred wedding of the final symbolic tableau. The triumph of joy arises from the fact that the male hand plays out the serpent role, the female the bird's. One is reminded of the preliminaries of salvation as given in the Gospel of Thomas: 'When you make the two one, and when you make the inner as the outer and the outer as the inner and the above as the below, and when you make the male and the female into a single one, so that the male will not be male and female [not] be female, . . .then shall you enter [the Kingdom].'[31] The terms 'male' and 'female' are of course intended to refer to psychic endowments which are present – more or less dormant, more less realised – in every human being, and the full awakening of, and harmonious interplay between which is the goal of the Great Work: the *rebis*, the androgyne, the Stone (see Figure 9).

FIGURE 10

That the union of the polarities subsists in something more complex than a simple merging, that it involves for each a 'death' and the flowering of a specific potential, is suggested by the images in Figure 10. An exquisite image from the fourteenth-century *Aurora consurgens* renders the complex 'crossing' action involved with great clarity (see Figure 11).[32] Each potency postulates the other within the ground of its own being; each focuses on ('pierces', kindles) its own image in the other. The polarity in this representation is as balanced and harmonious as in the well-known T'ai Chi symbol, where Yin and Yang also each contain the seed of the other.

FIGURE 11

(c) To begin with, Lawrence knew well that his preoccupation with sexual relationship was largely a 'religious' one. In 1914 he wrote to Gordon Campbell, 'I believe there is no getting of a vision before we get our souls fertilized by the *female* – and this female is *not necessarily woman but most obviously woman*' (*CL*, p. 291; second emphasis added). In *Twilight in Italy* Lawrence differentiates between two ways to God (although dogmatism and a kind of irritable 'Cockneyism' interfere with the full working-out):

It is past the time to cease seeking one Infinite, ignoring, striving to eliminate the other. The Infinite is twofold. By great retrogression back to the source of darkness in me, the Self, deep in the senses, I arrive at the Original, Creative Infinite. By projection forth from myself, by the elimination of my absolute sensual self, I arrive at the

Ultimate Infinite, Oneness in the Spirit. They are two Infinites, twofold approach to God. And man must know both. . .

There are two opposite ways to consummation. But that which relates them, like the base of the triangle, this is the constant, the Absolute, this makes the Ultimate Whole.[33]

Lawrence's imagination was constantly active in this area, which he conceptualised as the relationship of the sexes. *Aaron's Rod* gives a brief representation of a full and mature realisation in the image of the mid-air mating of fully equivalent, complementary winged beings. The Hardy study already battles with the confusions arising when the fully awakened hidden other (anima or animus) conflicts with gender roles and sexual identity. Lawrence's analyses of Hardy's characters and, even more significantly, the conception of the leading characters in *The Rainbow* and *Women in Love* which emerges from this cogitation show that what fascinated and challenged Lawrence's imagination was precisely the degree of androgyny realised in his characters. He appears to have worked towards a celebration of ideal lovers who are fully potentiated both in their own sexual function and in their contrasexual potential. The men have to activate their intuitive anima, the women their assertive combative animus. (David Bowie puts it in a nutshell, in his lyric 'Heroes': 'and you / you can be mean / and I / I'll drink all the time / cause we're lovers' – lines which clearly suggest endorsement of the 'underworld' Plutonic–Dionysiac potential in the fully realised *rebis*.) Both have to accept the essential otherness of their lover before the twain can meet in an encounter where each becomes fully man or woman precisely because they are at peace with their contrasexual energies. This is the 'star polarity' which Lawrence always sought as the ideal basis for relationship.

As the serpent victory in 'Snapdragon' symbolically suggests, Lawrence's own orientation appears to have been towards the female way. Thus it is seen by Carter:

Man as he tells of him is instinctively distrustful of all outside himself, of all that endéavours to take him ouside his own entity. He has an integrity to protect. But he never gives his reasons for it . . . . He – in them – finds it hard to express feelings in speech. All their talk about the other sex has a faint inflexion of jeers. But his women discussing men are in earnest. . . . Yes, women he knew, profoundly. He felt like them and felt with them when he wrote. But the spirit of man he found elusive, it retired from him, secret and uncommunicative.[34]

Lawrence's own characterisation of proto-Birkin endorses Carter's perception:

> Although nearly all his living interchange went on with one woman or another, although he was always terribly intimate with at least one woman, and practically never intimate with a man, yet the male physique had a fascination for him, and for the female physique he felt only a fondness, a sort of sacred love, as for a sister . . . It was the men's physique which held the passion and the mystery to him. The women he seemed to be kin to, he looked for the soul in them.[35]

As time went on, his male characters continued to live out the divine energy of their inner femininity, but the full reciprocity which he strove to represent increasingly eluded him. Under internal and external harassment, the beauty and completeness of human realisation which he was, in his early work, ceaselessly labouring to define in the form of a full sexual relationship coarsened. His visions became laboured and conceptualised, his voice stridently dogmatic.

He became, as it were, enmeshed in his own metaphor. The women's divine inner masculinity is increasingly subdued and derided. Lawrence appears to have felt threatened by the female animus, and to have reacted – in his final works – with febrile hostility to the flowering of female androgyny which nevertheless kept 'evolving itself out' in his characters. But he would not have it. He subdued it. Lady Chatterley's man is a cripple; Kate is denied union with Don Ramon; the woman who rode away is sacrificed to the sun. At times he is vindictively destructive, against the grain of what he knows. Thus in *Fantasia* 'woman' is stigmatised as deviationist: 'The moon, the planet of woman, sways us from our day-self, sways us back from *our real social unison*, sways us back, like a retreating tide, in a friction of criticism and separation and social disintegration. That is woman's inevitable mode, let her words be what they will' (*F*, p. 192; emphasis added). Yet to Ottoline Morrell he had written, from a truer vision, 'Every strong soul must put off its connection with this society, . . . and go naked with its fellows, weaponless, armourless . . . And each man shall know that he is part of the greater body . . . that all souls of all things do not compose the body of God' (*CL*, pp. 311–12). *The Plumed Serpent*, so grand in its conception as the celebration of the female sanctities, so powerful in the surge of the 'something deep evolving itself out', founders on Lawrence's 'almost mystical mysogyny', as Kingsley Widmer terms it.[36] He came to confuse the sexes and their gender roles with the archetypes which are merely 'most obviously' represented by the sexes, and had to, it seems, uphold male supremacy even if it stifled his characters and denied his own daemon.

His own potency, as 'Snapdragon' celebrates it, is that of Dionysiac joy, the heroic potency of the son-of-woman. Too much rationalisation, too much argumentation and preaching, distorted even that. A supremacist power dream crept in, a dream of leadership at the tip of the heap – as witness his exposition of the 'three great phases of consciousness' in the *Apocalypse* material:

> The first was a far-off phase of purely collective consciousness . . . tribal, felt all at once by a mass of men, but culminating or focussing in some leader . . . aware of the immediate connection between itself and the vast, potent, terrible cosmos, that lived with all life . . . taking from the cosmos life, vitality, potency, prowess, and power: *pouvoir*, *Macht*, might. The tribe or nation culminated in one man, the leader or chief, the tip of the great collective body. . . . The second . . . did not arise till man felt himself cut off from the cosmos, till he became aware of himself apart, as an apart, fragmentary, unfinished thing.[37]

Strange how his metaphors *know* what the rattling argumentation bullies underfoot: that there was no *Macht* autocrat at the tip of the connectedness, but a dark goddess containing all. Strange how the bludgeoning frenzy of his polemic has stunned Lawrence's sensitivity. Brilliant as *Apocalypse* is in many of its passages, in the sheer intelligence of its apprehensions, in the range and health of its impulses, yet the conceptualisations are enslaved, bigoted, blind. It does not occur to Lawrence that his divinity might be female. Woman remains the sexual other, the negative. And yet he *knows*; the metaphors signal to him and to us: 'This is the Fall, the fall into knowledge, or self-awareness, the fall into tragedy and into "sin". For a man's sex is his fragmentariness. The phallos is the point at which man is broken off from his context, and at which he can be rejoined.'[38]

To a mighty leader? And what man ever dropped out of a chief? No wonder he wrote to his sister-in-law, 'I am so weak. And something inside me weeps black tears. I wish it would go away' (*CL*, p. 1206). It was his denied daemon, the genius of the underworld. In 'Bavarian Gentians' Lawrence returns to it:

> Reach me a gentian, give me a torch
> Let me guide myself with the blue, forked torch of this flower

Down the darker and darker stairs, where blue is darkened on
    blueness . . .
Among the splendour of torches of darkness, shedding darkness
    on the lost bride and her groom.
The breath of life is in the sharp winds of change
Mingled with the breath of destruction.
But if you want to breathe deep, sumptuous life
Breathe all alone, in silence, in the dark,
And see nothing.

Again and again throughout his work the stubborn potency breaks
through in his many celebrations of the 'dark self', the 'blood being'; yet
he lost the patience to 'let it find its way out'; instead he conceptualised
and intellectualised his profound intuitions, and, since he also lacked
patience for sustained study and practice in any of the esoteric
disciplines he sampled, any one of which might have loosened the knot,
he foundered in the cats-cradle of his argumentation.

    The early poem this essay has been looking at is more serene: its action
symbolises liberation, the triumphant birth of the self, the daemonic
hero, the *rebis*. The poem appears to embody accomplishment of the
'white' work of alchemy. Buber describes this first 'event' as follows:

> First, the soul may become one . . . the being stands alone in itself and
> jubilates, as Paracelsus puts it, in its exaltation. . . . This is a man's
> decisive moment. Without it he is not fit for the work of the spirit.
> Concentrated into a unity, a human being can proceed to his
> encounter . . . with mystery and perfection . . . but this one, deep
> down, is the primally secret decision, pregnant with the most powerful
> destiny.[39]

It also maps out the field of Lawrence's subsequent imaginative
attention: the interaction between man and woman, between masculinity and femininity, between the male and the female poles of human
consciousness. His full attention on the 'something deep evolving itself
out' later sometimes faltered. Opposition drew him into hardened
intellectual postures, and into the very 'Cockneyism and purplism'
which he himself knew well were the blights of his creativeness. But not
here.

NOTES

In this study, illustrations have been made by myself from the following sources: Figures 1–3 from J.-M. Simon, *The Marseilles Tarot* (Paris, n.d.); Figures 4, 9, 10 from Stanislas Klossewski de Rola, *The Secret Art of Alchemy* (London: Thames and Hudson, 1973); Figures 5 and 8 from Joseph O. Campbell. *The Masks of God*, III: *Occidental Mythology*; Figure 6 from Leo Frobenius, *Kulturgeschichte Afrikas* (Zurich, 1933); Figure 7 from Geoffrey Parrinder, *African Mythology* (London: Hamlyn, 1967). The following sources are cited in these works. Figures 4 and 9: 'perfectionis ostensio', Arnold of Villanova, *Rosarium philosophorum*, 16th century, in the Stadtbibliothek Vadiana, St Gallen, MS 349a, ff. 97, 92. Figure 5: Sumerian terracotta plaque, Moon-Bull and Lion-Bird, c. 2500 B.C., in the University Museum, Philadelphia. Figure 6: scratched shell tablet, Tello, Mesopotamia, in the Louvre, Paris, Mission Sarsec no. 220. Figure 7: Yoruba Gelede mask. Figure 8: early red-figured vase, Zeus against Typhon, c. 650 B.C., in the Munich Museum. Figure 10: Anon., 14th century, in the Biblioteca Mediceo-Laurenziana, Florence, MS Ashburn 1166, ff. 16, 17v. Figure 11: *Aurora consurgens*, late 14th century, Zurich, Cod. Rhenovacensis 172, f. 10.

1.   Christopher Butler and Alastair Fowler, *Topics in Criticism* (London: Longman, 1971) topic 579.
2.   Ibid., topic 551.
3.   Ibid., topic 236.
4.   William Empson, *Some Versions of Pastoral* (1935; London: Chatto and Windus, 1966) p. 119.
5.   The curious may be stimulated by correlating this duality with, for example, the metaphor/metonymy, paradigmatic-association/ syntagmatic-chain dualisms propounded by Lévi-Strauss and excellently summarised in Edmund Leach, *Culture and Communication* (Cambridge: Cambridge University Press, 1976) *passim*; or with recent investigations of the independent functioning of the two cerebral lobes of the brain: the left, 'male', 'propositional', being verbal, analytic, intellectual; the right, 'female', 'appositional', mediating superior kinesthetic functioning, spatial perception, interpretative and musical abilities. See Joseph E. Bogen, 'The Other Side of the Brain: An Appositional Mind', *Bulletin of the Los Angeles Neurological Societies*, 34 (July 1969); and Robert E. Ornstein, *The Psychology of Human of Consciousness* (San Francisco: Freeman, 1975) *passim*.
6.   Herbert Silberer, *Hidden Symbolism of Alchemy and the Occult Arts* (New York: Dover Books, 1971) p. 415. First published as *Problems of Mysticism and its Symbolism* (New York, 1917).
7.   D. H. Lawrence, *Psychoanalysis and the Unconscious* (1923; Harmondsworth; Penguin, 1974) p. 245.
8.   Sandra M. Gilbert, *Acts of Attention* (London and Ithaca, NY: Cornell University Press, 1972) pp. 51–9.
9.   The curious may be intrigued by the following analogy. I quote from Jacqueline and Nicolas Parkhurst, *Altered States of Consciousness and the Christos Experience* (Glen Forrest, Western Australia, 1976) p. 86:

'This transformation process represents a process . . . taking place, as it were, inside the Self and comparable to the carbon-nitrogen cycle in the sun, where a carbon nucleus captures four protons (two of which immediately become neutrons) and releases them at the end of the cycle in the form of an alpha particle. The carbon nucleus itself comes out of the reaction unchanged, like the Phoenix from the ashes.'

10. Gilbert, *Acts of Attention*, p. 56.

11. A further, typographical patterning I ignore here. This is the recessing of two five-line stanzas in the Phoenix edition of the *Complete Poems*. These stanzas introduce the bird-on-cup trimetric sections surrounding the eye of the poem. Which typographical arrangement was sanctioned by the poetic manuscript? I do not know. And for the present argument the ritual structuring *as such* is the significant cognisance.

12. Gilbert, *Acts of Attention*, p. 59.

13. The multivalency of symbols must be respected. To see in them allegorised concepts is to fix them and rob them of their fluid, energic character, which acts specifically but always in a manner dictated by the 'geometry' of the context. Thus the sword by itself may indeed 'mean' the 'life-urge'; in juxtaposition with the cup it polarises into the 'male' pole of this force; in conjunction with cup, club and coin it becomes something more specialised again – yet it never changes its essential quality. Silberer says, 'It is a peculiarity of the alchemistic authors to use interchangeably fifty or more names for a thing and on the other hand to give one and the same name many meanings . . . it is necessary, so to speak, to think independently of the words used and regard them only in their context' (*Hidden Symbolism*, p. 119). Figure/ground again.

14. The words used here are closely paralleled in another poem of the same period, the nostalgically potent 'Piano': 'A child . . . *pressing* the small, *poised feet* of a mother who smiles as she sings' – a coincidence which may betray the psychic source from which Lawrence drew his imagery.

15. Silberer, *Hidden Symbolism*, p. 119.

16. Emma Jung and Marie-Louise von Franz, *The Grail Legend* (1960; London: Jupiter, 1971) pp. 106, 113, 80.

17. Ibid., p. 89. The reductive tendency of assigning to these symbols no larger meaning than that of the biological instruments of sex must, I think, be resisted. Weston seems to come to this conclusion: 'They are sex symbols of immemorial antiquity and world-wide diffusion – their signification is admitted by all familiar with "Life" symbolism, and they are absolutely in place as forming part of a ritual dealing with the processes of life and reproductive fertility' – Jessie Weston, *From Ritual to Romance* (1919; New York, 1957) p. 75. The preoccupation in Western thought of the past 150 years with sex itself seems to be a result of cultural repressions. The human creative intuition which makes myths can surely rise to greater heights than a rutting brooding on the tools of procreation and their fertility. In a mythological perspective, these and their metaphoric analogies (so patiently listed by Freud) are themselves analogues of universal functions, as above so below.

18. Joseph O. Campbell, *The Masks of God,* IV: *Creative Mythology* (1968; London: Secker and Warburg, 1974) p. 459.

19.   Frederick Carter, *D. H. Lawrence and the Body Mystical* (London, 1932)
       p. 14.
20.   Jane Harrison, *Themis* (1912; London: Merlin, 1977) pp. 176–7.
21.   Joseph O. Campbell, *The Hero with a Thousand Faces* (1949; London:
       Princeton University Press, 1975) p. 216. This passage also clarifies the
       rather confusing definition of the sword as Mercurial water or *acetum* in
       Jung and von Franz, cited above. That definition ignores the *plunged*
       nature of the sword. The 'divine water' is better seen as male-seed-
       contained-in-female – that is, the male as zygote or son (anagogically
       speaking, of course).
22.   The curious may be amused to note that the bird is now in the
       predicament of 'the volatile fixed'. Cf., for example, Elias Ashmole,
       Theatrum Chemicum Brittanicum (1652) p. 423:

                          Aenigma Philosophorum

            Lo here the *Primar Secret* of this Arte
            Contemne it not but understand it right
            Who faileth to attain this foremost part
            Who never known *Artes force* nor *Natures might*.
              Not yet have power of *One* and *One* so mixt
              To make by *One fixt*, One *unfixidfixt*.

23.   *The Gospel According to St Thomas*, ed. A. Guillaumont, H.-Ch. Peuch,
       G. Quispel, W. Till and Yassah 'abd al Masih (New York, 1959) Log. 7.
24.   *Meister Eckhart*, ed. and tr. Raymond B. Blakney (New York, 1941) p.
       224.
25.   Silberer, *Hidden Symbolism*, p. 377.
26.   J. E. Cirlot, *A Dictionary of Symbols* (1962; London, 1971) p. 28.
27.   Joseph O. Campbell, *The Masks of God*, III: *Occidental Mythology* (1964;
       London: Souvenir Press, 1974) p. 54.
28.   Cirlot, *A Dictionary of Symbols*, p. 29.
29.   Campbell, *The Masks of God*, IV: *Creative Mythology*, p. 630.
30.   Cf. Carl. G. Jung, *Man and his Symbols* (London: Jupiter, 1964) p. 118:
       'The ego must eventually free itself from unconsciousness and
       immaturity; its "battle of deliverance" is often symbolised by a hero's
       battle with a monster.'
31.   *The Gospel According to St Thomas*, Log. 22.
32.   A version of the same image occurs as 'The Castle Siege' in Bodleian MS
       194 sg. t. 3r, and appears, illustrating the taking of the castle, in some
       versions of the *Roman de la Rose*.
33.   D. H. Lawrence, *Twilight in Italy* (London: Jonathan Cape, 1926).
34.   Carter, *Lawrence and the Body Mystical*, p. 10.
35.   Quoted in George H. Ford, 'An Introductory Note to D. H. Lawrence's
       Prologue to *Women in Love*', *Times Quarterly*, 6 (1962) 92ff.
36.   Kingsley Widmer, 'Lawrence and the Fall of Modern Woman', *Modern
       Fiction Studies*, 5 (1959) 47–56.
37   'Testament: Unpublished Passages from the Last Work of D. H.
       Lawrence', *Guardian*, 23, 24, 25 Oct 1978.

38. Ibid.
39. Martin Buber, *I and Thou*, ed. and tr. Walter Kaufmann (Edinburgh: T. & T. Clark, 1970) p. 134.

Index

182